AMERICAN PREACHERS OF TO-DAY

American Preachers of To-Day

Intimate Appraisals of Thirty-Two Leaders

BY

EDGAR DEWITT JONES

Essay Index Reprint Series

BOOKS FOR LIBRARIES PRESS
FREEPORT, NEW YORK

INTERNATIONAL STANDARD BOOK NUMBER:
0-8369-2279-4

LIBRARY OF CONGRESS CATALOG CARD NUMBER:
76-156667

PRINTED IN THE UNITED STATES OF AMERICA

TO THE UNKNOWN PREACHER

Whose Obscure and Sacrificial Life
Is Hid with Christ in God
And Therefore Fruitful For Ever,
This Book Is Reverently Dedicated.

ACKNOWLEDGMENTS

I AM deeply indebted to the subjects of the following chapters for generous response to my inquiries, and for liberal inroads upon their time, expended in leisurely interviews or lengthy correspondence. I wish also to acknowledge helpful suggestions made by a royal company of my brother ministers in all the denominations represented in this volume. I am grateful to Mr. F. W. Moore for valuable assistance in reading proof, and to Mr. James E. Mann for pertinent criticisms. My gratitude includes the Rev. Robert Freeman for permission to print his *My Father's House,* and the Rev. William L. Stidger for the use of *I Saw God Wash the World Last Night.* Likewise my thanks are due Mrs. L. A. Douglas for efficient secretarial service through many months. Special mention should be made of the fine courtesy of the A. N. Marquis Company, Chicago, for use of the biographical sketches from Volume 1932-33 *Who's Who in America,* which appear on the page facing each chapter.

E. DeW. J.

Detroit, Michigan.
April, 1933.

CONTENTS

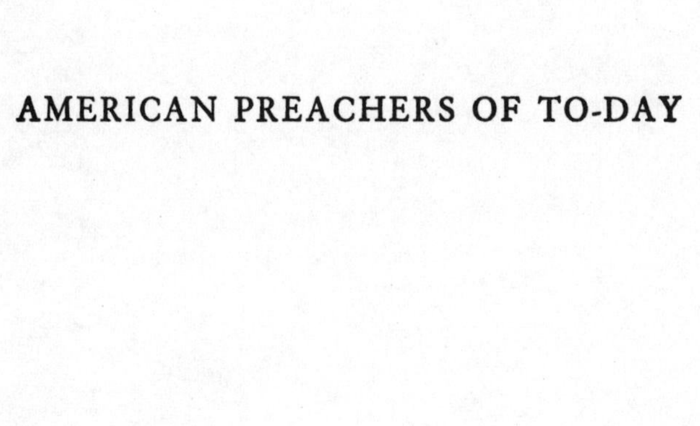

AMERICAN PREACHERS OF TO-DAY

AMERICAN PREACHERS OF TO-DAY

CHAPTER I

THE AGE OF PREACHING

OURS is an age of preaching and of able preachers. To be sure, there are no Henry Ward Beechers, Theodore Parkers, Phillips Brookses, Matthew Simpsons or George A. Gordons, towering above their preaching brethren, as heaven-kissing hills overshadow the lesser ranges. But a little lower than these Angels of Light there is to-day a shining company. And if those famed prophets of another age were with us to-day, perhaps the distance between them and their contemporaries would not be so great as it was in their own generation. It is doubtful if there has been another period in American history so opulent in the number of strong and brilliant preachers as our own. If this judgment seem extravagant or unwarranted, there are those competent to corroborate it.

Dr. Frederick Lynch, editor, preacher and internationalist, whose long and useful life impinges upon the "Golden Age of Preaching" when Beecher, Brooks, Spurgeon and Joseph Parker were going strong, should be heard. After examining a recent series of sermonic volumes by American ministers, Dr. Lynch wrote: "The reading of these sermons confirms a conviction I have often voiced that the days of fine preaching have not passed."

Dr. Gaius Glenn Atkins not only belongs to the elect company of living prophets, but he is also an accomplished writer and a teacher of homiletics in Auburn Theological Seminary, and in line with the late Dr. Arthur S. Hoyt whose works on preaching ranked him high. Dr. Atkins writes: "There is an amount of sound thinking and good writing touched by rare moral insight in the preaching of our own times which will strongly stand comparison with the preaching of any period and with the form and content of contemporaneous serious thinking and writing, whoever does it."

And again, in his foreword to a recent collection of sermons entitled *Voices of Living Prophets,* the compiler, the Rev. Thomas Bradley Mather, says: "That there are not such preachers today as yesterday is repeatedly asserted, and with some justification. Not all the truth of present-day preaching however lies in this statement. It has been my conviction for some years that our ministry of today is as excellent as the ministry of any age."

It would be an easy matter to multiply citations of a like tenor from others fully as competent to bear testimony to the strength and brilliance of the modern pulpit; but these will suffice. For at least their observations are arresting and suggestive. They invite attention to a fact that any one of an investigating turn of mind can discover for himself if he cares to do so. For twenty-five years I have been associating with ministers of the various communions, meeting with them in conferences and conventions, listening to them preach and reading their published sermons, and I have been amazed at the number and quality of gifted men in the preaching fraternity of America.

I incline to the belief that the average sermon to-day is more carefully prepared than was the average sermon of fifty and a hundred years ago. I believe this to be true despite the fact (or because of it) that the ministerial vocation to-day is much more complex and exacting than in former years. The modern minister is not only preacher, but pastor, executive and publicist as well. On the other hand, cultural facilities have greatly multiplied. Public libraries are larger and more available; good books are within the reach of the humblest salaried preacher; publications devoted to the technique of the preacher and pastor, magazines and periodicals, are abundant. Moreover stimulating conferences, convocations, institutes on preaching and the pastoral office, are widely established, and to these come the peers of the pulpit, to preach, lecture and confer. Such advantages can not but lift the standards of preaching, and influence the style and thought content of thousands of pulpit utterances.

More volumes of sermons are printed in a single year now than in a decade previous to 1890. This fact may not be an unqualified blessing. Over the radio, Dr. Cadman has expressed forcibly the wish that no more books of sermons be printed for twenty-five years, so that ministers might be driven to read and study the great old classics, as well as the best of modern works, and so be inspired to dig out their own sermons instead of utilizing material so easily pilfered from sermonic literature. There is something in this comment of Dr. Cadman, but the statement is extreme. One would like to believe that a slavish use of other men's sermons is not so general as some surmise, and it can not be otherwise but that the study of volumes of sermons written by able preachers assists young ministers to form an excellent pulpit style and encourages them to strive for lofty ideals of preaching.

When it comes to the content of contemporary preaching it is not nearly so doctrinal, expository and dialectic as the sermonic content of other generations. There has been loss here. There are not now many eminent theologians in the American pulpit. Dr. John A. Hutton, British preacher and editor, holds that no man is really great until he is a theologian. By such a standard, preaching in this country suffers, and few of us are great. But if there has been a loss in this respect there has been a gain in others. The preaching of to-day is not so obviously serious as that of the fathers, yet modern sermons do not lack seriousness, vigorous thinking, nor fail to come to close grips with stern realities. If the evangelistic note is not so trumpet-toned nor heard so often, the ethical and social note is strong and more often sounded. Modern preaching is on the whole more interesting, more entertaining and vivacious, and it is often simpler and more direct than the level of the older preaching.

Preaching to-day lacks somewhat the tremendous appeal of the grand old-time prophets in their address to the will and the conscience. The red-hot thunderbolts they boldly flung against iniquity and wrongdoing are missing. But that note is beginning to be heard again, and the thunder of God reverberates from many a modern pulpit as the preacher indicts powers, principalities, and denounces the deep-rooted evils that disappear in one age only to reappear in the next in another form. Thus, while the base of operations has shifted, it is likewise true that the enemy has shifted his point of attack. Our fathers were not plagued, as are we, by the scourge of an unseemly "jingoism" in a period of international perplexities; nor were their consciences tender on the subject of disarmament and an industrialized society, such as stir deeply the modern prophet. They had their own particular problems, and right royally did they meet the issues of their hour. All honor to them. They were mighty men of valor.

In delivery present-day preaching is mostly restrained, conversational, quiet and rarely declamatory or gymnastic. Abraham Lincoln once said that when he listened to a sermon he wanted the preacher to act like he was fighting bees. Mr. Lincoln would be disappointed in our best preachers, for with very few exceptions they could scarcely qualify as "bee fighters" in the pulpit. Mr. W. A. Sunday, who was so amazingly acrobatic on the platform of his tabernacles, had for a while a company of imitators who did picturesque stunts, such as mounting chairs, pulling off their coats and flinging aside their collars in a frenzy of fervor; but they did not last long, probably because they were palpably ineffective and lacked the red-blooded robustness and tremendous thrust of the famed evangelist.

So thoroughly is this an age of preaching that sermonizing is no longer the sole prerogative of the ordained minister.

Editors of the great dailies and "journals of opinions" preach; free-lance journalists, travelers and explorers preach; the scientists, psychologists and philosophers preach; sometimes the stage and the motion pictures preach; the poets, minor and major, preach; newspaper columnists preach; the cartoonists preach; and over the radio there are lay preachers not only for Sundays but for every day in the week. Such a volume as *If I Could Preach But Once* is a prophecy as to what might happen if thousands of able laymen were accorded the privilege of the conventional pulpit. It is indeed a preaching age.

Our American preaching lacks, of course, the painstaking preparation, close thinking and fine expository quality of the preaching of Great Britain, Scotland and Wales. Our ministry is not primarily scholarly, nor theological as is the case with our British brethren and the gifted ministers in the Scottish churches. But it is livelier, possibly more colorful, and to the masses of worshipers on this side of the Atlantic, more interesting, though it may not be so profound. I venture the observation that we are growing, deepening and greatening in sermonic methods and substance, despite a certain shallowness that sometimes appears in sermons by popular men of whom there was reason to expect something better. Still again, and this is important, the great depression has helped the preaching in this country, inspired a deeper note, evoked a latent power that some of the critics had not believed to be present. It has always been so. Dark and difficult times, periods of acute suffering and distress have produced the noblest preaching.

The richness and versatility of the American pulpit to-day becomes apparent when one attempts a survey of the field. I am of the opinion that the most caustic critic of the contemporary pulpit would wish to temper his criticisms after a "close-up" of the leading ministers of the various American communions, together with a scrutiny of the quality of their pulpit productions, as well as the diverse and varied activities of their pastorates. Who are the best preachers among the thousands of American preachers? I have asked men highly placed in the denominations, and of wide acquaintance with their ministry, to supply me with the names of their leading preachers. In making this request, which included my own communion, I stipulated that their choice be based upon preaching excellence rather than promotional activity, or unusual administrative qualities. The wealth of names that came in upon me was embarrassing, so much so that I was obliged to request that the lists be confined to groups of twenties, tens or fives, according to the numerical strength of the communions represented. To this my helpers acquiesced, much to my relief and gratitude.

In the lists supplied me some compilers saw fit to append to the names their honorary degrees, others omitted titles and degrees. With this explanation I have let the lists stand as submitted. I may further state that the names of the ministers who are subjects of chapters in the pages that follow are deleted from this roll to avoid repetition. Almost without exception the preachers interpreted in this book appear in the lists of names supplied me.

Taking this honor roll in alphabetical order, the Baptists head the grand review of the American legion of preachers. The Baptists have long been noted for their effective preaching. They have brought aggressiveness and forthrightness into their preaching. They have been assertive and strongly evangelistic. Illustrious names among Northern Baptist preachers are: Charles W. Gilkey, Dean of the Chapel, University of Chicago; Albert W. Beaven, President Colgate-Rochester Divinity School, Rochester, N. Y.; Charles Oscar Johnson, Third Baptist Church, St. Louis, Mo.; Harold Cooke Phillips, First Church, Cleveland, Ohio; William S. Abernethy, Calvary Church, Washington, D. C.; J. Whitcomb Brougher, Tremont Temple, Boston, Mass.; John Snape, Temple Church, Los Angeles, Calif.; Joseph M. Tomey, Baptist Temple, Philadelphia, Pa.; Isaac M. Haldeman, First Church, New York City. And among Southern Baptists, these: Carter Helm Jones, First Church, Murfreesboro, Tenn.; L. R. Scarborough, President Southwestern Baptist Theological Seminary, Fort Worth, Texas; C. W. Daniel, First Church, Richmond, Va.; J. M. Dawson, First Church, Waco, Texas; M. E. Dodd, First Church, Shreveport, La.; Henry Alfred Porter, First Church, Charlottesville, Va.; F. F. Brown, First Church, Knoxville, Tenn.; Leonard G. Broughton, evangelist and former pastor; Samuel Judson Porter, First Church, Washington, D. C.; J. E. Dillard, South Side Church, Birmingham, Ala.; Jasper C. Massee, pastor-evangelist, Atlanta, Ga.

Congregationalists from Beecher and Bushnell to Gunsaulus and Gordon have produced a noble company of high class preachers of the Word, and this historic communion is living up to its preaching heritage when it offers such men as: Rev. J. Gordon Gilkey, D.D., South Church, Springfield, Mass.; Rev. Hugh Elmer Brown, D.D., First Church, Evanston, Ill.; Rev. Russell H. Stafford, D.D., Old South Church, Boston, Mass.; Rev. Raymond Calkins, D.D., First Church, Cambridge, Mass.; Rev. Oswald W. S. McCall, D.D., First Church, Berkeley, Calif.; Rev. Albert W. Palmer, D.D., President, Chicago Theological Seminary; Rev. Jay T. Stocking, D.D., Pilgrim Church, St. Louis, Mo.; Rev. Charles H. Myers, D.D., North Church, Detroit, Mich.; Rev. Carl S. Patton, D.D., First Church, Los Angeles, Calif.; Rev. Rockwell Harmon Potter, D.D., Dean of Hartford Theological Seminary, Hartford, Conn.; Rev. Dan F. Bradley, D.D., Pilgrim Church, Cleveland, Ohio; Rev. McIlyar Hamilton Lichliter, D.D., First Church, Columbus, Ohio; Rev. Dwight J. Bradley, D.D., First Church, Newton Centre, Mass.; Rev. Robbins W. Barstow, D.D., President of Hartford Theological Seminary, Hartford, Conn.; Rev. Archibald Black, D.D., First Church, Montclair, N. J.; Rev. Miles H. Krumbine, D.D., Plymouth Church of Shaker Heights, Cleveland, Ohio; Rev. Warren Wheeler Pickett, First Church, Detroit, Mich.

The Christian Church, sometimes known as the Christian connection, now united with the Congregationalist, brought to that merger some strong preachers, such as R. C. Helfenstem, Dover, Del.; W. H. Haines, Irvington, N. J.; Frank G. Coffin, Columbus, Ohio; Warren H. Dennison, Dayton, Ohio; and Leon Edgar Smith, formerly of The Christian Temple, Norfolk, Va.

The Disciples of Christ, or Christian Churches, are comparatively a young body having had but little more than a century of separate existence. Strongly evangelistic and Biblical in their appeal, they have sent out a large number of excellent preachers and an elect company of gifted ministers. Among their pulpit leaders are: Alonzo W. Fortune, Central Church, Lexington, Ky.; Jacob H. Goldner, Euclid Avenue Church, Cleveland, Ohio; Frederick W. Burnham, Richmond, Va.; Cleo M. Chilton, Central Church, St. Joseph, Mo.; H. O. Pritchard, Secretary Educational Board, Indianapolis, Ind.; Pearl H. Welshimer, First Church, Canton, Ohio; Hugh McLellan, First Church, Winchester, Ky.; Roger T. Nooe, Vine Street Church, Nashville, Tenn.; George A. Campbell, Union Avenue Church, St. Louis, Mo.; John Ray Ewers, East End Church, Pittsburgh, Pa.; Geo. W. Knepper, High Street Church, Akron, Ohio; J. J. Castleberry, Walnut Hills Church, Cincinnati, Ohio; W. A. Shullenberger, Central Church, Indianapolis, Ind.; Chester B. Grubb, First Church, Bloomington, Ill.; L. N. D. Wells, East Dallas Church, Dallas, Texas; C. E. Lemmon, First Church, Columbia, Mo.; William F. Rothenburger, Third Church, Indianapolis, Ind.; Finis S. Idleman, Central Church, New York City; J. Warren Hastings, First Church, Savannah, Ga.; Edward S. Ames, Chicago, Ill.; Cleveland Kleihauer, University Church, Seattle, Wash.; George H. Combs, Country Club Church, Kansas City, Mo; Homer W. Carpenter, First Church, Louisville, Ky.; L. D. Anderson, First Church, Fort Worth, Texas; T. Hassell Bowen, First Church, Harrodsburg, Ky.; R. H. Crossfield, First Church, Birmingham, Ala.; Graham Frank, Dallas, Texas; Marvin O. Sansbury, Seattle, Wash; H. L. Willett, Chicago, Ill.

The Friends or Quakers, small numerically, have long

been powerful in influence and social passion. While they have not stressed pulpit gifts they have their full share of forceful preachers. Conspicuous are the following: Rufus M. Jones, Haverford College, Haverford, Pa.; A. Clark Bedford, Richmond, Ind.; David M. Edwards, Indianapolis, Ind.; Augusta T. Murray, Washington, D. C.; Morton C. Pearson, Detroit, Mich.; Francis W. Dell, Whittier, Calif.; Elbert Russell, Duke University, Durham, N. C.; Alexander C. Purdy, Hartford, Conn.; William K. Thomas, Philadelphia, Pa.; Charles M. Woodman, Richmond, Ind.; Willard O. Trueblood, Whittier, Calif.; William O. Mendenhall, Wichita, Kan.

The Jewish pulpit both liberal and orthodox is remarkably strong in eloquent and scholarly rabbis, and never more so than to-day. Witness this formidable list: Dr. Samuel H. Goldenson, Pittsburgh, Pa.; Dr. Abba Hillel Silver, The Temple, Cleveland, Ohio; Dr. Solomon B. Freehof, Chicago, Ill.; Dr. Samuel Schulman, Temple Emanu-El, New York, N. Y.; Dr. Abram Simon, Washington, D. C.; Dr. David Philipson, Rockdale Avenue Temple, Cincinnati, Ohio; Dr. James G. Heller, Wise Center, Cincinnati, Ohio; Rabbi William H. Finescriber, Philadelphia, Pa.; Dr. Louis L. Mann, Temple Sinai, Chicago, Ill.; Rabbi Louis Wolsey, Philadelphia, Pa.; Rabbi Jonah B. Wise, New York, N. Y.; Dr. Leo M. Franklin, Detroit, Mich.

The Roman Catholic Church, while it has not exalted the pulpit above the sacerdotal ministry, has her distinct orders in which preaching is paramount. Among her clergy and prelates who have achieved prominence as preachers of power are: Most Rev. John J. Glennon, Archbishop of St. Louis, Mo.; Most Rev. Joseph J. Shrembs, Bishop of Cleveland, Ohio; Rt. Rev. Msgr. Joseph M. Corrigan, President of Overbrook Seminary, Overbrook, Pa.; Rev. John J. McClorey, S.J., Detroit, Mich.; Rev. James M. Gillis, C.S.P., New York, N. Y.; Rev. Fulton Sheen, Washington, D. C.; Very Rev. J. W. R. Maguire, C.S.V., President of St. Viator College, Bourbonnais, Ill.; Very Rev. Charles L. O'Donnell,

C.S.C., President of Notre Dame University, Notre Dame, Ind.; Very Rev. Henry Ignatius Smith, O.P., Washington, D. C.; Most Rev. Michael J. Curley, D.D., Archbishop of Baltimore; Most Rev. Edward J. Hannah, D.D., Archbishop of San Francisco.

The Lutheran Church in this country has emphasized the pastoral office, yet nevertheless has its quota of competent preachers. Strongly given to doctrinal preaching, the Lutheran ministry includes in its long roll such eminent expounders of the Word as: Rev. Arthur J. Pfohl, D.D., Zion Church, Indiana, Pa.; Rev. Paul E. Scherer, D.D., Church of the Holy Trinity, New York, N. Y.; Rev. Carl C. Rasmussen, D.D., Luther Memorial Church, Washington, D. C.; Rev. Ross Stover, D.D., Messiah Lutheran Church, Philadelphia, Pa.; Rev. F. H. Knubel, D.D., Presbyterian United Lutheran Church, New York, N. Y.; Rev. Oscar F. Blackwelder, D.D., Christ Lutheran Church, Baltimore, Md.; Rev. H. W. A. Hanson, D.D., President Gettysburg College, Gettysburg, Pa.; Rev. R. A. Wentz, Ph.D., Professor Church History, Gettysburg College, Gettysburg, Pa.; Rev. George W. Englar, D.D., Bethany Lutheran Church, Pittsburgh, Pa.; Rev. C. P. Wiles, D.D., Editor, Philadelphia, Pa.; Rev. R. E. Tulloss, D.D., President Wittenburg College, Springfield, Ohio.

From the day of John Wesley to the present hour Methodism has had a galaxy of notable ministers whose pulpit gifts have been unique, and richly varied in intellectual acumen and sermonic style. This church maintains its great traditions with such names as these: Joseph M. M. Gray, Central Church, Detroit, Mich.; Ralph W. Sockman, Madison Avenue Church, New York City; Raymond L. Foreman, St. Paul's Church, New York City; William S. Mitchell, Wesley Church, Worcester, Mass.; Henry H. Crane, Elm Park Church, Scranton, Pa.; Albert E. Day, Mt. Vernon Place Church, Baltimore, Md.; Frederick B. Harris, Foundry Church, Washington, D. C.; Louis C. Wright, Epworth-Euclid Church, Cleveland, Ohio; Loren M. Edwards, Grace

Church, St. Louis, Mo.; J. E. Crowther, Trinity Church, Denver, Colo.; Richard C. Raines, Hennepin Avenue Church, Minneapolis, Minn.; Charles N. Pace, First Church, Duluth, Minn.; Dr. Frederick Spence, Jackson, Mich.; Merle N. Smith, First Church, Pasadena, Calif.; Roy L. Smith, First Church, Los Angeles, Calif.; Edwin H. Hughes, Washington, D. C.; Francis J. McConnell, New York City; and William F. McDowell (retired), Washington, D. C. And the Methodist Church, South, the following: Ivan Lee Holt, St. John's Church, St. Louis, Mo.; Bishop Edmund D. Mouzon, Charlotte, N. C.; Bishop Paul B. Kern, Nashville, Tenn.; Dr. Clovis G. Chappell, Birmingham, Ala.; Dr. Forney Hutchinson, Washington, D. C.; Bishop John M. Moore, Dallas, Texas; Bishop A. Frank Smith, Houston, Texas; Dr. Umphrey Lee, Dallas, Texas; Dr. C. C. Selecman, Dallas, Texas; Dr. George Stoves, Nashville, Tenn.

Presbyterianism, famous for its ministerial scholarship and fine training, has contributed to Christendom a brilliant fellowship of illustrious preachers. Names that shine like bright particular stars in the firmament of the preached Word. Glance through this roster of the Presbyterian Church, United States of America: Rev. J. Ross Stevenson, D.D., President Princeton Theological Seminary, Princeton, N. J.; Rev. John Timothy Stone, D.D., President Theological Seminary, Chicago, Ill.; Rev. Charles F. Wishart, D.D., Wooster, Ohio; Rev. Hugh T. Kerr, D.D., Shadyside Church, Pittsburgh, Pa.; Rev. Harrison Ray Anderson, D.D., Fourth Church, Chicago, Ill.; Robert E. Speer, D.D. (layman preacher), New York City; Rev. Cleland B. McAfee, D.D., Secretary Board Foreign Missions, New York City; Rev. Joseph R. Sizoo, D.D., New York Avenue Church, Washington, D. C.; Rev. William P. Merrill, D.D., Brick Church, New York City; Rev. Roy Ewing Vale, D.D., Woodward Avenue Church, Detroit, Mich.; Rev. Henry Howard, D.D., Fifth Avenue Church, New York City; Rev. William H. Boddy, D.D., Westminster Church, Minneapolis, Minn.; Rev. John M. Vander Meulen, D.D., Theological Seminary,

Louisville, Ky.; Rev. J. Harry Cotton, D.D., Broad Street Church, Columbus, Ohio; Rev. Herbert Booth Smith, D.D., Immanuel Church, Los Angeles, Calif.; Rev. Alvin E. Magary, D.D., Lafayette Avenue Church, Brooklyn, N. Y.; Rev. Stuart Nye Hutchinson, D.D., East Liberty Church, Pittsburgh, Pa.; Rev. John McDowell, D.D., Secretary Board National Missions, New York City; Rev. William Hiram Foulkes, D.D., First Church, Newark, N. J. And of the Southern Presbyterian preachers here are ten exceptionally gifted in the sermonic art: Rev. Samuel M. Glasgow, D.D., Savannah, Ga.; Rev. Teunis E. Gouwens, D.D., Louisville, Ky.; Rev. William Crowe, D.D., St. Louis, Mo.; Rev. J. Sprole Lyons, D.D., Atlanta, Ga.; Rev. Harris E. Kirk, LL.D., Baltimore, Md.; Rev. Dunbar H. Ogden, D.D., New Orleans, La.; Rev. Thos. K. Young, D.D., Memphis, Tenn.; Rev. Henry Wade Dubose, D.D., Spartanburg, S. C.; Rev. E. G. Gammon, D.D., Charlotte, N. C.; Rev. Hay Watson Smith, D.D., Little Rock, Ark.

The Protestant Episcopal Church, laying as it does much emphasis on the priestly function of the ministry, has its mighty prophets likewise, not perhaps quite in proportion to its numbers and prestige, but the communion that gave to America a Phillips Brooks continues to give to the nation illustrious interpreters of the everlasting Gospel. Here, indeed, are twelve preachers of eminence and assured position: Arthur L. Kinsolving, Holy Trinity Church, Boston, Mass.; W. Russell Bowie, Grace Church, New York City; George Craig Stewart, Bishop of Chicago, Evanston, Ill.; William Scarlett, Bishop of Missouri, St. Louis, Mo.; Edward L. Parsons, Bishop of California, San Francisco, Calif.; Samuel S. Marquis, Christ Church, Cranbrook, Bloomfield Hills, Mich.; Howard C. Robbins, General Theological Seminary, New York City; Samuel Shoemaker, Calvary Church, New York City; Karl Reiland, St. George's Church, New York City; Beverley D. Tucker, Jr., St. Paul's Church, Richmond, Va.; Frank Nelson, Christ Church, Cincinnati, Ohio; Lyman P. Powell, St. Margaret's Church, the Bronx, New York City.

The liberal pulpit is ably represented by the Unitarians and Universalists. Never large in numbers, the quality of the leaders is freely acknowledged by their brethren of the larger group. The Unitarian roll of honor is most interesting: Rev. Preston Bradley, People's Church, Chicago, Ill.; Rev. John Dietrich, First Society, Minneapolis, Minn.; Rev. George Rowland Dodson, D.D., Church of the Unity, St. Louis, Mo.; Rev. Frederick M. Eliot, Unity Church, St. Paul, Minn.; Rev. Samuel A. Eliot, D.D., Arlington Street Church, Boston, Mass.; Rev. Dilworth Lupton, First Church, Cleveland, Ohio; Rev. Charles Edwards Park, D.D., First Church, Boston, Mass.; Rev. William L. Sullivan, D.D., Germantown Society, Philadelphia, Pa.; Dr. Augustus P. Reccord, First Church, Detroit, Mich. Come now the Universalist preachers: Frederic W. Perkins, D.D., National Memorial Church, Washington, D. C.; William Wallace Rose, D.D., Los Angeles, Calif.; L. Griswold Williams, Barre, Vermont; Effie McCollum Jones, D.D., Webster City, Iowa; Roger F. Etz, D.D., General Superintendent, Universalist Churches, Boston, Mass.; Frank D. Adams, D.D., Oak Park, Ill.

The Church of the United Brethren in Christ is an aggressive body and growing. No roll would be complete of the preachers of this denomination that did not contain the names of: Bishop H. H. Fout, D.D., Indianapolis, Ind.; W. H. Todd, D.D., Terre Haute, Ind.; E. H. Dailey, D.D., Indianapolis, Ind.; Fred L. Dennis, D.D., Dayton, Ohio; S. B. Daugherty, D.D., Washington, D. C.; F. Berry Plummer, D.D., Hagerstown, Maryland; D. T. Gregory, Dayton, Ohio.

The Reformed Church in America lists these able proclaimers of the Gospel: Dr. Malcolm J. MacLeod, Collegiate Church of St. Nicholas, New York City; Dr. William I. Chamberlain, Secretary Board of Foreign Missions of the Reformed Church in America, New York City; Rev. Dr. Edgar F. Romig, West End Collegiate Church, New York City; Rev. Dr. W. H. S. Demarest, President New Brunswick Theological Seminary, New Brunswick, N. J.; Dr. John Van Ess, Basrah, Iraq (missionary of the Reformed Church); Rev. John W. Powell, Reformed Church of Bronxville, N. Y.; Rev. Dr. Norman Vincent Peale, Marble Collegiate Church, New York City; Rev. H. D. McKeehan, The Abbey Church, Huntingdon, Pa.; Rev. Daniel A. Poling, editor and reformer, Boston, Mass.

It is not easy to secure the names of the truly remarkable preachers who flourish among the Negro churches of America, but the four that follow are preeminent among their race in the Methodist and Baptist communions: Charles A. Tindley, Methodist, Philadelphia, Pa.; Mordecai Johnson, Baptist, President Howard University, Washington, D. C.; Clayton A. Powell, Baptist, New York City; L. K. Williams, Olivet Baptist Church, Chicago, Ill.; and John Knox, minister Fisk University, Nashville, Tenn. Among the Disciples of Christ, H. L. Herod, of Indianapolis, Ind., takes high rank.

Undoubtedly there are omissions in these lists—names of favorites that will occur to many a reader. But the good men who made the selections were limited in the number they might choose and have done the best they could in the circumstances. The lists are suggestive rather than inclusive. It is not likely that there would be entire agreement by a hundred typical churchmen of any communion as to their ten or twenty ablest preachers. Whoever assays to prepare such a list has his own preferences and must also consider the general opinion of his brotherhood. Putting these together enables him to prepare a fairly accurate roll, and that I think has been done.

The same difficulty was encountered in the chapters that follow where thirty-two American preachers appear in full-length portraits. Omissions of able men in each of the denominations represented will be noted but it would take a volume many times this size to include half the preachers who deserve a place in such a work. No one knows better than myself the inadequacy of the book in this respect as well as others. It was with extreme reluctance that I had to leave out of the picture many whom it would have afforded me pleasure and satisfaction to include. Nevertheless I am pretty firm in the conviction that two-thirds of the preachers portrayed in these pages would be selected by almost any one fairly well acquainted with the contemporary pulpit of America.

Practically every theological view is represented between the covers of this book. The extreme Fundamentalist and the extreme Liberal, the moderate or mediating school, the social prophet and the expounder of the great Christian doctrines, the dogmatist and the mystic, the teacher and the poet preacher—they are all here. The youngest preacher of the group is just turned forty, the oldest seventy-one. The average age of the group is about fifty-four. Thus the men are for the most part in the ripe maturity of the active ministry, holding responsible positions and in the flood-tide of their intellectual and spiritual power.

It has been a pleasure to prepare this work. The writing of it has afforded me many a fascinating hour and associations that have enriched me beyond my power to express. That those who read the pages that follow shall derive as much pleasure and profit as have I in writing them is my fond hope and fervent desire. Companying in the spirit with these prophets of our day, I have been made to feel the truth of Mrs. Browning's lines:

> "It takes a soul,
> To move a body; it takes a high-souled man,
> To move the masses, even to a cleaner stye;
> It takes the ideal, to blow a hair's-breadth off
> The dust of the actual."

FOSDICK, Harry Emerson, clergyman; *b.* Buffalo, N. Y., May 24, 1878; *s.* Frank S. and Amy I. (Weaver) F.; A.B., Colgate U., 1900, D.D., 1914; B.D., Union Theol. Sem., 1904; A.M., Columbia, 1908; D.D., New York, 1919, Brown, 1920, Yale, 1923, Glasgow (Scotland) U., 1924, Princeton, 1927, Union Coll., 1927, Boston U., 1929; LL.D., U. of Mich., 1923, U. of Rochester, 1925; S.T.D., Ohio U., 1925; *m.* Florence Allen Whitney, of Worcester, Mass., Aug. 16, 1904; children—Elinor Whitney, Dorothy. Ordained Bapt. ministry, 1903; pastor 1st. Ch., Montclair, N.J., 1904-15; instr. homiletics, 1908-15, prof. practical theology since 1915, Union Theol. Sem.; pastor Riverside Ch., New York. Trustee Colgate Univ., Smith College, Barnard College. Mem. Delta Upsilon, Phi Beta Kappa, Sons of the American Revolution. *Club:* Century. *Author:* The Second Mile, 1908; The Manhood of the Master, 1913; The Assurance of Immortality, 1913; The Meaning of Prayer, 1915; The Challenge of the Present Crisis, 1917; The Meaning of Faith, 1917; The Meaning of Service, 1920; Christianity and Progress, 1922; Twelve Tests of Character, 1923; The Modern Use of the Bible, 1924; Adventurous Religion, 1926; Spiritual Values and Eternal Life, 1927; A Pilgrimage to Palestine, 1927. *Home:* 606 W. 22nd St., *Address:* 490 Riverside Drive, New York, N. Y.

Chapter II

HARRY EMERSON FOSDICK

The most preeminent pulpit of the Christian faith in America, if not the world, is that of Dr. Harry Emerson Fosdick in Riverside Church, New York City. Given a ten-million-dollar cathedral, complete to the smallest detail, occupying a commanding site on a magnificent boulevard, a dynamic personality, possessing homiletic genius of a high order, safeguarded and empowered for the most efficient use of his preaching talent—and the possibilities stagger the imagination. Given another factor, the backing of a multi-millionaire, John D. Rockefeller, Jr., by name, and no strings or conditions attached, but on the other hand the full liberty of prophesying—given these, and you have the most extraordinary preaching opportunity of modern times.

Millions knew Dr. Fosdick through his books before the world knew him through his pulpit achievements. Those little volumes, *The Meaning of Prayer, The Meaning of Faith, The Meaning of Service, The Manhood of the Master* and *The Challenge of the Present Crisis,* had a ministry all their own, vital and inspiring. The writing of these books was something more than the preparation of manuscripts—a great man was in training for a mighty service. Baptist though he is, and of course an independent, Fosdick became the minister of First Presbyterian Church, New York City, whereupon his pulpit fame grew apace. His sermon entitled "Shall the Fundamentalists Win?" produced the livest kind of controversy. The newspapers gave the subject much space and played it up to the fullest. The denominational journals turned a barrage of criticism on the preacher, all of which but contributed to Dr. Fosdick's reputation and provided a sounding board that made his every utterance the more distinct and sent his name the world around.

As a preacher, Dr. Fosdick combines realism with idealism. His pulpit material is modern, and he has the courage to use accepted facts in Biblical criticism, sociology and economics. His power of clear statement is probably unexcelled in the American pulpit to-day. He can take a theme, say an appraisal of modern Protestantism, and in a series of pungent paragraphs bare to the bone every weakness, uncover and expose every blemish of organized Christianity, so that when he finishes there seems nothing left worth preserving. As you listen, you become alarmed, apprehensive, indignant. You say to yourself, "This man has gone too far; he has given his case away." You are humiliated and chagrined, when lo! Fosdick begins an assessment of the world's debt to Protestantism and what remains that is of priceless value, and marshals brilliantly the reasons for conserving the same. He becomes constructive; the man speaks with the fire of the crusader. Your heart beats faster, your cheeks are warm, something stirs within you in response to the preacher, and you feel that a real discipleship of Jesus Christ in these modern days is the mightiest challenge and the grandest thing in the world.

Listening to Dr. Fosdick, you do not think of the orator or the rhetorician. Yet his sermons are powerful and the result of painstaking toil. He does not go in for polish and literary beauty as does Joseph Fort Newton or Frederick F. Shannon. He does not range over so wide a field as Cadman, nor has he the charm of conversational eloquence of a Jefferson. He has not the serenity of a Gaius Glenn Atkins, nor the epigrammatical fire of Lynn Harold Hough. He is an able speaker who makes few gestures, talks right on and always to the point; comes to close grips with life; uses effectively illustrations taken not from books solely but from the daily experiences of men and women as they meet pain, disappointment and temptation. He is never "detached" or "remote" in his preaching. It is difficult to think of Fosdick as ever vague or "mystical." No hangovers of theology trouble him, no traditions weigh him down. He is a free man in a free pulpit. Physically, there is nothing extraordinary about him, yet he is an arresting personality. His hair, once so abundant, is beginning to thin a little, but still stands up like a mop. Dr. Fosdick exudes vitality. Much worn as the word is, "dynamic" best describes the man and his preaching.

How did Dr. Fosdick become the great preacher he is? By the hardest kind of work, unceasing, laborious toil, painstaking industry. For thirty years, approximately, since the days of his first pastorate in Montclair, New Jersey, he has spent the mornings of five days a week in his study. No messages get to him there, no telephone calls can reach him, no visitors are admitted. In such seclusion, he "toils terribly" over his sermons. This long practise, self-discipline, persistent, purposeful life program, is the answer to the question, how did Fosdick become the great preacher he is?

Does he do any pastoral work? Practically none; in fact, he regards social visitation as a waste of precious time. But he responds to urgent requests from ill and ailing parishioners who ask to see him personally. He writes numerous notes of commendation for services rendered, remembers to do the courteous deed in person, where no one could represent him or serve by proxy. Yet he is jealous of his time, duplicates no service, makes no unnecessary motion, is as finely disciplined as the head of a mammoth bank or industry, but keeps human, simple, patient, long-suffering.

Outside demands would crush this preacher if he permitted a tithe of them to sap his time and vitality. He goes from his pulpit only four times during the active preaching year, and then to speak at various colleges in the country, where he feels there is a special reason for his appearance. Yet Dr. Fosdick is not a scholarly recluse. He is accessible to those who have need to see him. The chinks of his busy afternoons are filled by carefully scheduled appointments, made at fifteen-minute intervals. Many of his evenings are spent with the organizational life of his church. Here he keeps in close and vital touch with the body of his congregation, assisted of course by an efficient and personable staff of expert associates, secretaries and staff visitors. He takes long and restful vacations, which are, however, devoted to reading, study and writing.

The budget of the Riverside Church is a wonder, both in its planning and carrying out, is indeed worthy of the most carefully directed business concern in the country. Here is an institution that balances its budget even in hard times. True, owing to the depression, the budget of Riverside Church for May 1, 1932, to April 30, 1933, was decreased one hundred thousand dollars, but nevertheless it totals three hundred twenty-two thousand dollars. Nor is this all: this budget is balanced to a penny between current expenses and benevolences and missions; thus one hundred sixty-one thousand dollars for self, and one hundred sixty-one thousand dollars for others—the ideal that thousands of churches everywhere have dreamed about but few attained. Dr. Fosdick preaches an annual budget sermon which in its own way is as pungent and masterful as any of his famous discourses that are heard by throngs and widely circulated through various publications.

I asked the Rev. Eugene C. Carder, Dr. Fosdick's able associate, to give me a "close-up" of the minister of Riverside Church. He told me that it was a joy for him to stress his admiration for Dr. Fosdick, as minister, first, last and all the time, assuring me that he never deviates from the main track, which is preaching. The heart of what Dr. Carder said in praise and interpretation of Dr. Fosdick is compressed in this most revealing paragraph:

> "The more I see of this man, the more convinced I am that he is essentially a conservative. He does not now nor never has owned an automobile. That is not due primarily to the fact that he lives in New York where taxicabs are to be had on every corner. Few

New Yorkers have resisted the temptation to join the great majority and buy a car some time or other. He just is not susceptible to the influence of the crowd. A circumstance connected with the furnishing of his study and its present equipment amuses me every time I go in there to talk with him. I was chairman of the committee that furnished the building here and had a hand in selecting all of the furnishings, furniture, lamps, etc., in his study. In due course the desk was set in place and the equipment put on it, bookcases arranged, table, and what-not. He has been working in that study for two years now and in so far as I can see there hasn't been a thing moved an inch from the place where it was put when we first set the room up. He simply moved in on top of the furniture we had placed there and went to work. Mr. Gandhi achieves his reputation for not being dependent upon things by divesting himself of all things, even his clothes. Dr. Fosdick achieves an even more significant independence of things by sitting down in the midst of all kinds of things, of everything he could possibly want, and proving himself to be absolutely independent of them by altogether ignoring them and doing his work, doing his work not because of them, but in spite of them. From this point of view, he is the most independent spirit I have ever known. I confess he is a great challenge to me at this particular point."

I put the inevitable question to Dr. Fosdick, "How do you prepare your sermons?" He answered with pithy brevity.

"I choose a subject early in the week, work on it hard, think about it all I can, write it out in full, draw off an outline of it for Sunday morning, and do as well as I can, talking from the outline."

Asked his opinion of present-day preaching, Dr. Fosdick placed in my hands a reprint of his article from *Harper's*

Magazine of July, 1928—"What is the Matter with Preaching?"—saying, "This will give you my idea about sermons, what they are for, and how to get at them." This pamphlet is solid stuff, made luminous by the use of short staccato sentences, direct and unconventional statements; the whole atmosphered with a buoyant enthusiasm for the preacher's task. Reading and reflecting on this treatise, for such it is, I speculated on the great good that might be accomplished if a copy could be put in the hands of every young man in America who is thinking of the ministry as a career. Two paragraphs, only, do I quote, but they are sufficient to indicate the style and the passion of the author, and something of the tang he has imparted to type.

> "Throughout this paper we have held up the ideal of preaching as an interesting operation. That is a most important matter, not only to the audience, but to the man in the pulpit. The number of fed-up, fatigued, bored preachers is appalling. Preaching has become to them a chore. They have to 'get up' a sermon, perhaps two sermons, weekly. They struggle at it. The juice goes out of them as the years pass. They return repeatedly to old subjects and try to whip up enthusiasm over weather-beaten texts and themes. Their discourses sink into formality. They build conventional sermon outlines, fill them in with conventional thoughts, and let it go at that. Where is the zest and thrill with which in their chivalrous youth they started out to be ministers of Christ to the spiritual life of their generation?
>
> "Of course, nothing can make preaching easy. At best it means drenching a congregation with one's life-blood. But while, like all high work, it involves severe concentration, toil, and self-expenditure, it can be so exhilarating as to recreate in the preacher the strength it takes from him, as good agriculture replaces the soil it uses. Whenever that phenomenon happens one is sure to find a man predominantly interested in per-

sonalities, and what goes on inside of them. He has understood people, their problems, troubles, motives, failures, and desires, and in his sermons he has known how to handle their lives so vitally that week after week he has produced real changes. People have habitually come up after the sermon, not to offer some bland compliment, but to say, 'How did you know I was facing that problem only this week?', or 'We were discussing that very matter at dinner last night,' or, best of all, 'I think you would understand my case—may I have a personal interview with you?'"

Somebody has said that Dr. Cadman is preaching to people over sixty, Fosdick to those over forty, and Niebuhr to those in their middle twenties. A statement of this kind needs to be qualified, and yet there is something in it. If Fosdick's appeal is to middle life instead of flaming youth, then I should say that those in mid-channel who continue to hear or read Fosdick will find it difficult to think complacently the thoughts they used to think, and are due for a rebirth at a period when most people are in a mental groove. I incline to the belief, however, that Fosdick, as was Beecher, is able to preach to all ages with almost equal power.

Has Dr. Fosdick no critics? What a foolish question. Anybody who ever does anything, and does it especially well, is a fair target. The very fact that he has achieved unusual prominence, and in his own field preeminence, would guarantee a crop of critics. But quite apart from the captious and the chronic critic there are of course the extremely conservative churchmen who look upon the minister of Riverside Church not as a rebel-saint but just a rebel. There are a few also among the radicals in the ministry who are disposed to chide Dr. Fosdick for not being radical enough. Some who read this will recall a rather caustic article in the *Christian Century* by the venturesome Reinhold Niebuhr, entitled, "How Adventurous Is Dr. Fosdick?"—a play of course upon the latter's book, *Adventurous Christianity.*

Another case at point is Mr. Douglas Bush's leading article in *The Bookman* for March, 1932, which refers to "Well meaning liberals like Dr. Fosdick present a faith so stripped of dogmatic encumbrance that they may be thought to have thrown out the baby with the bath water." Such criticisms are inevitable and do not matter. In truth they may render one valuable aid. Was it not Donatello who claimed that his art suffered when he worked in an atmosphere of constant praise?

It should be said to the credit of Northern Baptists that, while many of the conservatives among them fear and criticize Dr. Fosdick's liberalism, they do not rule him out of their list of great convention speakers. He appears occasionally on their national programs, and is accorded the fullest liberty of utterance. Salvos of applause greet his presentation and resound throughout the hall when he concludes his address. Many of his Baptist brethren, quite apart from doctrinal interpretations, seem to take a pride in this internationally famed preacher nurtured in their denomination, and who is a daring exponent of "soul liberty," a basic Baptist principle. Here indeed is a modern prophet not without honor among his own people, despite wide differences of theological opinion, culture and outlook. One could wish that all Christian communions were as wise and fraternal as to give a hearing on their platforms to able men quite regardless of their liberalism or conservatism. Until that time comes there is something farcical in talk of Christian unity, and sardonic in the passing of resolutions looking to the reunion of the divided house of God.

One of my preacher friends, who is also an intimate friend of Fosdick, confided to me that he never fails to pray each day for Harry Emerson Fosdick—prays for his success, his health, his ever-widening fame! Said this friend, "Modernism has its stake in Fosdick. If he should fall, Modernism would fall. If he keeps going, rising in power and influence, Modernism will rise with him and prosper even as he prospers. Therefore I pray daily for Harry Fosdick. He must not fail." Very fine, but I refuse to believe that any cause worthy of living depends upon any man, however potent his ministry, or necessary he may seem in the progress of emancipatory movements. Yet I can understand and appreciate this friend's concern and greatly admire his prayerful support of one of our day's most prophetic souls. Such support, I doubt not, means more to Dr. Fosdick than the pristine splendor of the cathedral in which he preaches and the terrible money power that encompasses him about.

RICE, Merton Stacher, clergyman; *b.* Ottawa, Kan., Sept. 5, 1872; *s.* Rev. Cyrus R. and Lucy A. (McCormick) R.; B.S., Baker U., Kan., 1893, M.S., 1896, LL.D., 1920; student law dept. U. of Mich., 1893-94; D.D., Upper Ia. U., 1901; D.Litt., Albion (Mich.) Coll., 1926; *m.* Laura Buckner of Baldwin, Kan., Apr. 3, 1895. Ordained M. E. ministry, 1894; pastor Westphalia, Kan., 1894-95, Fontana, 1895-96, Ottawa, 1896-99, West Union, Ia., 1899-1903, Iowa City, 1903-04, Duluth, Minn., 1904-13, Metropolitan Church, Detroit, Mich., Oct. 1913-. In Europe six months 1917-18, as spl. representative of Internat. Y.M.C.A. among soldiers. Del. Gen. Conf. M. E. Ch. five times. Mason (K.T.). *Author:* Dust and Destiny; The Expected Church; Preachographs; The Advantage of a Handicap; To Know Him; William Alfred Quayle; A Discontented Optimist. *Home:* 59, Alger Av., Detroit, Mich.

Chapter III

MERTON S. RICE

Dr. M. S. Rice has twice refused election as a bishop in the great Methodist Episcopal Church. This is not surprising considering his remarkable career in Detroit and his unique place in the life of that dynamic city. He has been a resident of the Fourth City for twenty years, during which time he has built up one of the most commanding churches in all Methodism, with a membership of about six thousand and an average Sunday-morning attendance of two thousand. The Metropolitan Methodist Church, of which he is pastor, occupies a strategic corner on Woodward Avenue, and was erected at a cost of one million five hundred thousand dollars. It is an enormous structure, with a seating capacity of three thousand and myriad rooms for classes, societies and the various organizations that make up a modern seven-days-in-the-week church.

Every spring, for a decade or more, Dr. Rice has preached for two weeks in a down-town theater at noon, and despite the fact that the Detroit Council of Churches brings the most eminent preachers in America in the Lenten series, Dr. Rice draws the largest audiences. "Mert" Rice, as William L. Stidger calls him, is burly of build, something of the type physically of Frank W. Gunsaulus or Charles H. Spurgeon. He pays little attention to his clothes, just about as little as his great and famous friend, William A. Quayle, whose biographer Dr. Rice is. He still clings to the Prince Albert for pulpit wear, lets his coat stay unbuttoned most of the time, puts his hands in his pockets, follows his own sweet will in mannerisms that are distinctly masculine. Rice loves a western type of broad-brimmed felt hat that suggests Kansas or Texas. He is decidedly midwestern, and Vachel Lindsay held that nowadays the Midwest is the typical American section of this republic.

The first time I heard Dr. Rice speak I was disappointed. He seemed "logy" and not at all equal to his great reputation. Just the same, he interested me by his mannerisms and I liked his frank open face, and the "cut of his jib." The next time I heard him he was in better form and I said to myself, "This is more like it." The third time I listened to him preach he made me laugh till my sides ached and then had me crying, much against my wishes. Before the sermon was over, he captured me completely and carried me up on a high mountain of irresistible eloquence and left me on some high peak where I sat gazing through misty eyes upon the Promised Land. Rice's type of preaching is his own. Sometimes he sticks pretty close to manuscript, often he ventures forth without so much as a scrap of paper or a single note. His voice is strong though scarcely remarkable, his enunciation at times is muffled, and unless you follow him closely you will lose a word every now and then. All the same, he is powerful, and a born preacher. He is the most anecdotal of famed preachers of this generation to whom I have listened. He is a master in the use of stories. He picks them up everywhere, some from books, others his experiences. Most of them are humorous, all of them told with consummate skill and vast effect.

Dr. Rice is Rooseveltian in more ways than one. He likes to hunt. He loves to be with men. He gets excitement out of a ride on a motor-boat with the famous Gar Wood at the wheel. One of his hobbies is snakes. He picks up rattlesnakes with a strange disregard for their fangs, as is eloquently indicated by the little finger on his right hand, which is crooked, almost bent double, the result of a rattler's fangs. Once when Dr. Rice and I were talking snakes, the subject was the hog-nosed snake, sometimes called "spreadhead viper" or "hissing adder," depending on the locality. This snake, commonly believed to be venomous, is quite harmless but the ugliest and most vicious-looking reptile we have in this country. Said Dr. Rice, "You know what I do when I come across spread-heads? I pick 'em up and stick my finger down their throats." That's M.S. for you—odd, humorous, masculine, eccentric. Out-of-doors or indoors this preacher is never dull or uninteresting, though he varies in pulpit power according to his moods.

Here is a preacher who disregards nearly all the rules of public speaking. His sermonic sins of commission and omission are numerous; yet he succeeds nevertheless in achieving results both dazzling and solidly rewarding. When he is in the full tide of his rugged eloquence, many of his sentences would be difficult to parse. He speaks pretty much as Thomas Carlyle writes in his *French Revolution*. A minister who used to reside in Duluth, Minnesota, Dr. Rice's former field, is my authority for this story. Rice, he said, was preaching on a Sunday night to a large audience. He was going good and strong. Suddenly he lifted his arm on high, clenched his fist, and bent his arm as if to strike a body blow, a favorite gesture, and exclaimed:

"I tell you, men, there's a tidal wave of sin stalking across the country burning everything in its wake."

Musing on this delectable sentence it is profitable to remember that Henry Ward Beecher once remarked that when a little thing like the English language got in his way something was bound to happen to it.

Sampling Dr. Rice's preaching through his published sermons is not altogether fair to him or satisfactory to the sampler. His sermons do not read as well as those of Joseph Fort Newton or Frederick F. Shannon, for instance; yet they reveal something of his originality, force and ingenuity of illustration. I have been examining his *Diagnosing Today,* Dr. Rice's fifth book of sermons, and find it stimulating. The author takes the Seven Deadly Sins of modern life as summarized by Canon Frederick Lewis Donaldson of Westminster Abbey and makes a sermon out of each. Preaching on "Worship without Sacrifice," Dr. Rice embodies in the heart of the sermon a characteristic anecdote:

"A story which I told in an Eastern city some time ago was picked up by a reporter for the Associated Press, and came back to me from many cities. It wore for an inelegant head-line in one of the New York papers this rather startling title, the truth of which I will not vouch for, 'No Deadbeats in Doctor Rice's Church.' The story was of an incident that happened in our city during the calling days when we were engaged in building a new and somewhat costly church. The money that was available was the money brought forward by those who belonged to the church. We had no claim upon any one else. In one of the offices of the city was a man who was a persistent worker for personal decision in the religious question, too persistent for the comfort of some of his near-by workers. One of them, wearying one day of the constant solicitation, was rather abrupt in his refusal, and coupled with the refusal a request not to be bothered any more about it. The conscientious, but not very tactful, brother, distressed over his failure, was greatly surprised and interested when some days later the one he had seemingly insulted came in saying boldly, 'Well I have decided to give my heart to God and join the church.' The earnest worker, expecting of course to be soon reporting him as a new recruit for his own church, asked in a rather patronizing way.

"'What church are you going to join?'

"He was again disturbed by the quick reply, 'I am going to join this church where Dr. Rice preaches.'

"In a convinced argumentative protest he was answered: 'I wouldn't join that church. If you do, they will soak you.'

"The challenge startled the young recruit, but it struck him where a real religious impulse never flinches, and he replied, 'I never thought of that. I will go and ask Rice.'

"He came directly to my study and told me the story.

When he had finished—and I had listened with very great interest—I replied to him just as flatly as I could find hard words with which to speak:

"'Yes, sir, he is right! If you join this church, we will soak you. If you do not want to be soaked, don't join this church. And may God have mercy on the cheap gate you seek to enter.'

"He looked straight into my eyes and said, 'Give me a card for admission.'

"He joined the church on the challenge of its cost. Of course, he did. He would have slunk in disgust from the door of a church that would wear the name of Christ and try to wear it cheaply."

"Mert" Rice is the "folksy" kind. As he travels up and down the land he engages all sorts of people in conversation, Pullman porters, taxicab drivers, newsboys, policemen, waiters, check-stand operators. He gets a lot of sermonic material this way, although that, I should say, is a by-product. The minister of Metropolitan Methodist Church talks to people because he loves them. He is always bubbling over with good humor, has time to swap stories, and make solicitous inquiries about the wives and babies. A book could be written of Dr. Rice's adventures of which this one is a fair specimen:

The doctor was returning from a lecture tour; as he left the railway station a man of seedy appearance accosted him, asked for enough money to buy a cup of coffee and a sandwich. "Sure," said Dr. Rice, "come right along with me. I haven't had breakfast. Let's eat together." The seedy one agreed. They went into a near-by eating-place, consumed the kind of breakfast that most men love, a stack of wheat cakes and plenty of sirup, ham and eggs, and a couple of cups of coffee apiece. When the time came to pay the bill, Dr. Rice discovered that he had given his last quarter to the Pullman porter. He was about to introduce himself to the cashier and make some sort of arrangement when his guest said, "Look here. You needn't do that. I'll pay the bill." Dr. Rice, a little surprised, thanked him, the bill was paid, and again they were out on the street. "Now," said the minister, "I am going to hail a taxi. You get in with me, ride up to my church and I'll pay you what I owe you." The stranger looked Rice over coldly, and exploded, "See here, mister, you caught me once; you got a breakfast on me, but you won't get a free ride off of me." Then he turned on his heel and walked away in a huff. Rice shakes with laughter every time he tells this story.

In front of Dr. Rice's church there stands a life-size statue in bronze which attracts the passer-by. It is the tense figure of a man about whose leg a venomous serpent is entwined. The man has grasped the reptile around the neck and is winning the terrible struggle. The serpent is in the throes of death. The man's face is upturned and his expression is one of triumph over disaster. On the base of the statue in front is the inscription from Psalms 42:5, "I shall yet praise him," and on the side these words, "Impression from a sermon by M. S. Rice."

This statue has a story. During a Lenten week, Dr. Rice was preaching in a down-town theater from the text quoted above. In the course of the sermon he alluded to the famous painting by George Frederick Watts in which Hope is depicted as a woman blindfolded, head bowed, clasping a harp with the strings broken, a picture the preacher declared that might better represent Despair. Then he gave his own idea of Hope—a man struggling courageously with a venomous serpent, which had entwined itself about his leg, his face turned upward with a great light upon it—the light of victory. The passage was of dramatic power, and greatly impressed a sculptor who happened to drop in to the theater service that day, a man by the way who had not attended a church service for years. After the sermon the sculptor introduced himself to Dr. Rice and asked the privilege of fashioning just such a statue as had been described. Dr. Rice was greatly pleased. The statue was made, set up in front of the church and dedicated with appropriate ceremonies.

At Metropolitan Church Dr. Rice is the preacher, and Dr. C. B. Allen, the pastor. They make an unusual team, supplementing each the other. Dr. Allen is a financial genius, which helps to account for the fact that this costly and magnificent building was dedicated free of debt. He is also the shepherd of the flock, making myriad calls, performing hundreds of marriages annually, conducting funeral services almost every other day in the week, barring Sunday. There is a staff of secretaries, deaconesses, superintendents of departments. The School of Religion which this church carries on every winter averages more than a thousand in attendance. The best modern movies are shown on Friday nights, and the latest talking device has been installed. In fine, here is a church vibrant with activity, permeated with enthusiasm, freighted with missionary and evangelistic ardor.

Talking shop with M. S. Rice is to inspire his most serious mood. He is a rollicking sort of person usually. He laughs with abandon and relishes a witty tale. It is easy to understand why they call him "Mike" at the Rotary Club. But talk with him about preaching and he becomes serious and dead in earnest. "My friend," I queried, "some of us would like to know how you prepare your sermons? You are on the go so much of the time, how do you do it?"

Rice: "I must be honest enough to say, I do not know. I am scared every week of my life that whatever the method it will not work, and I have abandoned all plans. I have one custom however which I can recommend, having used it for enough years to satisfy myself of its wisdom. Whatever the method I struggle with any particular week, I always start the preparation of my sermons for the coming Sabbath on Monday morning, if I have not already got them pretty well shaped out. Very, very few of my all too poor sermons are the creation of any week. I keep a good many ideas pounding through my head and soul, but on Monday of each week I insist upon settling definitely what I am to preach about the following Sunday. I study carefully to pick up my illustrations from the well-known every-day occurrences about me, and for ever find in the commonest news columns the emphasis of the fact I am trying religiously to interpret."

Jones: "What is the preaching that will win in such times as these?"

Rice: "I, of course, must not be made to seem to sit in judgment upon any of my brethren, vast numbers of whom could easily tell me how and what to do. I am however personally convinced of the need of intense religious preaching, preaching of convictions we hold religiously. The pulpit never was a place for mere argument. It is the place for the declaration of conclusions. I leave the vast amount of my theology in my study. I do not suppose that I have any vast amount of theology, but I am little concerned to pour controversial things upon my people. I use my beliefs in theology as a means to arrive at the convictions I hold, and those are preachable. I never find salesmen eloquently discoursing upon the machinery in the factories from which their wares come. I do find them displaying and describing the product in their most convincing terms. I do not believe I have ever faced audiences as hungry for genuine religious preaching as the audiences of this day. Many foundations have been shaken. The great truths of the Christian faith never were more solid."

Jones: "What would you say is the most unsettling thing in the preacher's life to-day?"

Rice: "Again I answer, please do not make me seem to be judging my brethren. I fear the loss of the passion of our great task is the greatest liability. Passion, passion, to lose that, is to lose all. I go every time I can where I can catch the glow of the young beginning preachers because of that blazing fact so constantly evident among them. You will find me, every time I can get there, at the ordination of young men. I seek to get as close to them as I can that I may keep in my soul the new glow of their passion. I can not allow it to die out of my ministry. I believe I can say that I am increasingly Christian. The whole issue centers in Christ. It is Christ everywhere or nowhere in my way of thinking. There is no alternative for Christianity between universal dominion and universal collapse. While the passion of that fact burns in my soul I feel secure in the task it imposes upon me, to burn out my life absolutely to the socket for the Cause."

These are brave words and I wish every young preacher in the land could have heard them as they fell from the lips of this big, boyish, buoyant soul. There is nothing formal or ecclesiastic about this preacher of the Christian Gospel. His sincerity is not merely on the surface; though it is there, it is also the deepest thing in Dr. Rice's life. I never saw him gloomy, sour or crabby. He must have his difficulties, doubts, soul battles, but when he appears in public, whether before a vast audience or in the circle of his friends, he appears as one who is conqueror over himself and situations, not by his own power but by the spirit of the Lord Christ. Something in these words of Dr. Rice bearing upon his personal ministry suggest to me that sonnet of Wordsworth which the poet addresses to his youthful friend Haydon.

"High is our calling, Friend! Creative Art
(Whether the instrument of words she use
Or pencil pregnant with etheral hues)
Demands the service of a mind and heart,
Though sensitive, yet, in their weakest part,
Heroically fashioned—to infuse
Faith in the whispers of the lonely Muse,
While the whole world seems adverse to desert.
And oh! when Nature sinks, as oft she may,
Through long-lived pressure of obscure distress,
Still to be strenuous for the bright reward,
And in the soul admit of no decay,
Brook no continuance of weak-mindedness—
Great is the glory, for the strife is hard!"

AINSLIE, Peter, clergyman; *b.* Dunnsville, Va., June 3, 1867; *s.* Peter and Rebecca Etta (Sizer) A.; ed. Transylvania Coll., Lexington, Ky., 1886-89; traveled in Europe, 1898; D.D., Drake U., 1911, Yale U., 1914; LL.D., Bethany Coll., W. Va.; *m.* Mary Elizabeth Weisel, June 30, 1925; children—Mary Elizabeth, Peter. Temp. supply, Newport News, 1889-91; pastor Baltimore since 1891; under his administration new building erected known as Christian Temple, and 8 br. chs. established. Editor Christian Union Quarterly since 1911. Founder, 1899, Girls' Club, on self-governing basis, for girls from rural dists. Pres. Nat. Conv. Disciples of Christ, 1910; mem. Am. Soc. Ch. History; trustee Disciples Div. House (U. of Chicago); trustee Ch. Peace Union, founded by Andrew Carnegie; del. to Ch. Peace Conf., Constance, Germany, 1914, Hague, 1919, Geneva, 1920, Copenhagen, 1922; Life and Work Conf., Stockholm, 1925; mem. internat. com. of World Alliance for Promoting Internat. Friendship through the Churches; pres. Assn. for Promotion Christian Unity, 1910-25; pres. Christian Unity League, 1927; mem. deputation apptd. by P.E. Ch. to visit Great Britain in interest of World Conf. on Faith and Order, 1913-14; editorial board Encyclopedia Britannica, 1927. Lecturer on Biblical lit., Goucher Coll., 1925-28, also lectures at Pro-Episcopal Seminary of Virginia, and Yale Divinity School, etc. ***Club:*** Eclectic. *Author:* Religion in Daily Doings, 1903; Studies in the Old Testament, 1907; Among the Gospels and the Acts, 1908; God and Me, 1908; My Brother and I, 1911; The Unfinished Task of the Reformation, 1910; Introduction to the Study of the Bible, 1910; The Message of the Disciples for the Union of the Church (Yale Lectures), 1913; Christ or Napoleon—Which? 1915; Working with God, 1917; If Not a United Church—What? 1920; Christian Worship (with H. C. Armstrong), 1923; The Way of Prayer, 1924; The Scandal of Christianity, 1929. *Home:* Ten Hills, Baltimore. *Office:* 230 N. Fulton Av., Baltimore, Md.

Chapter IV

PETER AINSLIE

Dr. Peter Ainslie, of Christian Temple, Baltimore, would have made a famous cardinal. He is very much of an ecclesiastic, using the word in its higher and finer meaning. He is urbane, endowed with a great deal of Old-World charm, a diplomat of the first order. Furthermore, he is a master of the Conference idea, where the like- and the unlike-minded put their legs beneath a mahogany table and discuss leisurely the issues, both great and small.

No man among the Disciples has undergone greater theological transformation in the last twenty years than this unordained bishop of Baltimore. Some of us knew him when his hobby was the imminent physical return of Jesus, and he was the exponent of other views bordering on the Moody Bible Institute type. But it should be said that Dr. Ainslie was seldom dogmatic in presenting these views and that he infused into crass literalism a spiritual glow that was wholesome and charming. Gradually, however, this kind of theology receded from his preaching and writings until it has disappeared entirely. But first, last and all the time Dr. Ainslie has been the prophet and apostle of Christian Unity.

Ainslie is the logical successor of Thomas Campbell in his communion, the Disciples of Christ. One of my friends once said of an ardent follower of Mary Baker Eddy, "Why that man talks, writes and dreams Christian Science." Substitute Christian Unity for Christian Science, in this quotation and the description fits our "Saint Peter," ardent apostle of the reunited House of God. Here is the man who has kept the fire burning on the altar of Christian unity when most of us had permitted it to burn fearfully low, and in some instances to go out entirely. In books, editorials, addresses, correspondence and unnumbered conferences, Ainslie has had one "paramount issue," namely, Christian unity.

This Baltimorean parson has a deep-seated conviction that sectarianism is a sin against which is to be charged many other woes of the world. He speaks and writes of divisions among Christians as "cancerous sores upon the body of Christ," or "terrible wounds on the body of our blessed Lord," and again as "wounding Christ in His own household," and still again, perhaps oftenest, as "the scandal of Christianity." In public addresses when using these or similar phrases, Dr. Ainslie's facial expression and tone of voice register his concern and humiliation that bigotry and unlovely partizanship flourish among those who are supposed to cultivate the mind of Christ.

Some years ago when the Disciples were met in annual convention at Winona Lake, Indiana, Dr. Ainslie gave an address on "The Disciples and Christian Union" that fairly sizzled with rebuke, reproach, criticism of the slowness of his brethren to practise the unity they preached so zealously and continuously. The speech was couched in elegant diction, delivered in restrained and velvety tones, but its strictures were for that reason the more cutting, caustic. The huge audience sat silent throughout the verbal lashing, gave their flaming apostle of unity a mighty ovation of applause when he finished, and later accepted his resignation as president of the Association for the Promotion of Christian Unity.

Retiring from the presidency of the association, a sort of subsidiary of his communion, Dr. Ainslie expanded his plans for union. He created the Christian Unity League, the purpose of which he set forth in a single sentence, "A fellowship of adventurous Christians from nearly every communion in America, seeking a practical expression of equality before God in order to raise the standard of Christian brotherhood above every denominational barrier, and to win others into the brotherhood of Jesus." All who become members of the League are required to sign "The Pact of Reconciliation," which is another document from the brain and heart of Ainslie, prophet and apostle of the reunion of all Christians, worth examining. It is included here for that purpose in entirety. It is, I hold, something more than a mere gesture. The day may come when this pact will be included among the significant papers that have contributed to the cause of unity.

"THE PACT OF RECONCILIATION."

"We, Christians of various churches, believing that only in a cooperative and united Christendom can the world be Christianized, deplore a divided Christendom as being opposed to the spirit of Christ and the needs of the world. We, therefore, desire to express our sympathetic interest in and prayerful attitude toward all conferences, small and large, that are looking toward reconciliation of the divided house of Christ.

"We acknowledge the equality of all Christians before God and propose to follow this principle, as far as possible, in all our spiritual fellowships. We will strive to bring the laws and practices of our several communions into conformity with this principle, so that no Christian shall be denied membership in any of our churches, nor the privilege of participation in the observance of the Lord's supper, and that no Christian minister shall be denied the freedom of our pulpits by reason of differences in forms of ordination.

"We pledge, irrespective of denominational barriers, to be brethren one to another in the name of Jesus Christ, our Lord and Savior, whose we are and whom we serve."

There is a wideness in the spirit of Dr. Ainslie like the wideness of the sea. He is one of the few Protestant pioneers for unity who never fails in his dreaming of unity to include the Roman Catholic Church and to do what he can to soften the asperities that have developed through controversies between Catholics and Protestants. It was characteristic of this man to journey once upon a time to Notre Dame, that sturdy Catholic seat of learning in the Middle West, and spend a day of leisurely and brotherly conference with the priests and professors of that institution. In the first paragraph of a statement which Dr. Ainslie prints on the second page of *The Christian Union Quarterly,* he avers that his journal is the organ of no party other than those growing up in all parties who are interested in the unity of the Church of Christ. Its pages are free to all indications of Christian Unity and Ventures of Faith. This journal maintains that, whether so accepted or not, all Christians—Eastern Orthodox, Roman Catholic, Anglican, Protestant and all others who accept Jesus as Lord and Savior—are parts of the Church of Christ and the recognition of their Equality before God is the paramount issue of modern times.

A mutual friend once remarked to me that much as he likes to hear Dr. Ainslie preach, he would rather hear him pray. I can understand that remark. The devotional is highly developed in Ainslie's character. The phrase "talking to God" is threadbare, but it applies to the prayers of the minister of Christian Temple. He is the author of a little book entitled *The Way of Prayer,* and he prepared, in conjunction with his associate, H. C. Armstrong, a book of *Christian Worship* with a subtitle, "For Voluntary Use among Disciples of Christ and Other Christians." When he built his home in Baltimore, having married late in life, he saw to it that a prayer chapel was constructed in the home to which he took his bride. At the great conventions and conferences on the other side of the Atlantic to which he is so often a delegate, when there is an early-morning communion service, Dr. Ainslie will usually be found there, kneeling at the altar and receiving the emblems from the hands of a priest of the Anglican Church; or again, himself assisting in the distribution of the loaf and the cup in some plain, nonconformist meeting-house. In truth, he is always going about doing good for the Cause of Christian Unity.

Ainslie believes in total non-resistance, and I once heard him say that if Baltimore were invaded by an enemy threatening to conquer the city he would not lift sword or gun to defend native land or his own life. Through his anti-war addresses he has invited and received vitriolic abuse and detraction. Preaching a series of noon sermons through holy week for the Protestant Churches of Washington, D.C., in the First Congregational Church in 1930, he opened up on the subject "Has Christianity Accepted Christ?" It was a searching sermon and one paragraph in particular stirred up a nest of hornets which proceeded to sting the Baltimore preacher angrily. The Associated Press put the story on the front page of a thousand newspapers and for a week or more Ainslie's critics raged, and his defenders spoke out boldly in his behalf. Here is the offending paragraph:

> "Some years ago, when the late Bishop Potter of New York attended the opening of a saloon in the subway with prayer, he was severely criticized throughout the nation. I can not see any more impropriety in a bishop opening a saloon with prayer that the drinks be honestly mixed and the patrons keep sober than a chaplain praying that the soldiers would shoot straight and kill as many of the enemy as possible. Of course, I do not know that the bishop and the chaplains phrased their prayers as rudely as I have suggested—hardly not, for usually we are amazingly polite in our prayers—but that is what their prayers must have practically meant if they prayed for success. Anyway there is no more place for a chaplain in an army than at a speakeasy."

Professor Glover somewhere says of the early Christians that they were "perfectly fearless; absurdly happy; always getting into trouble." It is about this way with Dr. Ainslie.

Preaching the baccalaureate sermon before the graduating class of the most historic and influential military school in the South, the doctor closed a truly magnificent discourse in which he pled for justice, brotherhood and good will, with this illustration:

> "I was riding on a train in the South. The car was rather crowded. All the seats in the front part of the car, where the negroes were supposed to sit, were taken. A colored girl weighted down with a heavy suitcase and package boarded the train, and the white woman seated just ahead of me, with a vacant place beside her, spread her skirts emphatically, saying, 'No nigger shall sit by me!' A man across the aisle expressed himself in a similar manner. I beckoned the little girl to a seat by me, which she accepted reluctantly. I had hardly lifted my book to continue my reading, when a tornado of protests came from all parts of the white section of the car, and calls for the conductor. A big burly fellow two seats across from me shouted, 'If the conductor don't put this here dam' Yankee off, I am big enough to do it. No nigger gal shall sit beside a white man on a train that I ride.'
>
> "By that time the conductor had arrived. He asked me if I had asked the negro girl to take the seat beside me. I assured him I had, and explained the reason—there was no other seat except in the white section. He then reminded me that it was a violation of the law of Virginia. I expressed my regret that Virginia had such a law, and, turning to the negro girl, I assured her that she would not be moved by my request. Up to this time the conductor and I had spoken in modulated voices, but now the train had come to a water tank and stopped. Then I asked him, in a loud voice that everybody might hear:
>
> "'If Robert E. Lee had been seated where I am and this little negro girl had come down the aisle looking for a

seat, and he had refused this seat to her, would Virginia have had any respect for his memory?'

"The conductor bent down and whispered in my ear: 'No, and I'll lose my job before I put you off this train or make this girl move.'

"The next stop was mine, and as I alighted, I heard the big burly fellow say in a lower tone, and indicating that he saw dimly: 'What dam' Virginian do you suppose that is—thinking that he is as good as Robert E. Lee.' "

This may not be verbatim, but I have given the incident very much as Dr. Ainslie used it and applied it. Now, the point is that this illustration was offensive to his audience and they indicated it by the pained expression on their faces and a marked restlessness. But this modern Saint Peter purposely sacrificed his popularity that day for the sake of a principle that he believed was vital. Oh, these prophets! How disagreeable they can make themselves and how uncomfortable they can make others for Jesus' sake!

Ainslie has been a prolific author. He has published *Religion in Daily Doing, Studies in the Old Testament, Among the Gospels and the Acts, God and Me, The Unfinished Task of the Reformation, Introduction to the Study of the Bible, The Message of the Disciples for the Union of the Church, Christ or Napoleon—Which?, Christian Worship, If Not a United Church—What?, The Way of Prayer, The Scandal of Christianity* and *My Brother and I.* Reference has already been made to *The Christian Union Quarterly* which he founded and edits—the best-known periodical in that particular field. In addition to the above Dr. Ainslie contributes special articles to numerous journals of distinction and usually on one of the three subjects that lie close to his heart: Christian Unity, World Peace and the Devotional Life.

In a foreword to his newest book, *Some Experiments in Living,* Dr. Ainslie writes a revealing word. There is something of the confessional in it.

"No person can make experiments without being misunderstood and misrepresented, but one must be as little afraid of such things as the mariner is of a northeast wind. . . . Were my heart opened, it would show footprints of friends and enemies. Both have helped me, one intentionally, and the other unintentionally. These heart-paths cross and recross as memory and imagination make the heart the meeting place of those who love us and those who love us not. . . . I hold no unkindness for those who think adversely, nor will I allow any one, by word or conduct toward me, to take from me my sense of brotherhood with every man and woman and child in the world."

Dr. Ainslie has made his communion, the Disciples of Christ, known on three continents and introduced that body of believers where it was unknown, or belittled if known, and possibly despised. For that achievement Dr. Ainslie deserves the undying gratitude of an undiscerning brotherhood. Just now this delightful Virginia gentleman and thoroughly Christian personality is in eclipse among the Disciples. No longer does he loom big in their conventions. He is not now a headliner in their church programs, and his name seldom appears in their most conservative journals except as a gibe or coupled with censure. He is taboo, under suspicion, and why? Simply because following the gleam as God gave him to glimpse it, he has come out for "open membership" in order as he sees it to practise what his communion has preached for a century.

Alas, it has always been so. We penalize our prophets and pillory our pathfinders. But the day that Peter Ainslie is gathered to his fathers the reaction will set in. Forty years from now, possibly sooner, the Disciples of Christ will dedicate something or other to Peter Ainslie, Apostle of Christian Unity, and a gifted orator will speak of him as the Salt of the Brotherhood, the Prophet of the Grander Day, and a great chorus will sing:

"They climbed the steep ascent of heaven
Through peril, toil, and pain;
O God, to us may grace be given,
To follow in their train."

Instead of lilies—white lilies for Ainslie dead, I propose roses—red roses for Ainslie living!

JEFFERSON, Charles Edward, clergyman; *b.* Cambridge, O., Aug. 29, 1860; *s.* Dr. Milton and Ella (Sarchett) J.; B.S., Ohio Wesleyan, 1882, A.B., 1886; supt. pub. schs., Worthington, O., 1882-84; S.T.B., Boston U., 1887; D.D., Oberlin Coll., 1898, Union Coll., 1898, Yale, 1903; LL.D., Ohio Wesleyan U., 1905, Miami U., 1923; D.D., U. of Vt., 1921; *m.* Belle Patterson, of Cambridge, O., Aug. 10, 1887; children—Charles Frederic, Ralph Waldo (dec.). Ordained Congl. ministry, 1887; pastor Central Ch., Chelsea, Mass., 1887-98, Broadway Tabernacle, New York, 1898-. Fellow Yale Corpn., 1902-24. *Author:* Quiet Hints to Growing Preachers in My Study, 1891; Quiet Talks with Earnest People in My Study, 1898; Doctrine and Deed, 1902; Things Fundamental, 1903; The Minister as Prophet, 1905; Faith and Life, 1905; The World's Christmas Tree, 1906; The Old Year and the New, 1907; The New Crusade, 1907; The Character of Jesus, 1908; My Father's Business, 1909; The Christmas Builders, 1909; The Building of the Church, 1910; Why We May Believe in Life after Death, 1911; The Minister as Shepherd, 1912; The Cause of the War, 1914; Christianity and International Peace, 1915; A Fire in the Snow, 1916; The Land of Enough, 1917; Forefathers' Day Sermons, 1917; Old Truths and New Facts, 1918; What the War Has Taught Us, 1919; Soldiers of the Prince; Quiet Talks with the Family; Under Twenty, 1922; The Friendship Indispensable, 1923; The Character of Paul, 1923; Five Present-day Controversies, 1924; Cardinal Ideas of Isaiah, 1925; Cardinal Ideas of Jeremiah, 1928; Christianizing a Nation, 1929; Other Nature Sermons, 1931. *Home:* 121 W. 85th St., New York, N. Y.

Chapter V

CHARLES E. JEFFERSON

I HAVE reasons for believing that Charles E. Jefferson is, by his brethren of the cloth, the most envied of living preachers. By "envy" here I mean something less than the "green-eyed monster" and something more than admiration—I mean the quality of intense longing to achieve what another has nobly done. Why do ministers envy Dr. Jefferson? There are more brilliant orators in the American pulpit, more spectacular "pulpiteers," and possibly more magnetic personalities. The cause for this ministerial envy of the higher type, I think, is this—for thirty years in the nation's metropolis, Dr. Jefferson has maintained the finest ideals of pulpit decorum, dignity, sermonic standards, and has never once sought to pander to the populace, which, like the Athenians, "spend their time in nothing else, but either to tell or to hear some new thing."

Most ministers down deep in their souls despise cheap pulpit devices to win an audience—despise them even while they employ them, justifying their use by the sophistry that it is better to fill your church by sensational methods than preach to empty pews. Is either horn of the dilemma necessary? Dr. Jefferson thinks not. Nay, he knows better. He has held himself unflinchingly to a straight, hard pulpit course, and if he has not had the largest night audiences in his city, he has always had four or five hundred thoughtful people to preach to Sunday evenings, and that is no small accomplishment in season and out in a down-town city church. Never sensational nor spectacular, his pulpit methods have always been fresh, stimulating, well conceived and ably carried out. His topics have been timely, and sometimes striking, both in subject-matter and treatment.

The Jefferson style is simplicity itself. His sentences are invariably short, terse, epigrammatic. They tingle in the memory. Sometimes they stab. They flash. They are packed with thought. Jefferson is as direct as sunlight and as clear. His simplicity is not wholly artless, but it is so skilful that the hearer or reader is likely to conclude that such a style is native, not acquired. Actually, Dr. Jefferson has labored long and arduously to perfect the quiet, tense, invigorating fluency which distinguishes his preaching. Sometimes he uses, but not often, a sentence of more than a dozen words, and when he does, again there is clarity of expression. He can put much in a single sentence. For example, "A sermon is a rose." Now, that is of itself interesting. But listen: "The text is the bud, and the preacher, breathing on the bud, causes the folded petals to open on the air and fill with fragrance the place where the saints of God are sitting." Then follows the advice: "Go to the bee, young friends, consider her ways, and be wise." Sorry I can not go on here with the bee, for it is very good.

In his ministry of more than thirty years at Broadway Tabernacle, Dr. Jefferson has rounded out his pulpit message as few ministers have been able to do. He has dealt with the great doctrines of the Church, such as Atonement, the unique nature of Christ, the New Birth, the inspiration of the Scriptures, and so forth. He has presented these themes in full-length sermons, treated them with intellectual integrity, at the same time imparting to them a modern interpretation, yet always constructive, helpful. He has preached many sermons on Christ, and his volume, *The Character of Jesus,* is a good example of popular preaching that is informative and absorbingly interesting. Dr. Jefferson has done the same thing with the Apostle Paul, also with at least two of the Prophets, Isaiah and Jeremiah, making these strong men of Israel real personages of flesh and blood, analyzing their messages and interpreting them to our day with skill and vigor.

I recall a Sunday evening in New York when I was free

from engagements and went to hear Dr. Jefferson preach. It was an evening in early spring and Broadway was thronged with people. The Broadway Tabernacle was comfortably well filled, the audience numbering, I should suppose, in the neighborhood of five hundred. The doctor appeared in the pulpit with two associates, young men, who shared the preliminary services. His sermon was on the odd subject "Grasshoppers and Stars," based on two obscure passages in which it appeared that the Creator was concerned with the most trivial as well as the weightiest of His creation. It was a helpful sermon, eminently practical, and reached us down where we live. The preacher scarcely looked his years, and while his delivery was restrained there was a kind of subdued vigor in it and one got the impression that he was tapping his resources only lightly. That was the impression given the first half-hour by the preacher. After that he drew more heavily upon his wealth of experience, spoke with more freedom, closing in a paragraph that was filled with gripping sentences. There was not a false note struck in the entire service. Nothing was obtruded, out of harmony with the dignified simplicity and the reverent program.

I wanted to know Dr. Jefferson's method of sermon preparation:

"I prepare my sermons by preparing myself. Self-preparation is the most difficult work a preacher has to do," he replied. "If the preacher does not prepare himself, it matters little what else he does. A preacher who is spiritually anemic, or intellectually improverished, or morally depleted, will wish often for a juniper tree. Milton contended that if a man wishes to write a good poem, he himself must be a poem. It is equally true that a preacher to create a living sermon must himself be a sermon. The preacher's fundamental job is working on himself.

"But I work on my sermons too. I work on them all the time. I work on them through my waking hours and probably I keep right on working in my sleep. But I have a queer way of working. I do not build sermons as Ford builds automobiles or architects build sky-scrapers. My sermons are not manufactured products. They are more like apple dumplings. I usually have a half-dozen of them in the pot at the same time. I keep the water boiling and now and then I stick in a fork to see which one should be served next. Some dumplings must be cooked longer than others.

"But my favorite figure for my sermons is a flower. My sermons grow. They unfold. I never 'get up' a sermon. I suspect the genuineness of a sermon which must be 'got up.' A sermon of the right sort gets itself up. If I supply the soil and the seed and the sun and the rain, the sermon will come up of itself. My soul is a flower-garden. My business is raising sermons. The tragedy of a preacher's life is that so many of his sermons must be picked too soon. Sundays come so close together and the preacher has so many things to do that often he can not find those nooks of leisure in which lovely things come to blossom."

The way a master preacher outlines a sermon is of interest to other preachers. How does he go about it? Does he use copious notes or a mere skeleton of divisions? Here is an outline of a sermon by Dr. Jefferson prepared for his own use, taken into the pulpit and only glanced at now and then in the course of a half-hour's delivery.

Subject: THE RICH YOUNG RULER.

Text: "What lack I yet?" Matthew 19:20.

I. Introduction:
   1. He appears in three Gospels.
   2. Each of the three tells us something not told by the other two.

II. A Vivid and Unforgettable Figure in the New Testament.
   1. He impressed the Evangelists.
   2. He impressed Jesus.
   3. He impresses us.

III. His Fascination Explained.
   1. He is lovable.
   2. He is unsatisfied.
   3. His question is a puzzle because he is young, rich, honored and good.

IV. Jesus' Answer:
   1. A false interpretation.
   2. The correct interpretation.

V. Application.
   1. We are not good enough.
   2. Our conventional goodness is tame and feeble.
   3. A higher type of man is demanded.

Dr. Jefferson is a peacemaker who has valiantly served the cause of Christian internationalism. His preaching against war is notable both in content and bulk. He has at least a dozen volumes on war and peace, and even in print these sermons stir the reader deeply. Take this flashing phrase from his pen as an epitome of his judgment on the so-called romance of war, "The heroisms of war are but the glancing sunlight on a sea of blood and tears." He has published in all twenty-five volumes and not one of them shows indications of haste or careless preparation. His books on preaching take a place at the top of preacher literature. His volume in the Yale series ranks with Beecher, Brooks, Horne and Jowett. My two Jefferson favorites are *The Minister as Shepherd,* and *The Minister as Prophet.* As I see it, these are the best and most helpful books on the two hemispheres of a minister's calling, of which I have any knowledge. They are practical, ideal, brilliant and immensely readable. They reflect the man who wrote them—his stature, spiritual and intellectual, his passion for preaching, his ideas of the shepherding vocation.

Not every young minister can hope to be a Charles E. Jefferson, but no young minister can make a mistake if he takes this marvelous preacher as his model. Jefferson's ministry in the "city of seven million" is monumental.

WISE, Stephen Samuel, rabbi; *b.* Budapest, Hungary, Mar. 17, 1872; *s.* Aaron (rabbi) and Sabine de Fischer (Farkashasy) W.; Coll. City of New York, 1887-91; A.B., Columbia, 1892, Ph.D., 1901; hon. degrees Temple Univ. and Syracuse Univ.; *m.* Louise, *d.* Julius and Justine Mayer Waterman, of New York, Nov. 14, 1900; children—James Waterman, Mrs. Justine Tulin. Pastor Congregation of Madison Av. Synagogue, New York, 1893-1900, Beth Israel, Portland Ore., 1900-06; founder, 1907, and since rabbi Free Synagogue of New York. Founder and 1st V.P. Ore. State Conf. Charities and Correction; founder, 1st sec. Federation of Am. Zionists; late commr. child labor State of Ore.; v.p. Free Religious Assn. America; founder Zionist Organization of America; chairman in succession to Justice Brandeis, of Provisional Exec. Com. for Gen. Zionist Affairs; mem. Am. Jewish Relief Com. and Joint Distribution Com.; v.-chmn. Jewish Emergency Refugee Relief Com.; mem. com. on labor of Council Nat. Defense. Rep. of Am. League to Enforce Peace; chmn. commn. of Zionist Orgn. America, and mem. delegation of Am. Jewish Congress (pres.) at Conf., Paris; v.-chmn. exec. com. World Zionist Orgn. Chevalier Legion d'Honneur, France, 1919. V.P. Open Forum Nat. Council; dir. Peace Soc. of New York; founder Eastern Council of Liberal Rabbis; trustee, Nat. Child Labor Com. Founder and pres. Jewish Inst. of Religion (training of men for Jewish ministry); chmn. United Palestine Funds Appeal, 1925-26; founder and trustee Near East Relief; vice chmn. New York City Affairs Com. *Author:* The Ethics of Solomon Ibn Gabirol, 1901; Beth Israel Pulpit (monthly sermon publ.) 3 vols.; Free Synagogue Pulpit (monthly sermon publ.) 10 vols.; How to Face Life; Child Versus Parent; The Great Betrayal (with Jacob de Haas). *Home:* 27 W. 96th St., New York, N. Y.

Chapter VI

STEPHEN S. WISE

To be a great orator, three qualities are necessary—an imposing presence, an impressive voice and an opulent imagination. Rabbi Stephen S. Wise possesses all three. His stature is not notable, but it is impressive. His dark piercing eyes are eloquent. His outthrust chin, well shaped head, cameo-like profile, contribute to a personality vibrant with power, a sensitive vehicle to stir, instruct and inspire an audience. He has that oratorical flair that fascinates, that something which we call magnetism plays upon his hearers as a master musician plays upon his favorite instrument.

I heard Dr. Wise during the World War at a meeting in Music Hall, Philadelphia, refer to Turkey as an Assassinocracy." He released the word with catapultic force; as a cannon releases a hurtling shell. There was a vocal explosion. You felt the impact and looked about you for casualties. No dud was that shot. It struck home fiercely and did damage all around. And he followed the explosion with a raking fire of sentences enlarging, intensifying, his opinion of the government of Turkey and its attitude toward the oppressed and long wronged. He was volcanic, torrential; his fluency was flaming and marvelous. From the first to the last word there were fire and fury, but also reasoned argument relieved here and there by humor, sometimes savage, and then again of the lighter sort. His sentences rang out as clear and convincing as when a blacksmith strikes his anvil blow upon blow, then bends the heated iron according to his wish. What an orator is this New York rabbi whose raven black hair is now streaked with white, but whose voice is as resonant as when a youthful speaker he achieved his first pulpit and platform conquest.

I listened to Dr. Wise when he offered prayer at the Democratic Convention in Madison Square Garden in 1924. I think he read the prayer, but I am not sure for my head was bowed. Anyhow, the phrasing was noble. There was a strain of the Hebrew prophet's diction and passion. It made you feel that God was mightily concerned in our national affairs and that it is His will that every political party should purge itself of all dross and try to experience a new baptism of high-minded patriotism. Praying over that convention was not the easiest thing in the world; it was turbulent, confused, and the poison of prejudice was at work, but for the time being, the brief period as Rabbi Wise prayed, you forgot what had happened and what might yet happen in a mob, and felt that only God is great.

Rabbi Wise is courageous. Many of his friends are of the rich and the highly placed, but he has never hesitated to speak his convictions regarding the responsibility and obligations of great wealth. He is a champion of the disinherited, an enemy of corruption in municipal government, of child labor, of intolerance, bigotry and narrow nationalism, a bitter and unrelenting foe of war and armaments. Institutional religion has always had its defenders as well as bitter enemies. Rabbi Wise is not blind to the weaknesses of synagogue and church. Witness this paragraph from his tribute to Lincoln, delivered at Springfield, Illinois, on the one hundred and fifth anniversary of the Emancipator's birth:

> "Such as fear God! Fearless before men, Abraham Lincoln feared God. Lip-piety was not of the substance of his religion, nor was he given to many professions of faith, but he walked in the fear of God. Not only was he a profoundly religious man, the content of whose life was rooted in religion, whose religion flowered in the beauty of the good and the true, but his was a conscious faith in a supreme purpose. Almost might one say in paraphrase of the word of Schiller, that the churches were not religious enough to command his allegiance.

The question touching his day is not so much whether Lincoln was a churchman, but whether the churches of his time were Lincoln-like. Only to a God-fearing man could have come the inspiration with which he closed his second inaugural address: 'With malice toward none, with charity for all, with firmness in the right as God gives us to see the right, let us strive on to finish the work we are in.' Such fear of God is a nation's strength."

Rabbi Wise regards Jesus with reverent affection. He thinks of Him as the greatest of the prophets. Perhaps no rabbi in America, of the modern school, has so endeared himself to Christian ministers and laymen of the various churches as this twentieth-century Jew who speaks as one with authority and in behalf of the inarticulate masses as well as the voiceful cultural minority.

Of all the men whom I have asked for information regarding their habits of study, sermonic preparation and reading, this busy rabbi of the Free Synagogue, New York, gave fullest answer. So valuable are the rabbi's "confessions," so original, as for instance his view that his sermons go best when preached six, eight or ten times—that his breezy, stimulating paragraphs are included in full, and just as a stenographer took them down.

"First: How do I prepare a sermon or speech? I need hardly tell a preacher how difficult it is, in any reasoning and coherent way, to answer that question. Some sermons come as if by a flash. A theme presents itself, and then the one thing to do is to sit down and think it through and work at it, so that one gets a good part of it done without delay. That happens sometimes, but not often. I usually let themes simmer for a long time—the time varying from a month to a year or two. I ought to add, however, that I preach on themes rather than on texts. I use texts but in an unorthodox way, namely, as illustration rather than as a peg on which to hang things. Sometimes I cite a word of Bible early in an address, but as a rule, I like to save it until the close and let it clinch the thing I have tried to say.

"I do not know that I ought to say this,—but I find (as I think some eminent preachers have said long before me) that the sermons or addresses that I think seem worth-while are those which I have spoken again and again. I sometimes say in jest to my students at the Jewish Institute of Religion, of which I am president, that a sermon does not ripen under my hand, or, perhaps I should say, in my mouth, until after I have preached it six or eight, or ten times. I know there is the feeling on the part of some men that one is in danger of falling into 'stale fervor' if one repeat an address. But the fact is, at least for me, that I never preach about a theme that does not interest me deeply. I do not preach because it is Sunday. I preach, as a rule, nine times out of ten or nineteen times times out of twenty (if one may resort to mathematical percentages) because I have something to say and not because I have to say something. That being so, and preaching as I uniformly do on subjects and themes and issues that interest me deeply and hold me tremendously, my interest in my word and theme does not wane because I have once said a thing to one community.

"As for preparing a sermon and speech,—I have twenty to thirty and perhaps even more envelopes on my desk containing material on things about which some day I am going to preach. As I read and think, I make memoranda and put the items into the different envelopes. A great deal of this material I shall never use, but again it is a case of sermon ripening rather than of being delivered and prepared *ad hoc* or delivered impromptu, save for a few days' preparation. I ought to add, after having preached for thirty-five years, that while I read and read, as I shall tell you after a moment,

I depend more or less upon myself. I use quotations less, not because I have come to think less of those whom I read, but because the only way I can help people is by uttering the things that are in and that grow out of my own soul.

"The final preparation of my sermon runs like this: By Wednesday or Thursday preceding the Sunday morning of my sermon (and, incidentally, I make it a rule not to preach more than three times a month on Sunday mornings), I work at my material and then try, though I do not always succeed, to dictate an abstract of the address by Thursday or Friday. If I can not do that, I try to stay in my study all of Saturday, usually unto late in the night, leaving it for early Sunday morning to map out a five-hundred to one-thousand-word summary of what I am going to say. I rarely, if ever, read a sermon in its entirety, though upon a few great occasions I have done that. The difficulty about reading, for me, as the members of my family tell me, is that I am a wretched reader, except of the Bible, and that when I read I might just as well be reading another man's output as my own. It does not seem, they claim, a part of me. It is not I.

"On the other hand, there is this to be said—if I may go on interminably—with respect to the method of finishing a sermon completely earlier in the week. I have found, upon the few occasions when an address or sermon was finished, days or weeks before delivery, that my mind ceased to occupy itself with the problem or the sermon once the thing was written out. There is, for me, a finality in the typewritten form of a sermon which somehow seems to call a halt to the creative power of one's spirit.

"You ask about my habits of study. I try to do as much studying as I can. There is an enormous amount of material for the intelligent and thoughtful person in the ministry to read in these days. For one thing, there are the old precious sources with which to remain familiar, and, in addition, there is a vast amount of contemporaneous literature. I try to make it a rule never to go through a day without reading and studying something worth-while. No matter how hard the day may have been, if, late at night, I find I have gone through the day without reading or studying, I devote from eleven to twelve-thirty or one in the morning to study of something of permanent value, even though I have to arise as early as I usually do the following morning.

"I think it a great mistake for men in the ministry not to be students. Most of us can not be scholars in the technical sense—I mean creative scholars—but we can be students, and we can not really be helpful thinkers and teachers unless we know and are familiar with the best things that are being said and done in the world.

"You ask whether, in my work as rabbi, I have done pastoral calling. When I was in Portland, Oregon, from 1900 to 1906, I did a great deal of pastoral calling. I was a very young man and the congregation consisted of two hundred or three hundred families, and the burden of the community lay rather lightly upon me. I must be forgiven if I say I am in a unique position now with respect to pastoral calling. I did not come to a finished congregation. I founded the congregation, I chose my congregation. My congregation did not choose me. I established and created and have developed it for twenty-five years. My people have been kind and generous to a fault, and they know that my public life, if I may use that term, includes so many responsibilities, including the Presidency of the Jewish Institute of Religion, the active leadership of the American Jewish Congress, the vital and constant participation in the leadership of the Zionist Organization, that not only do they not expect me to do pastoral calling, but they are kind and thoughtful enough to ask me not to call upon them.

"I do this—upon occasions of joy and upon occasions of sorrow, I go to my people. I perform marriage ceremonies and officiate at funerals for members of my congregation and, even beyond that circle, for friends. I conduct the service for one or two nights in homes of sorrow—which is our custom. Whenever I feel I am needed or can be of help to people, I go to them, or often I send for them, for, I must repeat, my people are so generous and so hyper-considerate that they wish to spare me (and I am nearing sixty) as much as they can.

"Finally you ask me, 'What, in your judgment, is the high duty of the ministry, both Jewish and Christian, these days?' Again, it is a question that it is not easy to answer. Still, I venture to say that the first duty of the ministry is to have in mind always that we who are ministers purport to represent an order of life the significance of which it is our business to bring to the life of others by everything we are and say and do. No man can be an ambassador of heaven-high-things and, at the same time, bear himself as a being without vision of and passion for the highest. The business of the man in the ministry is to bring the vision of God the Father to man and the vision of men as brothers to men. The business of the minister is to do what my Fathers have always taught—that religion means, above all things, holiness, that Jewish term which long preceded the Imitatio Dei—holiness—which can not be without equity and righteousness in the relations between man and man.

"Forgive me this very long screed. Paraphrasing a Frenchman, I have not had time to draft a short letter, and so I have rambled on at length."

Most of us crystallize mentally with the passing years, and radicals even have been known to take surprising conservative positions as age steals over their brains and bodies. It is not so with Stephen Wise. If anything, he seems bolder and less mindful of his critics as he passes his sixtieth birthday. Wherever there is a fight for freedom, be it theological, political or economic, there is he in the midst of the fray. Witness his recent frontal attack on the governmental corruption of his own New York City. Read his most recent pronouncements against the awful scourge of war. It is another William Lloyd Garrison speaking: "I will not equivocate, and I will be heard!"

Dr. Wise has his captious critics. One of his fellow rabbis in a Middle West city, remarked to me, "Wise is a spellbinder, and loves to play to the galleries." I have heard that remark before. It has been made of almost every able and brilliant public speaker who has won a vast popular following. Is "playing to the galleries" an unpardonable sin? The "galleries" as used in this connection, represents the masses, the people, if you please. Now an agitator or crusader must win the rank and file if he is to succeed. It is a triumph of no mean sort to be able to command a popular hearing. I have only praise for a man who can win a great hearing for a mighty cause, through the use of commanding platform talents. "Spellbinder, player to the galleries," indeed! Saint Paul might have been judged as "playing to the galleries" when he sought to win King Herod Agrippa by that direct and dramatic appeal on a certain memorable occasion described in the twenty-sixth chapter of Acts. Beecher, Webster, Clay, Wendell Phillips, Bryan, all the great speakers in every age played magnificently to the galleries in the sense that they used every ounce of oratorical appeal to sway the multitudes, produce conviction, win converts to their cause.

It is worth going a long way and at considerable expense to hear a preacher who plays to the galleries of popular emotion for the sake of liberty, truth and justice. Write me down as one who would willingly miss breakfast, dinner and supper, if necessary, to listen to Rabbi Stephen S. Wise in a sermon from that famous text in Isaiah 2:4, "And he shall judge among the nations, and shall rebuke many people;

and they shall beat their swords into plowshares and their spears into pruning-hooks; nation shall not lift up sword against nation, neither shall they learn war any more."

ATKINS, Gaius Glenn, clergyman; *b.* Mt. Carmel, Ind., Oct. 4, 1868; *s.* Thomas Benjamin and Caroline (Morris) A.; A.B., O. State U., 1888; LL.B., Cincinnati Law Sch., 1891; Student Yale Div. Sch.; (D.D., Univ. of Vermont, 1904, Dartmouth, 1906; L.H.D., U. of Vt., 1923); *m.* Adaline Haynes, of Bellbrook, O., Aug. 25, 1892; children—Helen, Morris Haynes, Laurence Porter, Robert Huntington, Richard Annesley. Head dept. of history, Mt. Hermon Fitting Sch., 1892-95; ordained Congl. ministry, 1895; pastor Greenfield, Mass., 1895-1900, Burlington, Vt., 1900-06; First Ch., Detroit, 1906-10; Central Ch., Providence, R. I., 1910-17; again First Ch., Detroit, 1917-27; Hoyt prof. homiletics and sociology, Auburn Theol. Sem., 1927. Mem. Phi Beta Kappa. *Author:* Things That Remain, 1911; Pilgrims of the Lonely Road, 1913; The Maze of the Nations, 1915; The Godward Side of Life, 1917; Jerusalem Past and Present, 1918; The Undiscovered Country, 1922; Modern Religious Cults and Movements, 1923; Craftsmen of the Soul, 1925; Reinspecting Victorian Religion, 1928; The Making of the Christian Mind, 1928; The Procession of the Gods, 1930; Life of Cardinal Newman, 1931. Contbr. to religious journals. Awarded Church Peace Union Prize for essay on International Peace, 1914. Am. Dir. Foyer du Soldat with French Army, 1918. *Home:* Huntington House, Seminary Campus, Auburn, N. Y.

Chapter VII

GAIUS GLENN ATKINS

If I were asked to name the ten ablest preachers in the United States of America I would put Gaius Glenn Atkins in the list and rank him high among that ten. I will agree that Atkins is not a preacher for the masses, that he is too intellectual, too profound, too much of a mystic to be what is known as a "popular preacher." But of his ability, scholarly mind, chaste and beautiful style, his capacity to interpret the things of God to needy mankind, no competent judge will gainsay. He is, to my way of thinking, the premier preacher's preacher on this side of the Atlantic. Speaking of Dr. Atkins' thoughtful style of sermons, a competent critic remarked, "You have to bring something to Atkins' services in order to take something away." Of course, that is true of any preacher, but especially true of this man.

Dr. Atkins is a quiet preacher, speaking mostly in a conversational tone. No one ever heard him storm or rant in the pulpit. He is not oratorical, as that term is popularly understood, nor interested in the mechanics of speech, although the master of an exquisite style, his rhetoric being quite flawless. He is in truth much of a poet, thinks in images, delights in rare and beautiful phrasings. You seldom listen to him without visioning the sweep of old ocean, the majestic range of mountains, the wonder of sunrise, the splendor of the afterglow which comes when "the sun has slipped his tether and galloped down the west." He is a philosopher who looks at life in the large, sees things from the long perspective, is never narrow, seldom dogmatic, yet constructive always. No one can listen to Dr. Atkins or read his books without realizing that back of the sermon are the reading of innumerable books, the brooding and musing ministry of reflection, meditation and prayer, the observations of a tireless traveler in many lands.

Dr. Atkins has a shepherd's heart; his tenderness is unmistakable. He has suffered deeply and is sufficiently acquainted with pain to know how to sympathize with those who are going through the valley of the shadow. There is an undertone of sadness in him even when his fine eyes sparkle and his sensitive mouth is bracketed with the parenthesis of a smile. The artistry of cultural generations is in this man's speech, his innate gentility. He is the inheritor of rich traditions, the product of a long line of ancestors who indulged in plain living and high thinking. He is a conversationalist of parts, but never loquacious, sometimes even laconic. He gives you the impression of a public speaker who never lets words run away with him. He is the thinker before he is the spokesman. He knows how to touch things lightly if the occasion requires, but he is never oratorically frivolous or flippant. Moreover, there is a touch of timidity, a shyness in this prophet of God.

Dr. Atkins values aright the effectiveness of a climax or peroration and achieves the same, sometimes with telling artistry. In a brilliant and discriminating speech on Woodrow Wilson, made on an anniversary occasion when I happened to be presiding, Dr. Atkins finished his forty-five minute address thus:

> "They buried Woodrow Wilson in Bethlehem Chapel, Washington, and Bethlehem is the place where things are born!"

The effect was electric . . . a full minute passed in impressive silence and then came a tumult of applause.

Would you like a specimen of Dr. Atkins' sermonic style? Here is a paragraph from his sermon, "The Road We Travel But Once," built upon the text, "Ye shall henceforth return no more that way." Deuteronomy 17: 16.

"No, the dreams of youth are irrevocable. Ecstasies and pains alike, once we have had them, are irrevocably gone. What the unknown gives to a first experience is so lost in the sheer having had it as to make it never afterwards what it was before. Life drives us on, baptizes us in its happiness, sobers us with its responsibilities, metes out to us our appointed measure of experience, saddens us, wearies us, teaches us, changes us, and though, to repeat, we come back to the old ways again, we who come are not the same and, therefore, the old ways themselves are not the same. Whether we will or no, we are always directed into new regions, once by virtue of the changes which take place about us, once by virtue of the changes which take place within us."

I asked Dr. Atkins for a sermon outline, and he offered me the following, remarking: "There is nothing original about it, but it happens to be the last I used."

THE UNSHAKEN THRONE

Isaiah VI:I

A time-worn text: a timeless theme.

King Uzziah had filled all the foreground of Isaiah's life. Now he was dead and Isaiah saw his state and his future against horizons empty of what had heretofore assured him. His world was empty; he looked for a little into a void.

* * *

Our own lives like that: their foregrounds filled with assuring forces, comfortable possessions, dear comradeship; the pleasant habits of established station.—What they give; what they hide.

* * *

Then in some change of Fortune they are gone; carried away on the tides of time and all our horizons are empty. What do we see when they are gone? A man's destiny may depend upon that vision. For he may see one of four things:

(a) Anarchy
(b) Fate
(c) Inexorable and Impersonal Law
(d) or God.

A consideration of the meaning of each of the first three.

Isaiah saw God, high and lifted up.
That is the supreme and saving vision—but not a mystic's escape.
It is *illuminating*—God seen in causes of change.

When Uzziah is dead, or King Prosperity, an order shaken, the happy habits of our lives confounded——Light may be a terribly disconcerting thing—but life is confusion without it.
Practical application to-day.

It is *demanding:* God seen in new duties, readjustments. Also practical application to-day.
It is *assuring:* We do not go on unhelped, unguided.—The sovereign Steadfastness, the blessed Constancies are still here. There is a Power above and beyond us in whose keeping are the issues of the Soul and Society.
It is *compensating:* A true vision of God is worth any price a man pays for it. Worth a king's death whether Uzziah's or prosperity's, the final Secret of Peace and Power.—Our horizons are no longer empty. They are bright with love, and guarded by the Eternal.
Note: In the full development of this theme and text I would take great care to keep it close to the actual experiences of troubled folk to-day. The illustrations would be in the applications.

A caustic and able preacher critic said of Atkins in my hearing: "He is not dogmatic enough; as a preacher, his style is beautiful but fails to grip the realities that the average man must battle with all his life. He is a preacher to the cultured, the charmed circle, university audiences, sequestered souls. I enjoy hearing him, but his preaching would never save my soul." Granted, but it takes all kinds of preaching to save all kinds of souls. I have not the slightest doubt that Apollos reached some souls that were impervious to Paul's preaching, which put at least one hearer to sleep. Or maybe Eutychus (see Acts 20:9) was so terribly tired that even the eloquent Alexandrian could not have kept him awake.

Dr. Atkins is an author of established reputation. His *Pilgrims of the Lonely Road, The Undiscovered Country, Modern Religious Cults and Movements, The Making of the Christian Mind* have found, delighted and fed the minds of an ever widening constituency. One of his recent books is entitled *The Procession of the Gods,* a most alluring theme and certain to attract a multitude of readers who have learned that Dr. Atkins never publishes until he has something worth publishing. His latest volume is a discriminating life of *John Henry Newman,* which has been highly praised by the reviewers. That out of the way, Atkins is now at work on another book of an entirely different nature and busy gathering material.

Having held conspicuous pastorates in Burlington, Vermont, Providence, Rhode Island, and Detroit, Michigan, two periods in the latter city, he resigned from First Congregational Church, Detroit, to become professor of Preaching in Auburn Theological Seminary, New York. Since Dr. Atkins went to his new field, his productivity as an author has been increased. He has more time for the brooding necessary for creative work. Visiting him in Huntington House on the campus at Auburn, the environment seems ideal. It is a comfortable, rambling sort of place and his library with its open fireplace and log wood burning there on a winter's day, is most inviting. Near by are the classrooms where he meets his students who are dreaming of careers as ambassadors of the spiritual life. Could anything be more attractive to a minister who knows full well the anxieties, endless tasks of a city church and has been relieved of the uncongenial chores of "serving tables"?

Pastors of large city churches who have passed fifty love to dream of retiring at sixty to some less exacting post of duty where they may write books, lecture and do occasional preaching, thus escaping the burden of administrative and pastoral duties. It is an alluring dream, but the reality is not always paradisiacal. Do you doubt this? Then hear Atkins:

"Jones, no preacher who has long been in the pastorate knows until he has experienced it, what it means to be without a congregation. At first he has a sense of release, of immense liberation; he is free at last. But that soon gives place to a feeling of loneliness, terrible loneliness. It is as if the head of a household should suddenly find himself without a family—children, wife, grandchildren all gone. One has to get used to it and that takes time. I enjoy my professorial work, authorship, occasional preaching, talking to and with young men who are preparing for the ministry, but I miss something, and that something is the sense of a congregational comradeship, the knowledge that I have a church, that I am shepherd of a flock. There are compensations, of course, but I miss my church."

Dr. Atkins refers whimsically to his authorship:

"The average religious books pay the writer very little. One publishing house which specializes in such literature pays no royalty at all on the first thousand and there is rarely a second thousand. All my own sermons—which went into books—were published on that highly remunerative basis. There were four volumes of them. I doubt if I received three hundred dollars for the lot. Other houses do better, and pay a royalty on the first thousand—ten per cent. They can not be priced over one dollar and fifty cents—and with a few exceptions—rarely go over one thousand. There you are: one hundred and fifty dollars. If the sermons have already been written and preached, that is, I suppose, mostly to the good, since the church has carried the preacher's overhead. In return he expects his congregation to buy—and read—the sermons.

"I used to see mine conspicuously on center tables with the pages uncut. After that I always arranged with the publisher to have the pages cut. It saved everybody's face.

"Religious books—or books about religion—are another matter. Even then a sale of two or three thousand is exceptional unless they are taken by the Religious Book Club. Rabbi Silver's book sold almost ten thousand. My *Procession of the Gods* has gone to about eight thousand, but it has a text-book use. My *Life of Newman* which was very widely received has not yet gone to one thousand. The labor of a research book like the *Procession of the Gods* is very great. I spent three years on it. I doubt if I got the wages of unskilled labor per hour from it—when unskilled labor got thirty cents an hour."

There is food for reflection in this humorous yet wise commentation. I question the likelihood that men of the caliber and character of Gaius Glenn Atkins sever those exquisitely tender pastoral relationships or circumscribe their prophetic careers, when they do as this minister has done. Rather, they extend their parish through their books, lectures and preaching ministry to college and university audiences. In a true sense they multiply their usefulness. If young men are to be trained for the ministry as of course they must, then there is every need that the training be done by men of unusual parts who have made a conspicuous success as preachers, pastors and administrators in charge of important churches. Did the late Dr. John A. Broadus make a mistake when he resigned a conspicuous pulpit to teach multitudes of young men how to preach? Give us Elishas, trained by Elijahs. What a privilege to study preaching under Atkins, mighty master of that art of arts!

Visiting Atkins once when he was in an expansive mood, I was vastly entertained as he spoke of men and movements. "Extremists and fanatics have made most of the world's trouble," he mused. "The extreme abolitionists and pro-slavery extremists provoked the Civil War; fanatical prohibitionists and radical evil-minded liquor advocates combined to put prohibition in the organic law of the land before we were ready for such drastic action, and behold the result—nation-wide disrespect for all law, liquor obtainable everywhere, and the bootlegger and racketeer flaunting their crimes in our faces. Extreme fundamentalists and intolerant liberals keep the churches in a stew. The moderates in politics, whether of state or church, are seldom heard; they get caught between the contending forces led by immoderates, and are squeezed into action on one side or the other. The extremists of Jesus' day sent Him to the cross. I do not deny the place of extremists in the grand scheme of things, but I maintain it is out of proportion and destructive. Preach a sermon, Jones, from the text: 'Let your moderation be known to all men.' It's needed."

G.G.A. loves the beautiful, is in rapport with crimson skies at sunset, deeply moved by a sight of the long roll of the surf on a wild stretch of seashore; glories in the bespangled heavens on a clear winter night. A garden of old-fashioned roses casts a spell over him, and lilac bushes white or lavender lure him as the lust for gold lured Cortez. He is an amateur ornithologist to whom woodland and open fields at the season of migrations are enchanted ground. Talking birds with Atkins once upon a time and agreeing with his view that the day one chances to have a good look at a male scarlet tanager is a day to remember, he remarked: "The notes of a wood thrush resemble the sound of a farmer whetting his scythe."

This remark of G.G.A.'s may not be original but it was the first time I heard such a comparison and I still think it happy and revealing. Atkins is like that—interesting, refreshing, whimsical, full of sentiment though never sentimental; an ardent book-lover yet not bookish, intellectual but not ever a pedant; a very great gentleman of the best of schools and one of the oldest—the school of Jesus of Bethany.

TITTLE, Ernest Fremont, clergyman; *b.* Springfield, O., Oct. 21, 1885; *s.* Clayton Darius and Elizabeth (Henry) T.; A.B., Ohio Wesleyan U., 1906; B.D., Drew Theological Seminary, 1908; D.D., Ohio Wesleyan University and Garrett Biblical Institute; LL.D., Wittenberg College; *m.* Glenna Myers of Springfield, June 11, 1908; children—John Myers, Elizabeth Ann, William Myers. Ordained M. E. ministry, 1910; pastor Christiansburg, O., 1908-10; Riverdale, Dayton, O., 1910-13; University Ch., Delaware, O., 1913-16, Broad St. Ch., Columbus, O., 1916-18, 1st Ch., Evanston, Ill., Dec. 1918-. With Army Y.M.C.A. in U. S., 2 mos., in France 6 mos.; participated in St. Mihiel offensive. Trustee Northwestern University; mem. Federal Council of Chs. of Christ in America, Phi Kappa Psi, Phi Beta Kappa. Mason. *Author:* What Must the Church Do To Be Saved? 1921; The Religion of the Spirit, 1928; The Foolishness of Preaching, 1930; We Need Religion, 1931. *Home:* 1810 Hinman Av., Evanston, Ill.

Chapter VIII

ERNEST FREMONT TITTLE

"Who is the ablest preacher in Methodism to-day?" I put this question to an eminent minister of that powerful communion which owes its origin to the tireless genius of John Wesley. "It depends on the type of preacher you have in mind," he replied. "We have a score of men in our ministry who preach with brilliance and popular favor. Bishop McConnell is a prophetic voice. Lynn Hough is a scintillating scholar. Ralph Sockman is a charming fellow with a divine gift of homiletics. Joe Gray has a lot of pulpit ability, but for unique and all around preaching ability, I would put Dr. Tittle of the First Church, Evanston, at the top."

I asked another well-known Methodist leader, "Who is your denomination's most powerful preacher?" "Tittle, of Evanston. He leaves me cold but he has the goods: brains, courage and an extraordinary gift of adapting the old Gospel to present conditions. He is the preacher of preachers for your flapper college girl and gay freshman to hear. They have to think if they listen to him. He outsmarts them and they like it. They know too that he understands them. Tittle is Methodism's best gift to the university circles."

I sauntered one day into a book store that specializes in religious literature, browsed around and not seeing anything that appealed to me, was on the point of leaving when a salesman I knew hailed me with the query; "Have you seen *The Foolishness of Preaching?*" "No, but I have heard a deal of it, and done some of it, I fear. What's on your mind?" "This volume," he rejoined, placing in my hands a book bound in black cloth with gold letters reading, *The Foolishness of Preaching, and Other Sermons,* by Ernest

Fremont Tittle. "It is great stuff," he assured me, "fresh, thoughtful, well phrased, very much alive." "What a salesman," I thought as I parted from some money, left the store, and on a ten-mile bus ride read with absorbing interest three of the twenty-one chapters.

This was not the first volume by Tittle that had come to my notice. Some years before I picked up somewhere his Mendenhall Lectures given at DePauw University and published under the title, *What Must the Church Do To Be Saved?* I liked the frank and fearless way the author dealt in these lectures with certain "touchy" subjects, his ungloved handling of institutionalism and antiquated theology. He seemed to be wearing new mental clothes, and I admired his garments. So I lived with *The Foolishness of Preaching* for the good part of a week, at odd hours, and after the day's work was done. Such chapters as "The Modern Jonah," "An Adequate National Defense," "Christianity in a Machine Age," "Reformer, Reform Yourself," kept me awake far past the curfew hour. I especially reveled in Chapter One, "The Field of the Pulpit—Life," where Tittle gives his opinion of the *Chicago Tribune* which on its own confession is the "World's Greatest Newspaper." As I read on I resolved to hear this preacher who spoke so pointedly and with such courage. I resolved to hear this man Tittle at the first opportunity. It came shortly.

It was at Chicago and in the chapel of a University Church on an evening with three hundred in the audience, many of them students and ministers. I saw a man of slight build and extremely youthful-looking sitting on the platform at one side of the pulpit desk. It was Tittle, of Evanston. He sat quietly throughout the brief preliminaries led by another and an older minister. When the time came for the sermon, he stepped quickly to the desk then moved to one side and began talking in a conversational tone on the subject of "Christianity and Internationalism." His sentences were short, pithy. Occasionally he was mildly sarcastic. He chided the so-called Christian statesmen, the servile clergy and other religious leaders, who love to ring the changes on Decatur's famous slogan, "My country, right or wrong." He wondered how patriotism could be saved, and just what constituted an "adequate defense" for the nation. It was an intellectual treat and a prophetic strain ran through the speech. The address, for it was not a formal sermon, sparkled. It was more of the head than of the heart, if you know what I mean. The quality uppermost was intellectual vigor, saturated with a bold liberalism. It was not fervid but there was an incandescent glow in the mind of the speaker.

Returning to the book *The Foolishness of Preaching,* Dr. Tittle employs no texts at the head of his chapters; all the familiar earmarks of published sermons are missing; but they are sermons not essays. They are all so good that it is difficult to select a particular sermon for analysis, but after some hesitation I chose the thirteenth sermon, "The Modern Jonah," as typical of Dr. Tittle's style, method and treatment. He plunges at once into the subject with these strong sentences:

> "The book of Jonah is the first great missionary tract ever written. It is one of the greatest books in the Old Testament. Its unknown author appears to have possessed the vision of a St. Paul, the satiric power of a George Bernard Shaw, and the delicious humor of a Gilbert Chesterton. Is this great little book a true story? As well ask is the parable of the Prodigal Son a true story? Neither the one nor the other represents an actual occurrence; yet how persistently true they are, how utterly accurate as portraits of a multitude of human hearts! In that prodigal son who gathered all together and went into a far country and wasted his substance in riotous living, and began to be in want, how many a man has recognized himself! And if in that disobedient prophet whose racial prejudices led him to refuse a divinely appointed task many another man does

not recognize himself, it is only because the everlasting meaning of the book of Jonah has been lost sight of in the dust of a foolish, futile controversy over the ability of a fish to swallow a man, and the ability of a man to live three days and three nights in the belly of a fish."

Now this is getting off to a good start. Curiosity is piqued, interest stimulated. Next he tells the story of Jonah, using seven robust and vivid paragraphs for that purpose. Then he gives in a brief paragraph what he terms the "abiding message of the book of Jonah," Thus:

"God cares for the Jew, but also for the Ninevite. He cares for the native born, but also for the foreign born. He cares for the white man, but also for the yellow man, and the brown, and the black. The love of God is broader than the measure of prejudicial people's minds. The concern of God reaches farther than hooded klansmen suppose."

And how masterfully the preacher links this Old Testament story with nowaday affairs. There is nothing academic or detached in this sort of preaching. It is so much alive that it glows, pulsates, and almost, but not quite, burns. Listen:

"What is pictured in Hollywood is seen in Tokio, not always to the moral advantage of the Japanese. What is spoken in Chicago is heard in Shanghai. What is whispered in the ear in the chancelleries of Europe and of America becomes a topic of conversation for the educated portion of the Orient, and after a little, even for the coolies and the jinrikisha man. The day of isolation is forever past; the day of world-wide contact has arrived. More and more the peoples of the world are going to mingle. Old King Canute standing on the beach and commanding the tide to stand still is a no more ludicrous figure than the man who supposes that by any number of kinds of exclusion acts, the intermingling of racial groups can be permanently checked."

What kind of human being is the man who can preach with such penetration and intellectual clarity? Dr. Tittle is not physically robust and has had to wrestle with a number of "break-downs." But his resilience is good and he recoups loss of strength and energy rapidly. His is an agreeable voice, deep and sonorous, a voice not naturally effective but made so by careful training. His gestures are few and more often made by a nod or a shake of the head than with his hands. For the most part his hands grip the lapels of his coat or gown; or they rest on the pulpit desk. One who knows him intimately writes: "There is no taint of snobbery about him. There is no bitterness in his soul, not even when 'The world's greatest newspaper,' questions his patriotism or cruelly lampoons him for his pacific stand. . . . His people love him, almost worship him." One can readily believe it. His hold on college young people is remarkable. His preaching brethren like and admire him even when they disagree with him. But not many, I fancy, are given to slapping him on the back and calling him "Ernie." Before this man's courage and sincerity most of his critics, but not all of them, bow reverently. Dr. Tittle acknowledges no hobby. Golf and cards he thoroughly dislikes but he enjoys climbing mountains, and like Thomas Jefferson he derives a vast deal of pleasure from playing a violin. He has the gift of sketching, and a charming landscape or lovely sketch of shore and sea he skilfully transfers to canvas for his own enjoyment; though friends who are fortunate enough to see these sketches share with the amateur artist the joy that is his. He reads widely and constantly, is always preparing to preach, though not given to exacting the sermonic pound of flesh from everything he reads or experiences, as is the custom of some ministers of parts.

I asked Dr. Tittle his opinion as to the content and objectives of preaching for our times. He answered, "I believe that preaching to-day should of course retain its ethical and social emphasis, but should also place behind it a profoundly religious conception of life and the world. Something must be done to help people recover their vanishing faith in God."

"You preach to hosts of young people, Dr. Tittle. Do you prepare and preach your sermons with these young folks in mind?" His reply was characteristic I thought.

"I do not often preach a sermon with young people only in mind. I do, of course, remember that hundreds of students are in my congregation and I try to keep their needs, both intellectual and moral, continually in mind."

"Where do you get your sermon themes, from books or people? How do you prepare for the pulpit?"

"Generally speaking," replied the doctor, "I get suggestions for themes from conversations which reveal urgent needs of one kind or another."

I was anxious to know what Dr. Tittle considered the besetting sin of the ministry. He told me in exactly eleven words, to wit: "Intellectual laziness. I am afraid cowardice ought also to be mentioned." The phrase "I am afraid" is revealing. This man loves his fellow ministers and is reluctant to criticize their frailties. But he is likewise a lover of the truth and knows that there are men in the ministry as there are in other vocations who side-step unpopular issues and trim their speech to serve the hour.

An organization calling itself the Paul Reveres addressed a letter to the ministers of Evanston, saluting them as "Reverend Sirs" and demanding a categorical answer "Yes" or "No" to three questions, namely: "Would you be good enough to indicate: whether you favor the leaning of some of our Evanston churches toward socialism and communism? Have you made a pulpit statement on your opinion of the end results of these leanings in the church of Jesus Christ? And if you have not, will you?"

Unmistakably this scurrilous questionnaire was an attack on the pastor of the First Methodist Church of Evanston and the official board of that body so construing it, called a special meeting and unanimously endorsed the following ringing statement:

> "For some time a campaign of insinuation, misrepresentation and slander, much of it anonymous, has been directed against our pastor, Dr. Ernest F. Tittle. We believe that we owe it to him and to our church and to this community to assert unmistakably our loyalty to him and our protest against such un-American and unchristian procedure.
>
> "After fourteen years of intimate association with Dr. Tittle as our minister, we would express our absolute confidence in his Christian character and his deep and unselfish devotion to his country, to the church, and to humanity. He is unalterably opposed to the methods of violence advocated by communism, and steadfastly committed to the orderly processes of democratic government.
>
> "We stand for a free pulpit and a free church. We do not expect or desire a minister simply to echo the opinions of the congregation, and we do not assert our individual agreement with all our minister's utterances. But we vigorously resent the effort of outside organizations to dictate to the church or to prescribe its message.
>
> "We hold it peculiarly important in this day that the church should stand apart from all appeals to passion, prejudice, and partisanship, and that our nation should have in the Christian Church a clear strong voice rising above all divisions, speaking in the name of God for justice, mutual understanding and good will.
>
> "This statement is authorized by the governing board of the First Methodist Episcopal Church of Evanston, Illinois."

I asked Dr. Tittle how it felt to be called a "Communist." His reply supplies material for a half-dozen sermons, or indeed a book: "Notwithstanding the fact that I am unalterably opposed to the methods of violence advocated by Communism, the accusation that I am a Communist has caused me seriously to ask, What would I be saying and doing today if I were a thoroughgoing Christian?"

A thoughtful pause followed. Then he went on:

"To-day I am more than ever convinced that Jesus is indeed the Way, the Truth and the Life. History, which has so often vindicated Him, is certainly vindicating Him now. They that took the sword *are* perishing with the sword. They that selfishly sought to save their own lives and investments *are* losing them. A society divided against itself is *not* standing. A society which laid up for itself treasures upon the earth—and none in heaven—is going to pieces. And behold what is being added unto a society that sought first not the kingdom of God but wealth, pleasure and power! Jesus is no longer on trial. What is on trial is a civilization which has piously called him 'Lord! Lord!' but refused to do the things which He commanded."

It was no occasion of surprise to Dr. Tittle's friends, though it was of rejoicing, when the announcement came of his selection as 1932 lecturer in the most famous series on preaching in the world—the Lyman Beecher Foundation at Yale. Established in 1871, this lectureship has been graced by the most distinguished preachers on both sides of the Atlantic and it would seem that everything worth saying on preaching had been said, and said superbly by the masters of modern pulpit discourse. Dr. Tittle's series, now available in book form, is in keeping with the noble line in which he appeared. It is entitled, *Jesus after Nineteen Centuries,* and there are eight lectures beginning with the theme "Light For Men" and ending with "A Creative Faith." The same clarity of style and high courage characterizes these lectures, as do Dr. Tittle's sermons. The thought is, I fancy, more closely woven than in his regular preaching, and the illustrative material bulks less. In his chapter on "The Larger Loyalty" this prophet of the twentieth century has this flaming paragraph:

"But, oh, a challenge is now presented to the souls of men; to prevent industrial paralysis, starvation, anarchy—the collapse of civilization; to lay at least the foundation of a social order that shall be more just, and therefore more secure; to beat all swords into plowshares and build institutions of peace; to abolish poverty, and unemployment, banish disease, disseminate knowledge, lift the masses of men to a higher material and spiritual level; to achieve new victories through science, new glories through art, new insights through religion, new discoveries through God. What a challenge it is—the challenge of a dream! But it is the only dream worth dreaming, the only madness that borders on sanity, the only fanaticism that is in accord with reality, the only ambition that will not eventually hurt the man who has it and tear his world to pieces, the only salvation for society, the only happiness and peace for the individual, the only end that is worth living for."

A truly Websterian paragraph and filled with pith and point, the creed of a modern Amos, Micah, Isaiah rolled into one, a courteous, lovable, minister of Jesus Christ, human to the core, a little aloof intellectually, enraptured with the gospel of social justice, a personality touched with an incandescence that glows and glows. Verily, Ernest Fremont Tittle could say with Lucifer in his dialogue with Festus:

"It is time that something should be done for the poor
The sole equality on earth is death;
Now rich and poor are both dissatisfied.
I am for judgment; that will settle both.
Nothing is to be done without destruction;
Death is the universal salt of states . . .
I should like to macadamize the world;
The road to heaven needs mending."

SHANNON, Frederick Franklin, clergyman; *b.* Morris Co., Kan., Feb. 11, 1877; *s.* James W. and Kate P. (Sullivan) S.; ed. Webb Sch., Bell Buckle, Tenn.; Harvard Univ., 1898-99; Litt. D., Syracuse U., 1924; LL.D., Lincoln Memorial Univ., Harrogate, Tenn., 1929; *m.* Effie Grace Myers, of York, Pa., May 3, 1903; 1 son, Frederick Nighbert. Ordained Methodist Episcopal Church, South, 1899; pastor Logan, W. Va., 1899-1900, Grace Ch., Brooklyn, 1904-12, Ref. Ch. on Heights, Brooklyn, 1912-19, Central Ch., Chicago, since Jan. 1920. *Author:* The Soul's Atlas and Other Sermons, 1911; The New Personality, 1915; The Enchanted Universe, 1916; The Breath in the Winds, 1918; God's Faith in Man, 1919; The Economic Eden; The Land of Beginning Again; The Infinite Artist; The Country Faith; A Moneyless Magnate; The New Greatness; The Unfathomable Christ; Doors of God; The Universe Within. *Home:* 6933 Oglesby Av., Chicago, Ill.

Chapter IX

FREDERICK F. SHANNON

Dr. Shannon, of Central Church, Chicago, is the artist in the pulpit. I agree with the writer of a brief biographical sketch of this preacher that "No Velasquez ever mixed his colors with greater skill than Shannon reveals in the use of his winged words." There is more than a suggestion of the rich style of Newell Dwight Hillis in Shannon's sermons, to wit: wealth of literary allusion, splendid rhetoric and a homiletic genius expressed in apt and unusual phrasing of topics as well as cumulative and striking divisional arrangement. Also, this preacher is a master user of illustration and poetical quotation.

The physical presence of Dr. Shannon is not particularly impressive. He is slight of build and on first sight when compared with his immediate predecessor he suffers considerably. You miss the large and sturdy frame, the Atlantean shoulders, the noble head and powerful personality of Dr. Gunsaulus. Shannon doesn't quite look the great preacher part as he comes into the pulpit or participates in the preliminary service. But once in the sermon, the artistry of his preaching, the beauty of his rhetoric, the sheer brilliance of his sermonic art, captures and holds you captive to the end.

An interesting feature of Dr. Shannon's pulpit power is his posture, the attitude of his body in the delivery of the sermon, which helps to drive home his points. It is a shame to put a gown upon some preachers for the reason that their bodies preach: shoulders, arms, legs, feet, all preach. This was true of Beecher and to a certain extent it was true of Talmadge. Shannon strikes dramatic attitudes in the course of the sermon. Standing out on the rostrum in full view of the audience, it is fascinating to watch his apparently unconscious attitudinizing. His postures fit the particular part of the sermon and seem to be quite unintentional. Listening to him in a sermon preached in a Detroit theater during a pre-Easter series I observed at least four different dramatic postures in which head, hands, feet—his entire body—coordinated perfectly with the theme, and climactically so.

I incline to the belief that Dr. Shannon has the most remarkable gift of any American preacher when it comes to the titling of his sermons, though Dr. Halford Luccock is not far behind. I think I should rank Hubert L. Simpson, on the other side of the Atlantic, as equaling him in this art although differing somewhat in the choice of titles and the manner of phrasing them. Here are a few of Shannon's sermon subjects, gathered at random: "The Breath in the Winds," Ezekiel 37:9; "The Heavenly Human," Matthew 5:48; "The Enchanted Universe," "The Land of Beginning Again," "The Infinite Artist," "Some Friends of Mine in Paradise," Luke 23:43; "The Ultimate Riches," Genesis 13:2; "Fireproof Faith," Daniel 3:15; "The Priority of the Spiritual," Matthew 6:33.

Dr. Shannon broadcasts his sermons from Orchestra Hall regularly. Multitudes throughout Illinois, Indiana, Wisconsin and adjoining states, tune in for his half-hour discourses. "Did you hear Dr. Shannon Sunday?" is a familiar inquiry heard in Bloomington, Illinois, or Crawfordsville, Indiana. His radio mail is large and filled with sincere tributes to his words of comfort and good cheer.

Interrogating Dr. Shannon on preaching is an agreeable experience. "You are ranked among the leaders in the homiletic art," I began. "Tell me how you go about preparing a sermon."

"Frankly I am always going about sermon preparation," he replied. "That is, as I reflect, observe, read, converse, I am in a continuous process of sermonic preparation. Take the matter of text and theme; for me their relation must be definite, else I never successfully begin. This relation in nine cases out of ten is seen through what I call my 'inner flash,' a kind of insight which, however sudden, constitutes the solidity of the sermon itself. Without this flash, text and theme lack for me the organic relation of sermonic livingness."

"Sermonic livingness is good," I commented. "Do you ever repeat sermons, your best sermons, to your regular congregation? Jenkins of Kansas City does occasionally, likewise Clausen of Syracuse. The latter, you will remember, wrote a book entitled *Preach It Again*."

"So far as I can recall I have never, in thirty years' ministry, repeated a sermon to my regular congregation. Like most preachers I love certain texts and sermons beyond others and frequently use these in other churches and cities over the country. Though often requested to repeat sermons preached in Central Church, I never do it; it simply will not work for me. Socrates, you will remember, had his 'demon, or good genius,' well my 'sermonic demon' is hypersensitiveness in this matter. When I tell 'him' that 'he' is absolutely foolish 'he' says that even 'his' foolishness is due to association with me, and so the argument ends. Moreover I have scores of sermons I have never preached; they are as nearly complete as any of my sermons are up to Sunday morning; that is, text and theme, collateral reading, references, illustrations—all the sermonic work has been done. But one thing is needful; my own personal preparation—the mood, the irresistible feel, as it were, for a particular sermon. When these three—the text, the theme and I—get together, really understand each other, and are tuned in each to each, then 'we' have a going sermonic concern, but not until then!"

"Most interesting, Dr. Shannon, I thank you. But you haven't said a word as to your subjects—I mean the striking nomenclature of your sermons. You are unusually gifted in this respect. How do you do it?"

"I give much attention to this aspect of the sermon. Believing that a single clean-cut phrase should express the meaning of each discourse, I try to shape that phrase. Of course, there's no telling when or where the topic and phrasing will come. It may be while walking, reading, listening, talking, meditating. Most sermons come to me while reading the Bible for devotional rather than for sermonic reasons. The important thing is that I must seize the topic when it 'flashes,' so to speak. I have just counted twenty note-books covering a quarter of a century. They are filled with topics and sermonic material gathered from philosophic, scientific, historic, and poetic readings. These books are alive with sermonic stuff; but as I have one or two new ones always in my pockets I shall hardly be able, in this little life, to give the old material its due because the new is aggressively pushing it to the rear.

"I may add that I rarely write a sermon until it has been preached. Using the barest outline, to which I scarcely refer, my phrasing comes in the process of preaching. I have no memory for prose, but a somewhat unusual one for poetry. Memoriter preaching has always been, for me, out of the question; I simply am 'not there' in such a process; and I never read a sermon from the pulpit in my life."

"What of pastoral calling? Do you find time for visitation among your parishioners?"

"For necessary visitation, yes. Social calls are reduced to the minimum; there is neither time nor strength for them. The regular membership averages a distance of seven miles. Our members live not only in various sections of Chicago, but in Glencoe, Evanston, Oak Park, Wheaton and other places. Pastoral work, therefore, is largely confined to cases of sickness and death."

"And now if you are through quizzing me on the preaching subject, let's talk about Woodrow Wilson. Have you read Ray Stannard Baker's third and fourth volumes?"

I had, but that is another story.

The opinions of intelligent preachers concerning other preachers are a source of unending interest to me. Even when I am not wholly in agreement with their criticisms

I am fascinated by them. Talking with a Chicago preacher of analytical mind about Dr. Shannon and his preaching, he said: "Shannon is not a preacher. He is a skilful homilist."

"Explain the difference between a homilist and a preacher," I suggested.

"Certainly. It is easy. A homilist is a maker of sermons, an artist in sermonic construction whose first thought and last thought is the sermon, construction, delivery. A preacher is a proclaimer of the life spiritual, an interpreter of religion who is more concerned with the content of his preaching than he is with the artistry of the sermon. I will not say that homilists are never prophets. I will say that they seldom are. They entertain, delight and sometimes comfort their hearers, but rarely stir the hearts of men deeply and move them to repentance."

Reflecting on this rather severe criticism, I recall what a fellow minister once said to me as we lunched together with a dozen or so other parsons. "Jones, your trouble is that you are tempted to care more about the way you say a thing, than what you say." If he had whanged me over the head with the big spoon with which he was helping himself to a supply of buttered beets, I wouldn't have been more surprised or hurt. But I am sure the robust Presbyterian prophet who so addressed me did me a service, and that he meant to do just that.

Every preacher has his peculiar temptations and I suppose that Dr. Shannon has to watch himself lest the very artistry of his sermons weaken their appeal to the will of man and do not stir him to repentance unto salvation. Almost before one knows it, to so gifted a sermonizer the sermon becomes an end in itself. I do not say this is the case with Dr. Shannon; I say it might become so to any man who loves beautiful rhetoric. This I know: I heard him once in a sermon full of color and charm, flawless in composition, exquisite in phrasings. Yet in the midst of it, even while I was admiring the art everywhere in evidence, there came a swift sentence that stabbed me wide awake and made me question a certain phase of my own religious experience. Moreover, I carried away with me that day that conscience-quickening thought. It filled me with a kind of divine discontent and I feel sure profited me greatly. As long as Dr. Shannon carries such arrows in his sermonic quiver he is immune from serfdom to lovely diction.

A sermon by Dr. Shannon which I first read more than a decade ago still haunts me, and I take down the volume in which it appears and reread it, from time to time. The title is "Life's Last Thirty Minutes." The text is James 4:14, "What is your life?" I fancy Shannon preached this sermon on a Sunday either at the end of the old year or the beginning of the new. He introduces the subject by a reference to Canon Liddon's celebrated discourse on "The First Five Minutes after Death." Dr. Shannon bases this sermon upon a dream. He dreamed he had but thirty minutes to live and so began at once to figure how he could make the most of that tremendous half-hour. There are five divisions. 1. He received an unforgettable impression of the value of time, and thought of Henry Vaughan's memorable lines, "I saw Eternity the other night." 2. He experienced a quickened sense of the beauty of the world, the sky at sunset time, the grass, the water, the trees, the birds, the clouds. 3. He decided to make use of his last thirty minutes doing some things which he might have done but which had been left undone. He wanted to whisper something consoling into the ear of the heartbroken. He wanted to help carry the load of the overburdened, to make certain calls, to write certain letters. 4. He decided he must have five minutes just to gaze into human faces, the face of a little child, the face of an aged woman, the face of a hod carrier, faces, human faces. 5. And now with only ten minutes remaining of the fleeting thirty he wanted to read for five minutes, and being told he could have any book that he wished from any library ancient or modern, he chose the Bible and opened it at the twenty-third Psalm, and then again at the fourteenth chapter of St. John. As for the last five minutes, let the preacher himself speak:

> "And now there were just five minutes more! But that feeling of terrible solemnity had already passed into an experience of unutterable joy. Had the Little Book triumphed again? I am sure it had; for I was not so much in tune with the infinite as I was in soul-deep communion with God. I saw the everlasting miracle and power of prayer. It seemed the mightiest, subtlest force in the universe, passing through matter and space with inconceivable velocity and irresistible momentum. It went straight to its mark—the Heart of God. Some of the answers were instantaneous, some were ages and ages in being answered, but all were answered. And then—I woke up."

As poet-preacher, rhetorician and sermonizer superb, Frederick F. Shannon's name is rightly emblazoned on the scroll of popular American preachers.

MATTHEWS, Mark Allison, clergyman; *b.* Calhoun, Ga., Sept. 24, 1867; *s.* Mark Lafayette and Malinda Rebecca (Clemmons) M.; acad. edn. at Calhoun, Ga.; D.D., 1900; LL.D. Whitman Coll., 1908, Huron Coll. 1912; *m.* at Seattle, Wash., Grace Owen, *d.* Rev. Owen Jones, of Wales, Aug. 24, 1904. Began preaching at 19; ordained Presbyn. ministry, 1887; pastor First Ch. (which he built), Calhoun, Ga., 1888-93, Dalton, Ga., 1893-96; Jackson, Tenn., 1896-1902; First Ch., Seattle, since 1902 (membership over 7,500, 25 branch Sunday schs.). Admitted to bar June, 1900. Trustee Whitman College, Walla Walla, Wash., Whitworth Coll., Spokane, Wash., San Francisco Theol. Sem., Seattle Chamber of Commerce. Mem. Federal Council of Chs. and Ministers Assn. York and Scottish Rite Mason. *Clubs:* Commercial, Rainier, Arctic, Union League, Masonic; Japanese (New York and Seattle). Moderator Gen. Assembly Presbyn. Ch., Louisville, 1912. *Home:* 726 Harvard St. N., Seattle, Wash.

Chapter X

MARK A. MATTHEWS

It is surely something to be the minister of the largest Presbyterian Church in the world. That church is the First Presbyterian parish of Seattle, Washington, and the minister is the Rev. Mark Allison Matthews, D.D. The church numbers seventy-five hundred members and operates twenty-five branch Sunday-Schools. The building in which this congregation meets is a monstrous affair, and it is comfortably filled twice a Sunday almost the year around. The church is a beehive of activity, with a large staff and myriad organizations, but the dominating personality that keeps the institution moving and over the life of which his lengthened shadow falls is the tall, slender, gray-templed preacher-pastor, Dr. Matthews, known as "The Tall Pine of the Sierras," a man of force and unwearied energy.

Practically everybody in Seattle knows Mark Matthews. His tall gaunt figure, swathed in a long-tailed coat, a broad-brimmed western hat crowning his head, hair curling over his collar, is a familiar sight to citizens of Seattle. He is as much at home in the metropolis of his state as is King George in London, and as sure of his divine right to rule his congregation and instruct a General Assembly of his brethren, as the British Sovereign his subjects, with this difference: England's king never interferes with politics of the realm, Dr. Matthews frequently mixes in with the politics of Presbyterianism. When there was some talk of omitting the annual General Assembly in 1933 because of the financial depression, or at least reducing the quota of delegates by half, Dr. Matthews thundered: "No Presbytery has a right to elect less than its full quota. . . . If there is not enough money for expenses, let them walk. If they can not walk then something is the matter with their feet as well as their heads. This is the time when the Presbyterian Church should function at its radio of power, the reason being that the nation has gone crazy." And that's that!

A mentor of orthodoxy is Dr. Matthews. He is a militant fundamentalist and proud of it. He is dogmatic in his preaching and glories in it. He is a defender of the faith once for all delivered to the Presbyterian saints and willing that every one should know it. He loves a good old-fashioned fight with his brethren of the liberal school and never asks for quarter. He believes in the verbal inspiration of the Bible and loves to give his reasons for such belief. He is a fiery evangelistic preacher and always preaches for a verdict. He is postive in his convictions, positive he is right, positive that world redemption is only possible through the acceptance of the Gospel as he interprets and expounds it. And Dr. Matthews' positiveness largely accounts for his extraordinary success.

Matthews, of Seattle, is not a middle-of-the-roader. He certainly is not "on the fence." The following verses were not written of him:

"There was once a preacher of sense
Who sat very tight on the fence.
When the folks of the town
Said, 'Preacher, come down!'
He replied with a feeling intense,
'The question is Whither, not Whence!' "

His preaching is theologically severe but not personally so. His doctrines cut deep and do not admit of compromise or evasion, but the man himself is genial, loves a good story, and tells one admirably. His sermons do not read as well as they sound when he preaches them. They are quite devoid of rhetorical finish or elaboration. They are direct and clear, simple in construction though interlarded with the conventional theological phrases. In a sermon on "The Seven R's of the Full Gospel," Dr. Matthews' style and theology are typically presented. Taking as texts Matthew 28: 19, and II Timothy 4: 2, the preacher discusses: "1. Ruined by the Fall. 2. Redemption by Jesus Christ. 3. Regeneration by the Holy Spirit. 4. Reformation by Regeneration," and under his fifth and sixth divisions he discusses "Resurrection by Jesus Christ and Return of Christ," of which I submit a fragment:

> "The soul has always been immortal. It cannot be touched by death. Christianity is a present day power and force. Men are saved now, not hereafter. Men are lost now. Therefore, Christianity is presented to them at this time, and the Gospel is brought to them in their lost and ruined condition. Jesus Christ came after them and offers them salvation now. It is for this world, and the world to come. Therefore Christ arose from the dead and became the first fruits, consequently there must be a harvest. He arose for our justification. He ascended for our glorification. By His resurrection He guaranteed the resurrection of every human body in the world. He was the first fruits; we are the subsequent fruits. I speak reverentially when I say that God cannot keep this body from being raised again. I do not care what you do with the body when the soul leaves it. You may bury it, cremate it, feed it to the birds, or give it to the fishes. There is no power to prevent God from bringing it back a resurrected, glorified body. He makes it over anew every seven years. Why can't He make it over again after the soul has left it? At the resurrection my mortal body shall put on immortality; it shall lose its corruption and become immortal. Into that immortal body the soul will again enter and live with Christ forever and ever.
>
> "Christ came into this world to establish His Father's Kingdom. When He ascended to Heaven and began His mediatorial work it was with the distinct promise that He would return and gather the Church unto Himself.

Christ is coming again in the manner in which He ascended. I do not know when He will return, am not interested in the date, do not care, would like to see Him at once. Whether He comes before my death or after it, makes no difference to me. He has said that no man knew, not even the angels, when He would return. Only His Father knows the time of His second advent. I know He is coming, and I rejoice in the fact. When He comes He will gather the Church unto Himself. He has said to His disciples, to His children, to His church, 'Where I am there you shall be forever and ever.' Wherever Christ is that is Heaven.

"You now see that the full Gospel includes the sovereignty of God, the deity of Christ, and the redemption of Man. God the Father, Christ the Son, and the Holy Ghost, the second Paraclete, the Three-in-One combine their powers to save a lost soul.

"The love of God is explained to us in His infallible Bible—His love-letter, His own Word indited and written by the Holy Ghost. The incarnate Christ came because of the Father's love. Therefore, the full Gospel includes the seven great R's. Ruined by the Fall; Redeemed by Christ; Regenerated by the Holy Ghost; Reformed by Regeneration; Resurrected by Christ; Return of Christ to receive His own, whom He will gather unto Himself where they may reign with Him triumphant forever and forever.

"Receive Christ and experience the glories of this full Gospel. Go into the world and preach it, and testify that you have been redeemed and regenerated by Christ, the eternal Son of the eternal God."

Now, you may or may not care for this kind of preaching, but you are not at a loss to know just what the preacher believes. He preaches facts, accepted truths, that have the support of credal statements forged out of fire and blood, and based upon a rather literal interpretation of the New

Testament. His appeal is always to the Book. Here is the Word; take it or leave it, but don't try to explain it away. The Book! The Book! Always the Book!

Dr. Matthews enjoys talking shop. He answers questions as to the technique of his pulpit and pastoral ministry in the same assertive fashion that he employs when he preaches. Here is the lordly way he disposed of my interrogations as to sermonic preparations, habits of study, pastoral calls, views of contemporary preaching:

"When I began the ministry I wrote every word I uttered and used the manuscript, but soon discovered I was spending too much time on the flowers of speech and not enough on the fruits of the Gospel.

"That method was followed with profuse notes, but I soon discovered that the notes were a crutch. I then tried three methods—writing fully, making profuse notes, or intense preparation before speaking without either notes or manuscript. I can now use any one of the methods. If using a manuscript I always hold it in my hand so the audience can see it and you could not tell whether I was speaking with or without it. I prefer, however, to speak without manuscript. Better work can be done.

"Young ministers, however, ought not to follow that method. It takes years of experience, hard study and work to be able to use all three methods, or any one of the methods.

"The basis of all my preaching is doctrinal. Sometimes it is topical, sometimes expository, sometimes textual, sometimes a whole chapter, sometimes a book of the Bible.

"My usual method is to preach a strictly doctrinal sermon in the morning, expounding the Bible, unfolding the truths, teaching the great fundamentals, and explaining the Gospel, the full Gospel, and Christ's vicarious atonement.

"The evening sermon is the application of those doctrines to the practical, personal and every-day life of the people.

"You say you fancy most of my sermons are Biblical.

They are all Biblical. No man has a right in the pulpit if he does not use the Bible. No man has a right to enter the pulpit if he is going to omit the Bible.

"I believe God's Infallible Word. It is my only text-book and it is the only text-book of the church. It is the only book any minister has a right to use in the pulpit.

"The papers, magazines and current books are read only for superficial purposes. The books that expound the truth, defend the faith, advance the cause and magnify the vicarious atonement of Christ, are incessantly searched. I haven't time to read the trash. Life is too short. Time is too precious, and I am too disgusted with the so-called book writers.

"I have no hobbies, except the hobby of work. I work about sixteen hours every day, and I work for work's sake. I do not care anything about sports, waste no time on them. My exercise, my joy, my pleasure, my happiness, my progress, my amusement, are all found in the course of duty, in the field of service, at hard labor.

"The besetting sin of preachers is laziness, indecision, lack of 'stick-to-it-iveness.' A minister ought to work about sixteen hours a day, and he ought to put in ten days each week. He ought to know how to work and be master of every detail.

"I visit frequently all the sick, the shut-ins, the poor, the needy, the distressed, or anybody else that needs my attention. Of course my assistants, I have ten or twelve of them, have to visit every day, doing the routine, perfunctory, pastoral calling. The essential, remediable calling I do. Every visit made by the assistants has to be reported to me and the whole work is manned, planned and managed by me.

"The preachers of to-day ought to return to their pulpits and preach Christ and Him crucified, the Infallible Bible and the fundamental doctrines. They should be found incessant in prayer and labor. The people will then come back to their pews. You can not get people to come to an empty table."

Again, that's that! You do not have to guess where this

preacher stands—you *know!* It is Mark Matthews' way, mind you! His forthrightness reminds one of the comment of Oliver Goldsmith with reference to his friend old Dr. Samuel Johnson. Of that Prime Minister of Literature and one of the tallest talkers who ever lived, this crony said: "There is no use arguing with Johnson for if his pistol misses fire he knocks you down with the butt end of it." Dr. Matthews' theological pistol seldom misses fire. His aim is accurate, his hand steady and he does a deal of shooting.

It will be a lonelier Seattle when Dr. Mark Allison Matthews goes to his long home and his eternal reward and the mourners go about the streets.

JENKINS, Burris Atkins, clergyman; *b.* Kansas City, Mo., Oct. 2, 1869; *s.* Andrew T. and Sarah Henry (Baker) J.; A.B., Bethany Coll., 1891; S.T.B., Harvard, 1895, A.M., 1896; *m.* Mattie Hocker, of Lexington, Ky., May 23, 1894; children—Katherine Baker (dec.), Burris Atkins, Paul Andrew, Logan Hocker. Ordained Christian (Disciples) ministry, 1891; pastor, Indianapolis, Ind., 1896-1900; prof. N.T. lit. and exegesis, 1898-1900; pres. 1899-1900, U. of Indianapolis; pres. Ky. U., 1901-07; pastor Linwood Boul. Christian Ch., Kansas City, since Sept. 1907. Also editor and pub. Kansas City Post, Jan. 1, 1919-21. *Author:* Heroes of Faith, 1896; The Man in the Street and Religion, 1917; Facing the Hindenburg Line, 1917; It Happened Over There, 1918; The Protestant, 1918; Princess Salome, 1921; The Bracegirdle, 1922; The Beauty of the New Testament, 1925; The Drift of the Day, 1928; The World's Debt to Protestantism, 1930; American Religion As I See It Lived, 1930. *Address:* 3529 Charlotte St., Kansas City, Mo.

Chapter XI

BURRIS JENKINS

There are about one hundred and fifty thousand preachers of the Protestant faith in the United States. To the superficial observer these parsons seem as much alike as cherries picked from the same tree. They prate about a Carpenter who lived nineteen hundred years ago in Syria, and was put to death for his non-conformity; marry the love-lorn, pronounce funeral orations, butt into myriad affairs and wear white collars seven days in the week.

As an item of fact, however, clergymen in the mass are pretty much the same as their brethren of other vocations. Most of them are average men—faithful plodders, conformists, creatures of custom, hedged in by many a peccadillo, with here and there a virile personality, aggressive, fearless, and unbroken by the dead terrible hand of traditions. To this last named group, small in the nature of things, belongs Burris Atkins Jenkins of Kansas City.

In the home where Jenkins was brought up the Puritan and the cavalier contributed fifty-fifty, the result being a brand of one-hundred-per-cent. Americanism worth shouting about. It was a family of ardent hospitality, whose menfolk hunted 'coons and went fishing when they felt like it; attended revivals—"protracted meetings" they called them; and voted the Democratic ticket straight.

The Jenkinses were Christian Church people—"Campbellites" the Presbyterians, Baptists and Methodists of that day called the heretical body which, inspired by Alexander Campbell and his compeers, had assayed the hard and thankless task of uniting a divided church that wanted to stay divided. The Jenkins home was the headquarters for the preachers, honored guests there always. One of those, Alexander Procter by name, an open-minded lovable seer who declared that he "believed nothing just because it was in a book," profoundly influenced the youth, decided him for the ministry, gave him his theological bent.

So it came about that the tall gangling boy of twenty went to Bethany College, West Virginia, the same founded by the great Alexander Campbell, polemic apostle of Christian unity. Later he became a student at Harvard where he won distinction under Thayer, learned professor of Greek. Jenkins is both a Bachelor and a Doctor of Divinity, and of course he has his A.B. and A.M.

Jenkins held churches in Indianapolis and Buffalo, and then was elected president of Transylvania College, Lexington, Kentucky (he used to be called in those days "the youngest president of the oldest college west of the Alleghanies"), the college of Henry Clay, James Lane Allen, John Fox, Jr., and a whole galaxy of celebrities.

As head of a church college in the blue-grass region Jenkins was popular with everybody except the hide-bound theologians. His oratorical gifts, which are of a high order, endeared him to a section where the shades of Henry Clay, Tom Marshall and the Breckenridges are still potent. But broken health and an immense weariness because of his orthodox handicaps induced him to resign his presidency and return to the city where "Baron Bill" Nelson's *Star* was scintillating merrily and a new mayor by the name of "Jim" Reed was making things hum. There he took a church small in membership; and from a modest beginning has grown in twenty-five years one of the most conspicuous congregations in Protestantism, the Linwood Boulevard Christian Church, now known as the Linwood Community Church.

Jenkins was a war correspondent of the *Kansas City Star,* in 1917-18; editor of the *Kansas City Post* for six years. He wrote *Princess Salome, The Bracegirdle,* novels, and a half-dozen volumes of a theological nature. He publishes *The Christian,* a liberal journal of religion, and keeps a column,

"The Drift of the Day," going in a dozen midwestern newspapers. Also he is a member of the state boxing commission of Missouri. But these are side-issues. Jenkins is first, last and all the time a preacher, and a preacher who doesn't dress, talk or think as the average parson is supposed to dress, talk, think.

The Linwood Community Church bears unmistakably the stamp of the spirit and mind of Burris Jenkins. It is a big stone structure with an auditorium seating comfortably fifteen hundred and into which eighteen hundred are crowded at least once a Lord's Day, and several hundred would-be worshipers turned away. For several years, during the fall and winter two major services in the forenoon were held, one at nine-forty, which was broadcast, very simple and limited to one hour; the second at eleven o'clock with vested choir, liturgical music and communion. At this service Jenkins repeated the sermon preached at the earlier hour. There are two Happy Sunday evening services at three and five o'clock, identical, with community singing, a talking picture show, occasional special entertainment features, a sermonette and an invitation to join the church; and an open forum at eight o'clock, presenting the ablest speakers on the American platform.

The three thousand men, women and children who compose Jenkins' church are a cosmopolitan lot. Every shade of social strata is represented except the excessively rich and the fanatical. Millionaires there are none, but plenty of well-to-do folks, bevies of clerks and small merchants. Of doctors there are enough to staff a hospital. Lawyers and school-teachers abound. Some of Kansas City's best known names appear on the rolls. It is an intelligent if not an intellectual membership with a sprinkling of highbrows and a dash of the local literati. John G. Niehardt, the poet, asked to have his name enrolled in this church, and there are other out-of-the-city members of renown.

An important aspect of this church's work is the "body and soul" or "trouble" clinic. A highly skilled psychiatrist, a graduate of Johns Hopkins, who has had two periods of special study in his field in Europe, is in charge. In the years the clinic has been held hundreds of persons have been served. Most remarkable reconstructions of life have been effected in several cases.

The Linwood Community Church is not only what is known in denominational nomenclature as "open membership," by which is meant it does not require baptism by immersion of those who seek its gates, but it is still wider open. Any man, woman or child who expresses a desire to take the Carpenter of Nazareth as Friend and Teacher is welcomed and made to feel at home. It is the widest open church of its size and prestige in the world.

Theologically Jenkins avers that he is neither Unitarian nor Trinitarian, a position identical with that taken a century ago by Alexander Campbell, battling crusader for a Christian unity minus ecclesiastical and credal encrustments. In some other views, however, Jenkins and Mr. Campbell are as far apart as the poles. As Campbell was to his generation, so Jenkins is to this—a denominational rebel. Jenkins is a liberal, not an ultra-radical; a voice in the wilderness, not a bitter iconoclast. He is a modernist who is also incurably religious. He is not a lecturer merely, nor an entertainer primarily, not even a teacher chiefly. Jenkins is a preacher.

For a sample of Jenkins in a lusty mood, take the sermon on "The Kid Brother," the occasion being the recognition of the opening of Boys' Week. Three troops of Scouts from the Linwood Church were the guests of honor. The text announced was Matthew 5:21-22, "Ye have heard that it was said by them of old time, . . . but I say unto you." The entire sermon is worth quoting if only for the benefit of two classes, those who hear no sermons and those who hear only one kind:

"I venture to make a new set of ten commandments for boys. So many people have been making new sets of ten commandments of late, I'll just have a fling at it myself. I couldn't make one for girls. I don't know enough about them; but I do know boys, having watched three of them grow up to manhood, and having feebly, at least, understood the difficulties of their paths.

"For example, ye have heard that it hath been said: Thou shalt not play billiards, or pool, or cards, or other games that have had bad association. But I say unto you: They are great and skilful games and at some period in your life you will want to play them. Go to it and play hard at them while the impulse is on you, for after a while they will no longer interest you. I don't know anything that has not had its bad associations and its bad phases. I have seen as much money change hands over golf as I ever saw over cards—yes, more—yet nobody has any prejudice against golf because of its associations. My young son and I, while motor touring in the West a few years ago, played pool every evening in the pool halls of Colorado towns. It was the only thing to do at night. At the beginning of the summer I beat him every game, but by fall I couldn't win once. In one town where we stayed several weeks, the Methodist preacher dropped in to watch us, then he took a cue, then came the Baptist, and all the other preachers, and some of the deacons and elders; and for once in a blue moon they became human beings, like boys. My son told me the other night he had not been in a pool hall since. It's an extremely scientific game, good exercise and good relaxation.

"Ye have heard that it hath been said: Thou shalt not hit another fellow on the jaw. But I say unto you: Learn to box. It is a manly art, much less dangerous than football or baseball. It will train you in self-control, in judgment, in courage. The instinct of pugnacity, that is, the desire to fight, is one of the primal instincts of humanity. Soft gloves will keep us from fighting to the death, from war. William James wants moral substitutes for war; boxing is one of them.

"Ye have heard: Thou shalt not dance. But I say unto you: You can't help it. I saw some of you dancing up the sidewalk on the way here this morning. Dancing is instinctive. You can't sing a lively Billy-Sunday-brighten-the-corner-where-you-are type of jig-time evangelistic tune without the old ladies patting their feet and the old men keeping time with their fingers or their hands. That's dancing, though they don't know it. I tell you: Go ahead with it, learn to do it right, with decent and beautiful postures and movements. It is one means of cultivating you for society, and it is the best possible path of safety for many young people. Far from exciting dangerous sex manifestations, it is a means of expressing and getting rid of those very manifestations.

"Ye have heard that it hath been said: Hush! Hush! Don't talk about your intimate concerns, your sex life, and such difficulties, which are the greatest difficulties you have to confront in your adolescent age. But I say to you: Talk! Talk! Talk! Not to the family hired man or chauffeur or the wayside tramp stranger, but to your father. If he is ashamed and embarrassed, as he is nine times out of ten, through an ancient prejudice, make him talk; take him by the lapel of the coat and say, 'Here, Dad, I want to know all about this. Now tell me.' Get it out of your system! Don't bottle it up, that's dangerous. 'Hush, hush, naughty, naughty,' is the wickedest old maxim that we ever had.

"Ye have heard: Thou shalt not own a dog. But I say unto you: Get one at some period in your life. No boy is complete without a dog, and no dog without a boy. If you can't keep him in your apartment-house, keep him on the roof, or farm him out in the country.

"Ye have heard: Thou shalt not go into the woods to camp and to sleep overnight. But I say to you: Go ahead, for at least a few times—best thing you ever did.

"Ye have heard: Thou shalt not run away from home.

But I say: Run whenever you want to and as far as you want to, at least once in your boyhood. But tell your dad you are going so that he can stock you up with enough money to buy cheese and crackers and sardines for three or four days or a week; and when you run out of money go to the police wherever you are and you'll find them your best friends.

"Ye have heard: Love your school and love your teachers. But I say unto you: Under existing conditions ninety-nine times out of a hundred, no boy can. Your school is too big and too much like a jail; and as for many of the teachers, what can you expect for seventy-five or a hundred dollars a month? We've got a lot to learn about schools and boys before this ancient command can be fulfilled.

"Ye have heard: Make a pal of your dad. But I say to you: It can't be done. You can't make a pal of anybody who is a different age from your own. It is just an impossibility to bridge the chasm of the years. Your dad is your best friend; he'll sacrifice more for you than anybody else will; so if ever you are in trouble go to him and most of the time he'll be fair and square with you and help you out. Dads and boys should cultivate the closest friendship; but as for being buddies, and pals it just can't be done.

"Finally, Ye have heard all your life: Don't! Don't! Don't! But I say: Do! Do! Do! Live life positively. Experiment. Try."

Burris Jenkins resembles no other preacher of my acquaintance. He is the most original man in the American pulpit of whom I have any knowledge. Moreover, his originality has grown with the years; he is at his sermonic best now. The modernity of this man's preaching is startling. It is down to the minute, yet it is far from sheer sensationalism. It is practical, venturesome, and in a very true sense devotional, certainly not pietistic. Here is a sheaf of Jenkins' subjects with the texts subjoined, preached in the winter of 1931-32: "Don't Be Silly": text, "A foolish man . . . built his house upon the sand" (Matthew 7:26); "An Old Bronze Door-Knocker": "Behold, I stand at the door, and knock" (Rev. 3:20); "What Would You Do If——": "As ye would that men should do to you, do ye also to men likewise" (Luke 6:31); "The Man Who Played God": "Not a sparrow shall fall on the ground without your Father" (Matthew 10:29); "The Godsakers": "My Father worketh hitherto, and I work" (John 5:17); "The Wisdom of Will Rogers": "Call for Samson, that he may make us sport" (Judges 16:25); "Kidnapers and Kidnaping": "Whoso shall offend one of these little ones . . . it were better for him that a millstone were hanged about his neck, and that he were drowned in the depths of the sea" (Matthew 18:6); "My Job": "It pleased God by the foolishness of preaching to save them that believe" (I Corinthians 1:21); "Amos 'n' Andy": "And Jonathan loved him as his own soul" (I Samuel 18:1).

Study this list if you would know how skilfully a famous liberal preacher of our times links the Eternal with the Now. Here are nine subjects taken at random. They touch upon a popular motion picture in which George Arliss starred; two popular phrases on the lips of millions, half-slang, half-serious; the most widely favored radio feature of the times; the most beloved wise-cracking philosopher; a kidnaping case of international moment and tragic interest—and every one of these themes is related to the life spiritual, couched in clear, pungent, easily remembered phrases, set off here and there by good old-fashioned oratorical periods, and lit up by a quaint midwestern humor.

Liberal that he is in theology and tolerant to an amiable degree of the opinions and habits of others, Jenkins holds tenaciously to views that are stigmatized by some as old-fashioned. Politically he is a Wilsonian Democrat and a champion of the League of Nations. He is convinced that monogamy is best for men and women and is given to exalting the home and family life. He has debated companionate marriage with Judge Ben Lindsay, arguing strongly against the Denverite's views on this particular issue, although agreeing with Judge Ben on other subjects and honoring him for his long fight in behalf of unprivileged youth.

Jenkins has been in the center of many controversies, one-sided affairs usually, for he rarely replies to his critics. The exception was at the National Convention of the Disciples at St. Louis in 1921, when he took the platform at a critical juncture and, to the surprise of the conservatives and the embarrassment of the liberals, indulged in personalities. There are those among the Disciples who regard him as a dangerous radical and believe him to have repudiated most of the cardinal positions of his communion. Others view his frank discussion of sex topics with concern. Yet, when the *World Call,* leading monthly of the Disciples, sent out a questionnaire to one thousand ministers asking that they name the ten most effective preachers in the Brotherhood, Dr. Jenkins' name appeared among the ten receiving the most votes. I think it can be said that criticism does not often so much as ruffle Burris Jenkins. He appears to thrive upon it, and goes on his own chosen way harboring no grudges.

"This business of preaching, what have you to say about it, Jenkins?" The Kansas Citian shifted his game leg, settled himself comfortably in his office chair and mused:

"A big job, this foolishness of preaching. Sometimes we feel the futility of it just because we do not comprehend the bigness of it. How delicate and fine an art, to take people in the midst of their every-day concerns and gently lead them on from the things they play with to the greater things they ought to attain! How much study and thought it demands to keep always a series of pictures flashing before the minds of hearers, Sunday after Sunday, pictures freighted with significance and world-wide importance. How essential not merely that a man practise what he preach, but that he be what he preach! If preaching is the projection of personality, if, as Father Taylor said, 'The business of the preacher is to take something hot out of his own heart and shove it into mine,' then first of all he must try to live inside himself the light that he tries to throw. No man can tell another how to do it. Each man must be himself, himself, and himself alone, sublimated, refined, incandescent with his message. The preacher, unlike other artists, can leave no pictures or symphonies or buildings behind. Like the actor, when he passes off the stage, there is nothing he can leave. His personality is gone. His published words can never be himself. This scientific time calls for scientific methods of treatment. This perplexed, bewildered and painful time calls for sympathy and understanding and encouragement. Never was a day which more needed this foolishness of preaching; for the same old world staggers along because it will not learn the simple rudiments of life: gentleness, kindness, love, the golden rule, the beauty of service, the willingness to sacrifice and to die for the truth, all the things which Jesus taught."

"How do you account for your success in Kansas City?"

Dr. Jenkins busied himself again with his new leg, got it adjusted to his satisfaction and speculated: "Well, you see, I'm a native, I belong here, and they put up with a great deal from native stock. In the second place, my economic independence must be taken into consideration, that also has helped."

Yes, it has helped, and there is something in the native-son idea; but Burris A. Jenkins, if born in the desert region of Utah, half a thousand miles from nowhere, poor as a church-mouse in hard times, would sooner or later have arrived somewhere and with a bang!

Jenkins is acquainted with pain, and suffering is his brother. His face is cross-checked with little lines etched there by pain. He has gone on the operating table twenty-two times, I believe, and in recent years lost his right leg and various parts of his anatomy, all of which he views humorously. Coming "out from under" after the amputation of his leg, he looked about him, grinned and remarked, "Well, it seems my kicking days are over." So it goes—pain, suffering, up and down, in and out, courage, fortitude—this minister of the Gospel of One who suffered more than tongue can tell, belongs to the fellowship of those whom pain has drenched but not discouraged. Possibly this is one reason why the man in the street understands Jenkins' language, appreciates his untheological ways of stating spiritual truths, hears him gladly, and seeks him out in time of trouble.

Some preachers are like that!

BROWN, Charles Reynolds, clergyman; *b.* Bethany, W. Va., Oct. 1, 1862; *s.* Benjamin F. and Sarah J. B.; U. of Ia., 1883, A.M., 1886; S.T.B., Boston U., 1899, S.T.D., 1922; A.M., Yale, 1911, D.D., 1928; D.D., Oberlin, 1912, Brown, 1914; LL.D., Wesleyan, 1915; L.H.D., U. of Vt., 1926; *m.* Alice Tufts, Sept. 23, 1896. Pastor First Congl. Ch., Oakland, Calif., 1896-1911; dean Div. Sch. of Yale U., 1911-28, emeritus dean since 1928. Professional study, Egypt and Palestine, 1897; spl. lecturer on ethics, Leland Stanford Jr. U., 1899-1906; Lyman Beecher lecturer Yale, 1905-06, 1922-23; spl. lecturer, Cornell, 1909, Columbia, 1911; Earl lecturer Pacific Sch. of Religion, 1924; Ingersoll lecturer on Immortality, Harvard, 1920; John Calvin McNair lecturer U. of N. C., 1926. Moderator Nat. Council Congl. Ch., 1913-15. *Author:* The Main Points, 1899; Social Message of the Modern Pulpit, 1906; The Strange Ways of God; The Young Man's Affairs; Faith and Health, 1910; The Modern Man's Religion, 1911; The Latent Energies in Life, 1912; The Quest of Life, 1913; The Master's Way, 1919; Living Again, 1920; The Religion of a Layman, 1921; The Greatest Man of the Nineteenth Century, 1921; The Art of Preaching, 1922; Why I Believe in Religion, 1923; What Is Your Name, 1924; Where Do You Live, 1925; Ten Short Stories from the Bible, 1925; These Twelve, 1926; The Making of a Minister, 1927; The Gospel for Main Street, 1929; My Own Yesterdays, 1931. *Home:* 233 Edwards St., New Haven, Conn.

Chapter XII

CHARLES REYNOLDS BROWN

For forty years Dr. Brown has been active in the Christian ministry—pastor, preacher, educator, lecturer and prolific author. Half of this period has been devoted to teaching young preachers how to preach, as Dean of the Yale Divinity School. Born in Iowa, of a father who was a Virginian, and studying in Bethany College when Alexander Campbell was its president, Dr. Brown was trained in the University of Iowa, had a brief experience in a law office in Illinois, also with an insurance company in Des Moines, decided for the ministry, and took theology in Boston University, with some months in Harvard Divinity School thrown in for good measure. He began as a Methodist, but soon passed on to the Congregationalists, that roomy fellowship which many ministers from other communions enter and few leave.

There are some so-called great preachers who are uninteresting and without popular appeal. One simply can not think of Dr. Brown as uninteresting. His popular appeal is direct and unfailing. He combines decent scholarship and a becoming dignity with a style that borders on the racy, in the sense that it is fresh, unconventional, warm, vivid. Think of a man preaching on Immortality from the topic "Where Do We Go from Here?" The versatility of Dean Brown is one of his strong elements of sermonic power. He is one of four men who have been called upon twice to deliver the Yale lectures on preaching, the others being Henry Ward Beecher, W. M. Taylor and Washington Gladden. His first series, *The Social Message of the Modern Pulpit,* was given in 1908; the second, *The Art of Preaching,* in 1922. This alone bespeaks the ability and genius of the man, and it is but one of many tokens that indicate Dr. Brown's brilliance and resourcefulness.

The life of Dean Brown has been populous with unusual experiences, contacts, episodes, events. During his pastorate in California, a man who was attracted to his church and became a regular attendant, although never formally enrolled, one day handed Dr. Brown a check for ten thousand dollars. Two years later the same man died, leaving the bulk of his estate, amounting to one hundred and sixty thousand dollars, to his friend and pastor. Dr. Brown turned over the ten-thousand-dollar check and the estate to the missionary treasurers of the Methodist, Congregational and Baptist Churches, according to his friend's request. He officiated at hundreds of weddings and received from one bridegroom as fee five twenty-dollar gold pieces and from another a quarter and a nickel—just thirty cents. So far as I know, the Dean is the only preacher who ever delivered a sermon in a church edifice while wearing his hat. This is what happened when Dr. Brown was the preacher in an Orthodox synagogue in California. The rabbi said to him, "We wear our hats in this synagogue, but you will not need to do that unless you choose." Dr. Brown assured him that if the rabbi came to speak in his church he would expect him to take off his hat; therefore it was his pleasure to conform to the Jewish custom. In 1924 the *World's Work* offered a prize of five hundred dollars for the best sermon, the contest being open to Catholics, Protestants and Hebrews. Dr. Brown won the prize with a sermon on the text, "Silver and gold have I none, but such as I have give I thee."

I once asked Dr. Brown what he considered to be the besetting sin of the preacher, then before he could reply, I varied the query: "What are the pitfalls that endanger the minister?" He seemed to relish the word "pitfalls." No wonder. It is a pictorial word and "besetting sin" sounds too theological. Here is the Doctor's answer:

"I feel that one of the commonest and easiest pitfalls into

which the young preacher is liable to drop, in these days, is that of failing to preach on the great themes of religion as they stand declared in the Bible. If the young minister would preach with interest and power, he can not do better than to 'read, mark, learn, and inwardly digest' his Bible, until his tongue and his mind are steeped in the language of Scripture and his heart saturated with the vital truths there outlined in terms of life. 'Grass withers; flowers fade; but the word of our God shall stand forever.'

"Hear this clear-cut word from Harris E. Kirk, pastor of the First Presbyterian Church of Baltimore, where he is now on his thirty-first year and still going strong! 'The modern preacher does not fully realize that most of his people are not at all influenced by mere intellectual phrasings of old truths, but are strangely moved when they feel the touch of life. There is a tremendous volume of life in these old Bible stories, and all of them lend themselves readily to the right interpretation of the Christian message.'

"People are not influenced very much by clever, epigrammatic orations and essays on 'the topics of the day.' What does the ordinary man of affairs think when he reads on the sermon-topics page of the Saturday newspaper that Brother Fifthly will preach the next day on 'The Superiority of the Psychological and Empirical Approach to Religion over the old Authoritative Appeal to Scriptural and Ecclesiastical Formulas'?

"I quote this topic from memory, as I once saw it in a church announcement, but I am sure that it is almost verbatim. What does the every-day man say when he reads that? I should rather not quote his remark in its entirety—my father and mother were godly people who taught me in early life not to use profane language. I might deplore the man's language, but the sentiment I would regard as sound. If the young minister would make his preaching interesting, stimulating, fruitful in its abiding influence for good, let him use his Bible for those truths which are 'spirits and life,' and let him manifest the fine flavor of a long-continued, familiar, sympathetic acquaintance with the very words of Scripture in all of his public address."

Dean Brown enjoys himself and his work always and everywhere. I think the word to describe this quality in the Dean is "gusto." He does not look especially robust; nobody would take him for an athlete; yet I once heard him say that he had never missed a preaching appointment in his life, and all because he had taken reasonably good care of himself. He's a hard hitter when he wants to be and he never spares those brethren of the Church who are continually apologizing for the Church. He's about the last man to ride a hobby to death or become enamored with a fad.

Once upon a time I had the temerity to write a group of representative American preachers asking that they furnish me with a list of the five books that had most influenced their life. I should have been bashed over the head, or disciplined in some other way for perpetrating such a questionnaire. Well, the Dean chided me beautifully when he replied to my letter as follows:

> "I have your night letter. I am not very good at that sort of thing. When these questionnaires come asking us to name the five outstanding moments in our spiritual experience, or the five articles of food which have brought us the greatest thrill and nourishment as they passed down our throats, or the five most impressive things we saw on a trip through Europe or the Far East—I came back from India last February—they find me as dumb as a lobster. Other men seem to be able to do it, but I am not quite up to it.
>
> "The Bible is the one book which has done me more good as a Christian and as a preacher than all the other books put together, and the King James version of the Bible (as opposed to these chatty modern translations in baseball English), and Shakespeare's plays have done most for whatever style I have in preaching. But this is

not the sort of thing you want. Here's hoping that you may get on better with the rest of the 'fourteen premier preachers' and my love to you and my hearty appreciation of what you write so well, always and ever!

"Heartily yours,

"CHARLES R. BROWN."

Sanity, humor and common sense distinguish Dr. Brown. He discusses helpfully and humorously the vexed questions that have troubled the ministerial brethren since time immemorial. As for instance, how long should a sermon be? Brown of New Haven disposes of this in short order. The sermon, he says, is nothing more nor less than a tool, What size should a tool be? How long should a scythe be? How heavy should an ax be? This can not be determined by certain fixed presuppositions, but altogether by the demands of the task to which the particular tool is applied. Sermons of thirty or forty minutes have no Biblical sanction. The question of length is a practical question altogether. A long sermon is a sermon that seems long. It may have lasted an hour, or only fifteen minutes. If it seems long, it is long—it is too long. Dr. Brown holds that you can not tell how long a sermon is by watching a clock—watch the people. See where their hands are. See where their eyes are. See where their minds are. By such signs will the wise parson conquer.

And as to public prayers—Dr. Brown may not agree fully with John Haynes Holmes that "much, perhaps most of the language of prayer in our day is abominable," but he pays his respects to the various kinds of atrocities that go by the name of prayer, the long prayer, the grandiloquent prayer, the too-familiar-with-the-Almighty prayer. The Doctor cites an experience of his own when he was to deliver a memorial address in an eastern city. The exercises were held in a park. The mayor of the city presided. A large crowd was present. The pastor of one of the city churches had been asked to offer the prayer. He prayed exactly eighteen minutes. He began with the Declaration of Independence, and ended up with the Emancipation Proclamation, pausing along the way to pay tributes to the heroic leaders who had sacrificed their all on the altar of freedom. He was eloquent, voluble, dramatic and most of all, pathetic. The man began by saying, "O Lord," and he concluded by saying "Amen," but he gave an address instead of offering a prayer.

Dr. Brown would have the young preacher study his pulpit prayers as carefully as he studies his sermons. He would have him take care of his health, guard his appetite. He would advise him as Thomas Jefferson, who was one of the most abstemious of men, advised his grandson, thus: "No man ever regretted having eaten too little." Dr. Brown would have the young preacher watch his voice, learn how to use it, master it, make it as agreeable an instrument as possible; avoid the rasping tone as well as any vocal mannerism that detracts from the thought of the sermon itself. He thinks there is a place for humor in the sermon though it must be used sparingly and with discretion, certainly in proper proportions. He cites the dry Scotch humor introduced now and then by George A. Gordon, in his preaching, by Henry Ward Beecher, Charles H. Spurgeon and even Phillips Brooks, who occasionally caused a smile to sweep over his congregation like a cool breeze on a summer day.

I would advise all young preachers to read Charles Reynolds Brown and Charles E. Jefferson on the subject of preaching. These two Charleses have given years to the study of sermonic art, written and lectured on preaching and preachers in season and out of season, and have reached the uplands as preachers of the Word.

In Dr. Brown's twenty-ninth book, *My Own Yesterdays,* he says at its close, on page three hundred and thirty-one:

> "If any word which I have written here serves to make that high calling (the ministry) seem more interesting and alluring in the eyes of any young man of

promise, I shall thank God and take courage and sing the Long Metre Doxology through again three times without stopping."

There you have the spirit of the man—great good humor, infinite zest, contagious enthusiasm, and a love and loyalty to the Christian ministry that burns like the fire on the altar of the Vestal Virgins.

COWIN, Frederick, *b.* Laxey, Isle of Man, 1878, *s.* Joseph and Sarah Cowin. Educated Dalton-in-Furness, Lancashire, College of Disciples, Birmingham, England, Wycliffe College, Toronto, Canada. Married Alice Perry of London, England, 1910. Children, Gladys, Jean, Fred, Douglas. Ordained to ministry 1900. Pastorates: Glasgow, Kirkcaldy, Scotland; Cape Town, Johannesburg, Buluwayo, South Africa; Toronto, Canada, eleven years; E. Grand Blvd. Church, Detroit, six years; Church of Christ, Ann Arbor, Mich., since 1928. President Michigan Convention of Disciples, 1925-27. Member, Commission on Ministry, Disciples of Christ. Student of Robert Burns and lecturer. *Home:* 1621 Granger Av., Ann Arbor, Mich.

Chapter XIII

FREDERICK COWIN

It has been said that the world knows little of her greatest men, an aphorism that contains fragments of truth. I would paraphrase the sentence to read "the world knows nothing of some of her greatest preachers"—men of genius who for one reason or other have never achieved a reputation equal to their gifts or fame beyond a loyal local constituency. Innate modesty helps to account for this in some instances, unfortunate environment in others, and then again there are cases where no explanations really explain. I know at least three preachers whose rare ability and sermonic excellence are such as to warrant their holding pulpits of prominence far beyond anything they have ever known. Of these three, a shining example is Frederick Cowin, minister of the Church of Christ, Ann Arbor, Michigan.

Cowin is a Manxman by birth, but his ancestry is Scotch, and his face is, I should say, a goodly map of the land of the heather. His accent carries just enough of the beloved brogue to give it a fascinating tang. One of my favorite conundrums, emerging from my friendship for this rare man, is as follows: "When is a Scotchman not a Scotchman?" Answer, "When he's a Manxman." I love to work this off on Frederick when we are at a public meeting together and things are in the lighter vein. Cowin is a lover of Robert Burns and has a lecture on that famous bard of such merit that I could wish it might be arranged for him to deliver it from coast to coast. I have heard two of the Lyceum favorites, justly popular twenty years ago, who had lectures on Burns; but to my way of thinking, not so able or delightful as Cowin's evening on "Robby," as he loves to call him.

As a preacher, Cowin is unusually gifted in expository

sermons. That kind of sermonizing, when it is well done, is the veritable cream of preaching. But it is difficult for most ministers, and much that passes for exposition is prolix and dreadfully dull. Not so with Frederick Cowin. He selects a passage of Scripture, backgrounds it beautifully, interprets it helpfully and illustrates it with consummate artistry. His style is simple, vocabulary mostly Anglo-Saxon, and he has a habit true of many English and Scotch preachers of finishing a sentence with a rising inflection. He rarely preaches longer than thirty minutes, never scolds, berates or rants. He stands quite still and makes few gestures, nor is he afraid of the use of occasional humor in the sermon.

This preacher looks not a little like the portraits of Principal Marcus Dods, only his expression is not severe, but smiling. Cowin's complexion is ruddy, and his hair, now thinning considerably, of the sandy sort and inclined to curl. Frederick's humor is rich and spontaneous. He is adept in the art of toastmastering and a most happy after-dinner speaker. He quotes poetry intelligently, and always good poetry, particularly Burns, whose most famous lines he knows by the hundreds. He is likewise gifted in public prayer. There is a simplicity and a singular tenderness in his prayers such as greatly gentle the hearts of those whom he leads in this art of arts.

Mr. Cowin began preaching in his early twenties. His work was among the fisher folk of the eastern and western coasts in Scotland. He also preached in the Hebrides, and for two years, practically all of his sermons were delivered out-of-doors, in market-places, on street corners and in public parks. Maybe this helps to account for his strong resonant voice. He was in South Africa for a while, preached in Cape Town and Johannesburg. The Bible was very largely his one text-book in those days, although he began in a modest way to gather a collection of good books and to pore over their pages in the days of his itinerancy. Very early in his ministry, he purchased the works of Samuel Cox who was the first editor of *The Expositor* and therefore the predecessor of Sir William Robertson Nicoll. He acknowledges a large indebtedness to Dr. Cox and often quotes him. For thirty years Cowin has been a subscriber to *The British Weekly* and has read it with avidity. He was long an ardent admirer of Sir William Ramsay and on the shelves of his study may be seen all of the sturdy volumes of that able church historian. Years before this preacher came to America he had heard most of the able ministers of England and Scotland. When in charge of a little church in Birmingham, he used often to be in attendance on the week night meetings held in famous Carr's Lane Church during those golden years of John Henry Jowett's ministry there.

For a memorable year Frederick Cowin was my associate at old Central Christian Church, Detroit. For twelve months we divided the pulpit responsibilities, and I always heard him with delight and profit. Some of his sermons, in my judgment, would rank with those of a Jowett, an Alexander Whyte, or Alexander Maclaren. Moreover, and this I hold to be vital, his life is finer than any sermon he ever preached. Lo! here is a paradox; Cowin is Scotch and generous to a fault. He tells stories of Scotch thrift and then gives them the lie by distributing with a lavish hand contributions to many worthy causes. He is a big man, big in his theological views, never a denominationalist or a narrow partizan. And such a pastor! I have seldom known a minister who could go into homes where death had come, bringing with him an atmosphere of faith and a ministry of comfort and consolation with the ease and compassion of my former associate.

Cowin's method of sermon composition is, I think, unusual. He does not write his sermons out in full. In truth, he writes little if at all. He reads, fills himself full of his subject and then walks, walks, walks. He does not pace his study so much as he paces the city streets and country roads when the latter are available. When he was preaching in Detroit, Frederick used to walk the three or four miles from his house to his church, and all along the way he turned over in his mind the sermon that he was soon to deliver. Some preachers like to come into the pulpit from a half-hour of quiet, absolute quiet. Cowin likes most to enter the pulpit after trudging for an hour or so through the streets. Joseph Parker was also famed as a pedestrian, and studied his themes as he strode along London thoroughfares.

This reminds me of an associate I had in my early ministry, an ambitious young person, who took the matter of his preaching seriously and rightly so. He, too, had a habit of studying on the street as he went to and from the church and his home. It was his custom to carry his manuscript with him and to consult it from time to time. One morning he came into my study not a little perturbed and told me that he had started for the church with the manuscript of a brand-new sermon which he carried in his right hand, stopping now and then to glance at a paragraph or a division heading, and that his arm went to sleep. "Now," he inquired, "if that sermon put my arm to sleep, what do you think will happen when I preach it?" I agreed with him that since "coming events cast their shadows before" maybe he had better choose another sermon. And he did.

In 1932 Mr. Cowin made his début as a speaker at the International Convention of the Disciples, meeting that year at Indianapolis. He spoke at the Christian Unity session taking as his subject "Broken Walls." Having been at one time or another preacher in three distinct theological groups among the Disciples he undertook to administer a good-natured spanking to us all for our tendency to talk Christian unity and fail to practise it within our ranks. In the course of the address "he broke some china" as one of those who heard him phrased it. And not even his wit and genial humor saved him from the wrath of some who thought they detected heresy. But there were those present who deemed Cowin's speech one of the most stimulating and searching of the whole convention. Frederick didn't sleep much the night that followed his speech, not because it had been criticized, he expected that, but because he feared it might embarrass a dear friend who had made the opportunity possible. That's Cowin for you, a considerate gentleman, always, courageous, yet withal tender and gentle, a shepherd of souls, a brotherly prophet of the Lord!

Mr. Cowin spends his vacations at Crystal Lake, northern Michigan, where he has a cottage, largely built with his own hands. Although he preaches a great part of the vacation season he spends most of his time between Sundays at this delightful spot. If you drop in on him there you will be sure of a cup of real tea brewed by the "wee wifie," and the sight of a few shelves of extra choice reading matter, probably a copy of Robert Louis Stevenson's Essays, the sermons of George Macdonald; very likely some of the writings of the Rev. George Jackson, D.D., maybe a new volume by James Black, minister of St. George's, Edinburgh, and, of course, the poetry of Robert Burns. There are a couple of small boys in that home who rightly regard their father as the greatest man ever, and a daughter who bears a name well beloved in bonnie Scotland. I am referring, you must know, to Jean. Aye, this is a preacher's cottage, simple and plain, yet fragrant with the spirit of things eternal!

Frederick Cowin is a bit indifferent as to his attire and loses no time trying to decide what necktie to wear or whether it exactly matches his socks. He is the sort of a dominie who would rather stop at a moderate-priced hotel and invest the saving in a first edition or some especially desired volume. It is a joy to loaf with this comrade of the high calling, fold my long legs and talk it out with him. I love to hear him say in broadest Scotch, "Aye, weel, we Scotchmen have a way not only of keeping the Sobbath but everything else we get our hands on, ye know." To which I reply, sans the rich brogue, "Hoot, Frederick, ye are jokin'; ye might have had a church o' a thousand members if ye had only caught and kept holdin' on to the system of sellin' yerself. Anyhow, Frederick, what's more important, ye are a-holdin' on to the Lord, and that's yon big thing, mind ye!" And it is—the biggest thing!

CLAUSEN, Bernard Chancellor, clergyman; *b.* Hoboken, N. J., Apr. 5, 1892, *s.* Bernard and Mary (Chancellor) C.; A.B., Colgate, 1915, A.M., 1916; Union Theol. Sem., 1915-17; D.D., Syracuse U., 1922; *m.* Mary Elizabeth Darnell, of Waynetown, Ind., Aug. 5, 1918; children—Mary Carolyn, Barton Randolph, Susan Elizabeth. Ordained Bapt. ministry, 1917; asst. pastor, Mt. Vernon, N. Y., 1915-18, pastor, Hamilton, N. Y., 1919-20, 1st Ch., Syracuse, since 1920. Chaplain U. S. Navy, on board U.S.S. North Carolina, Dec. 1917-June, 1919. Mem. Phi Beta Kappa, Delta Sigma Rho. *Author:* Preach It Again, 1922; The Miracle of Me, 1923; Pen Portraits of the Twelve, 1924; The Door That Has No Key, 1924; The Technique of a Minister, 1925; Pen Portraits of the Prophets, 1926; Pen Pictures in the Upper Room, 1927; Pen Portraits on Calvary, 1928; Tested Programs for Special Days, 1928. *Home:* 303 Berkeley Drive, Syracuse, N. Y.

Chapter XIV

BERNARD C. CLAUSEN

On a certain July Sunday I was due to supply the pulpit of the First Baptist Church, Syracuse, New York. That church is only a few blocks from the hotel where I was stopping but not knowing that I hailed a taxi. As I got out of the car in front of the church the taxi driver remarked, "You are going to hear this morning, the greatest preacher in the world." Somewhat embarrassed, I informed him that I was supplying Dr. Clausen's pulpit that day. This incident is chronicled here because it reflects a typical opinion among the rank and file of Syracusans with respect to Bernard C. Clausen, D.D., pastor of the First Baptist Church of that city.

Physically Dr. Clausen is winsome, attractive, most appealing, easy to look at. He is slight of built with a head of abundant wavy light blond hair which is never covered winter or summer, indoors or out. When he went to Europe with a Sherwood Eddy party in 1925, he carried the usual luggage but no head covering, not even a cap. He is always well groomed but not foppishly so, or of a Beau Brummel tendency. The Clausen voice is one in ten thousand, organ-toned, sweet and wonderfully flexible. Despite the fact that he does not indulge in games or sports he keeps in excellent physical condition and is rarely ill. Possibly his habit of buying his fire-wood in cord length so that he can have the fun of sawing it up in proper size, may explain Dr. Clausen's physical fitness.

In the pulpit, the genius of this preacher flowers continually, often gorgeously. His versatility and daring are constantly in evidence. In the midst of a sermon he is likely to introduce a popular song such as *Blue Heaven,* which he especially favors, or it may be one of the grand old hymns. His singing voice is as attractive as his speaking voice, and this is saying much. He is dramatic and effective in most any type of sermon and some of his subjects are frankly sensational, as for instance, "Thanks for the Buggy Ride." But one can never be sure from his advertised subjects what the contents of the sermon will be, as is the case with so many of the motion-picture titles that blaze in the electric-lighted signs. He strikes a much deeper note than do most preachers of the sensational type, the spiritual quality is strong, and the social note not muffled nor missing, but is forcefully sounded. The evangelistic appeal is always present, comes naturally, is not forced, or dragged in as though to level up or round out a sermon which on the surface appeared to be purely topical and even newspaperish.

Clausen is an amiable fellow, gentlemanly and studious far beyond the average preacher. He follows carefully laid out plans, trusts not at all to moods or the inspiration of the occasion. Here in his own words thoughtfully arranged is the story of how he carries on his conspicuous ministry.

"The broad general themes of my sermons in any given year are determined by a specific objective which we adopt each year and which focuses our attention as a congregation upon a single great intellectual field. During recent years, some of these themes have been: Faith and Health; Religion and Politics; What is a Christian Home; Catholics, Jews and Protestants; and this year, The Place of a Christian in a World of War. Next year I intend to set as our intellectual objective Baptism and the Baptists, and at the end of the year we shall be ready for a decision on the part of our church concerning our future policy regarding that rite.

"Approximately half the sermons preached drive away at this central idea.

"Every communion Sunday morning, once a month, I preach on Missions—geographical, biographical, historical, etc., devising in advance the series for the year, which we illustrate by pageants, lights, maps, etc. That leaves a margin of about thirty opportunities for occasional sermons, and the subjects for these arise in quite the ordinary way—out of my reading and experience.

"But I spend much time on titles, writing and rewriting, phrasing and rephrasing—striving to make the title not only definitive, but genuinely attractive and memorable. A sermon to me is always part of a debate. My only technique is the debater's technique. I preach against a weight of argument in order to obtain a change of mind and an ultimate decision. With this purpose in view, I arrange a typical debater's outline for each sermon, charting the course of the general argument in graphic form under heads and subheads, writing in the outlines of evidence and illustrations under these heads and subheads, and using the opposite blank side of the sermon outline paper for quotations, statistics, and poetic references—all written out in longhand.

"I try to gather my material as a debater does: by personal interviews, by deliberate reading, and by much mulling over the problem involved in these minds which I want to lead to my conclusion. At the end, I expect a verdict each time; not in terms of conversion or confession, but in terms of new convictions toward the truth which seems important to me.

"I never refer to these sermon outlines when preaching, but do my best to achieve a photographic memory of them before the service begins.

"I read about a thousand books a year, for I have excellent eyes and have deliberately cultivated the habit of swift reading. My favorite books are biographies, and the book which I have read more often than any other, except the Bible, is an old-fashioned volume which I do not believe you have ever seen, but a constant inspiration to me—William Cleaver Wilkinson's *Modern Masters of Pulpit Discourse.*

"I am the more delighted to cooperate in your venture because Wilkinson's efforts along a similar line have so greatly benefited me.

"I do no pastoral calling as such. I set aside every Monday to call upon all the sick, and take in my Monday round the infirm and shut-in. I set aside every Thursday for office hours, and invite anybody who can get to the church and wants to see me to use my time on that day. I make frequent personal visits to members of my congregation by telephone, send each one a birthday card with a personal message and invite a personal greeting for the following Sunday, and have within recent years used many consecutive weeks for neighborhood parties in the various sections of our city, inviting members from the neighborhood to be my guests at a home which I borrow for the occasion.

"The raising of the budget and the administration of the church's finances are kept completely under the supervision of our Board of Trustees. They have been taught to interview me freely on every problem where my judgment might be considered valuable, but they know that I take pride in their independent responsibilities. I do not even attend meetings of the Board of Trustees; instead, I take dinner with the Board on the night of their monthly meeting, and spend an hour or two in informal conversation with them about the problems of the church before their meeting is called to order. They understand, however, that none of my suggestions have any official weight and that my only special competence lies in my ability to sense the temper and the mood of the congregation and interpret it to those who are charged with the financial duties of the church."

Dr. Clausen has published numerous sermons but not one of them quite caught my fancy as revealing him at his unique best, so I asked him to single out for me one which he would be willing for me to use in this sketch. He obligingly sent me a sermon entitled "For Crying Out Loud." No text was attached, nor do I know what Scripture lesson he read in connection with it. Such a sermon, skilfully wrought, artistically turned, put together expertly! The introduction is complete in four brief paragraphs.

> "'Twenty-three, skiddoo!' This was the slogan of the Roosevelt era, when the tempo of our national life was quick and curt, and the temper of our national mood was strenuous and decisive.
>
> "'Applesauce!' was the watchword of the literary Wilsonian administration, when from the White House there poured a constantly increasing stream of phrases and official proclamations.
>
> "As the Harding administration waxed and waned, and our national life was characterized by official and personal carelessness, everybody began to say the slang phrase which is supposed to be derived from the original Hebrew, 'Ish Kabibble!'
>
> "And what is the most popular slang of to-day? What are young people learning to say in the Hoover years? What remark precipitates a giggle of appreciative recognition whenever it sounds out from a movie on Broadway or Main Street? To-day, everybody is saying, 'Well, for crying out loud!'"

And now for the milk in this sermonic cocoanut. It is here and it is not, to employ a New Testament phrase, "milk for babes."

> "Listen, for instance, to the ordinary conversation of women. What is the outstanding topic of their talk these days? Do you think it is bridge? No, bridge is second (a close second, I will admit), but outdistanced in popularity by a very peculiar topic,—'speaking of operations. . . .' It seems necessary to have four or five

horrifying symptoms to describe in order to get along well in social contacts these days. The more dreadful your illnesses, the more attractive your conversation. Irvin Cobb used to claim, 'I know that I am ugly. No one can flatter me. Even my photographer can not flatter me. The only flattering photograph I ever had taken was an x-ray of my gallstones!' There are many, many women who agree with that statement exactly. The most flattering things they have about them are their illnesses, and they exhibit them for inspection on all occasions. Yet it is true that when you have a headache and talk about it, you do your own headache no good and pass on the headache to every one who is forced to listen. Stop crying out loud!

"The same mental trait may be observed in business life. This is the mood which President Hoover is fighting during these valiant months. He knows that you can not build a bank, you can not build a city, you can not build a nation, and certainly you can not build success in the next national election, without an intangible thing called Confidence. And he knows that when crying out loud begins, confidence flies out the window. Yet business men by the hundreds take a certain pride in collecting the most heartrending disaster stories and in passing them on to their friends. They fondle tales of tragedy, whether they be true or not, as if they were gems, and hold them up to the light for every one to see. Stop crying out loud!

"'Oh, well,' you are saying, 'after all you must be willing to face facts. Pollyanna psychology will not take you very far through a real situation such as we face. You can't change circumstances by refusing to talk about them. Every one must be willing to face the facts.' Very well, then, I will face the facts, but I prefer to exercise some judgment in the choice of the facts I face. Suppose you let me select three out of three thousand facts that I could readily produce for your inspection. Do you realize that at the present depth of our depression, people of America are at a higher level of material comfort than any other nation in the world has ever been at the height of its prosperity? Do you realize that at the very depth of our depression, the average per capita buying power of the American citizen is six times that of the average citizen of Soviet Russia? I do not mean six per cent. more. I do not mean sixty per cent. more. I mean six times as much. Do you realize that the taxes paid by the ordinary American, even now when municipal and state and national budgets seem loaded to the breaking point, are less than one-fifth of the taxes paid by the Englishman who draws approximately the same income? Yet *we* are doing the whining. We boasted that we could teach the world how to be good sports in the midst of adversity. We must learn to stop crying out loud!"

There is a lot more like this, fully as good, or better, and buttressed with the incident of a prisoner, "one of my best friends and in a penitentiary for twenty years. You may marvel that he is in and I am out," Clausen moralizes; the passage is so gripping and vivid that to read it is to feel your nerves tingle and the muscles in your throat ache. And with that prisoner's thrilling witness for courage and fortitude, he concludes thus:

"I know how he is doing his best with the job he has—maintaining contact with the State libraries, getting the books the young convicts need for their studies, helping them to apply for courses of correspondence instruction so that they may be ready for the tests of the world when the prison doors open, and always keeping up a running fire of correspondence with men on the outside like myself, to whom he can send his young friends when they are discharged and have a chance at beginning life again.

"Remembering his letter to me, when the limitations of my own life cast their shadows like cell bars across my work and the future loses itself in gloom like the dank corridor of a penitentiary cell-block, I will do the best I can with the job I have. And by God's help, I will not cry out loud! Will you?"

This parson is courageous. When the wet interests of Syracuse announced they were staging a parade on the date that Mayor Walker of New York was putting on his big parade, Clausen announced he would organize a parade of the Sunday-School children to follow the wets with a dry demonstration. Again when the American Legion brought pressure to bear on the Public Library to remove certain peace posters from the display boards in the Library building, Clausen rushed into print, denouncing the Legion's action and gave notice that those same posters would be exhibited on his church bulletin-board so that all who passed might see them. These are typical incidents and could be multiplied many times. This preacher has convictions and never loses an opportunity to declare them; he courteously and powerfully declares his convictions to a public often hostile.

Dr. Clausen, who after ten years still draws the largest audiences both morning and evening in the city, has his enemies to be sure. And some of his most caustic critics are among his ministerial brethren. Probably this is to be expected. The subtlest of such criticisms and the most intelligent comes from another eminent preacher, able, wise and generous, the late Rev. Carl Wallace Petty, pastor of the First Baptist Church, of Pittsburgh, who, lecturing on "The Homiletical Mind," has this to say:

"We, as Protestants, in spite of our new worship emphasis, will probably always have with us the pulpit showman and ecclesiastical clown. In some of our churches the ushers will continue to pass out apples on Apple Sunday, and in our pulpits an occasional brother will preach on 'Singing in the Rain' as he stands under an umbrella. There will remain those of the preaching fraternity who find their highest conception of a prophet of God to be a sort of a Will Rogers who has substituted a white tie and a cutaway coat for the sombrero and the lariat. There seems to be a large portion of the American public that satisfy their dramatic instinct in Charlie Chaplin, their musical craving from the works of Irving Berlin, their political needs from the Hearst newspapers, and their religious urges in pious vaudeville. It may be lamented—in fact, we may be inspired with a holy zeal to correct the condition—but the fact nevertheless remains. These folk must be ministered to. In a criticism of how it is done we can decry methods without impugning motives. To call our ecclesiastical showmen mountebanks seems to me, for one, to elect to occupy a place in the pew of the Pharisees. God no doubt has often to cause the crudities of men, as well as their wrath, to glorify Him."

This is very much to the point with one exception, in so far as it bears on the subject of the chapter—there is no "crudity" in Dr. Clausen's pulpit productions. Rather there is an *elegance* in his platform conduct even when most eccentric. I do not know to whom to liken him among his contemporaries. There is, in a way, some resemblance to J. Whitcomb Brougher now the preacher at Tremont Temple, Boston, and famed for his long-time success in down-town Baptist Temple, Los Angeles. But Clausen is finer-grained than Brougher, more artistic and gentler even when he thunders; he is as original, though not in the same way as Burris Jenkins, yet not so daring a pioneer in modern interpretation of the teachings of Jesus as the Kansas Citian. In truth Bernard Clausen is difficult to classify, is not a copyist, has blazed for himself a new trail, and withal is helping to bring down to earth in Syracuse, New York, the city of God.

COUGHLIN, Charles Edward, priest; *b.* of Am. parents at Hamilton, Can., Oct. 25, 1891; *s.* Thomas J. and Amelia (Mahoney) C.; honor grad. U. of Toronto, 1911. Ordained priest R.C. Ch., 1916; teacher of philosophy, Assumption Coll., Western U., 1916-22; pastor Shrine of the Little Flower, Royal Oak (Detroit), Mich., since 1926. *Author:* Christ or the Red Serpent, 1930; By the Sweat of Thy Brow, 1931; Father Coughlin's Radio Sermons, 1931. Known for his radio sermons on communism, labor conditions, etc. *Address:* Woodward and Twelve Mile Road, Royal Oak, Michigan.

Chapter XV

CHARLES E. COUGHLIN

As a usual thing the priests of the Catholic Church follow a well-beaten path, deviating but slightly, and preserving an impressive unity of doctrinal appeal and sermonic content. The Catholic pulpit, for instance, while often distinguished by able minds, offers nothing like the diversity and variety of personality and sermonic presentation which characterizes the non-Catholic ministry. Yet there are exceptions, and Rev. Charles E. Coughlin, of the Shrine to Ste. Therese, the Little Flower of Jesus, is one such. He is colorful, spectacular and resourceful to a daring degree.

Motorists driving along the super highway which proclaims Woodward Avenue, north of Detroit, can not fail to see the crucifixion tower that marks the shrine and the church from which Father Coughlin reaches millions by his radio sermons. It is a noble and artistic creation in stone, and at night-time the flood lighting effect is of surpassing beauty. So great are the crowds that throng Father Coughlin's services that traffic on the super highway is often frightfully congested. Something unusual is always going on at the Shrine of the Little Flower. Excursions from distant cities are run to special meetings. There are picnics for little children, and at one of these, in which thousands of youngsters participated, it was estimated that six thousand quarts of milk, two thousand cakes, fifty-two thousand dishes of ice-cream and uncounted barrels of ginger ale, were consumed by the youngsters.

Father Coughlin is a robust man physically, good-looking, and the most unconventional Roman Catholic priest I have seen or heard. Usually the pastors of this powerful division of Christendom, while friendly and human enough in their relations with their fellow human beings, are extremely serious, often rigid and aloof, when conducting the ceremonials of their church or speaking on subjects that relate to their religion. Not so the pastor of the Shrine of the Little Flower. On Sunday afternoons he frequently talks to the children of the parish and these talks are broadcast. On these occasions he appears like a big rollicking boy rather than a priest of the church, and he says surprising things. Talking to the children of his parish, I heard him say, "If any of you Catholic boys and girls turn up your noses at some other boy or girl just because he is a Protestant, you are a flop. You are not a good Catholic. . . . Of course, we have bigots in our church, just as there are bigots in all churches, but a good Catholic can not be a bigot. . . . Every little boy or girl tells lies at some time or other. When I was a little boy I told lies, but I soon found out there was nothing in telling lies. Do you little boys or girls want to know what I think of anybody who tells lies? I'll tell you. Anybody who lies is a jackass. . . . Be honest. Learn to tell the truth. Say your prayers every day, say them morning and night. Treat everybody fair and square. Jesus loves you little boys and girls. Think of Him being right here now and calling you by your first names: Katherine, Mike, Bill, Mary, Freckleface." . . . And thus on and on for half an hour and closing with pastor and children repeating one of the prayers of the church.

The sermon subjects discussed by Father Coughlin cover a wide range, "Communism," "Capital and Labor," "Unemployment," "Birth-Control," "Prosperity," etc. He handles these subjects ungloved and with a tremendous zest. He goes far afield as compared with those of his same calling and communion. An arch foe of capital punishment, he spoke his mind on this subject when Michigan was facing a referendum as to whether the law forbidding the supreme penalty should be repealed. He took this position despite the fact that the great majority of his fellow priests, who took any public position at all, took the other side.

When he got into trouble with the Columbia Broadcasting System, who wanted him to omit his "Prosperity" sermon, it is said that nearly two hundred thousand letters of protest were received by the Columbia System and Father Coughlin against barring him from the air. His daily mail is enormous and it is not all commendatory, but mostly so. Father Coughlin has his critics among his own churchmen. Like every strong personality, he has ardent supporters and equally enthusiastic detractors. Like Gallio of New Testament times, Father Coughlin "cared for none of these things."

One of my Catholic friends, highly placed, a most devout churchman, and thoroughly acquainted with the fine points of Catholic traditions and procedure, objects to Father Coughlin's radio sermons on the ground that he discusses so many subjects upon which the Church has not officially spoken. My friend holds that this is confusing to the radio audience, since the pastor of the Shrine of the Little Flower does not distinguish clearly between those views which have the "imprimatur" of the church and his own views. This is interesting. Other Catholics have taken the same view, and since Father Coughlin's printed sermons bear the "imprimatur" of Bishop Gallagher, numerous critics of the Bishop's fold have asked him if he indorsed everything that this bold and unconventional priest said from his pulpit. The Bishop explained that his "imprimatur" referred only to the theology and doctrinal section of the sermons which were sound and had nothing whatsoever to do with other assertions, declarations, political or economic. Moreover Bishop Gallagher publicly approved of Father Coughlin following Cardinal O'Connell's veiled but unmistakable attack on the Royal Oak priest's radio sermons. The criticism of Coughlin by the Cardinal so far as my observation goes only magnified the radio ministry of the former and gave him colossal publicity in the press, such as could not have been purchased at a fabulous cost. It piques the curiosity of Protestants and multiplies their interest in a Catholic priest who can draw the fire of a "prince of the church" and continue to preach his convictions. The Cardinal's rebuke coupled with the Bishop's commendation, meant a greater and still greater radio audience for Coughlin, and added immeasurably to the gaiety of the nation. For I am stoutly of the opinion that the Protestants who listen in on Father Coughlin are, to a surprising extent, his champions and ardent admirers, and in the long run the wise old "mother church" that has an almost uncanny knowledge of human nature, will be the gainer by the heavy hitting of this sermonic batsman of the major air league of the U. S. A. She usually is!

During the winter of 1932 and '33, Father Coughlin delivered a series of sermons on economic and industrial questions that set the city of Detroit agog and engulfed him in bitter controversy. When the banking débâcle came affecting over seven hundred thousand depositors Coughlin's onslaught on the officials and financiers was terrific. He made vitriolic attacks on the bankers of Detroit calling some of them by name, and drew a devastating barrage of criticism from the *Detroit Free Press* which labeled him a "demagog," charged him with uttering "falsehoods," and called upon his ecclesiastical superiors to discipline him. This old and influential newspaper also threatened libel suits against the priest and the radio station that broadcast his sermon. Bishop Gallagher gave out an interview in which he said that some of the priest's remarks were intemperate, but refused to interfere with his broadcasting. The radio station likewise declined to censor the pastor's sermons. So Father Coughlin stayed on the air and reiterated his indictment of banks and bankers. But for ten days the controversy rocked Detroit and provided an endless topic of conversation.

Here is a specimen of the Coughlin attack on the banking situation, a paragraph from the discourse which drew the fire of the *Detroit Free Press,* and involved him in the fiercest controversy of his career:

"For twenty years or more the people of this nation

have been suffering from the slavery of Mellonism. Its policy was to protect the white carnation. Its program was occupied with gambling with other people's money, with the building up of false confidence that has come crashing down upon them.

"'Save the stockholders.'

"'Let the depositors pay on the line,' although sixty thousand families in Detroit are eating the dole bread of poverty at the table of the Lord.

"Meanwhile they did revive the old banks, revive the crookedness, protect the under-secured borrower, pamper the speculator, bequest to your children the financial sorrows which you have experienced—and above all, they did sustain their holding company, the den of forty thieves, the hideout, the blind-pig financial institution where shady transactions are perpetuated and where are printed the depositors' passport to doom.

"Thus the battle was waged.

"The defenders of the old system preyed upon the minds of the small depositors by telling them that if the United States plans of government-controlled banks were adopted our finances would fall into the hands of 'outsiders' of Wall Street. The business man was approached with the threat that his industry, his holdings, would be ruthlessly liquidated.

"How false and misleading!"

There follows the peroration to another of Coughlin's famous philippics against the bankers. It is a fairly good example of his style and method, though the dramatic fire and rich Irish brogue are sadly missing:

"In conclusion, may I state that we must look forward to new men among the citizens as well as among our leaders.

"Now is the time to put off the old leaven, the old habits, the carousing, the false pride, the intemperance, and the carelessness for virtue, which were the revered vices of yesterday.

"At last, my friends, we have found leadership. Now we are seeking followership.

"Oh, Washington! Oh, Jefferson! Oh, Lincoln! How have we failed to follow you in your leadership so strong, so true, so dedicated to political, to personal liberty!

"Oh, fathers! Oh, mothers, of this generation, how have we failed to follow you in those examples so dearly dedicated to generosity, to self-effacement and to humility!

"Oh, Christ, divine Teacher of the divine plan, how have we failed to follow your lessons of justice, of charity, of truth—willing indeed to follow up the mountain if the loaves and the fishes were to be again multiplied—unwilling to follow into the Garden of Gethsemane to spend one hour with Thee!

"Oh, Christ! To-day we implore Thee by Thy poverty of Bethlehem, by Thy flight into Egypt—we beseech Thee by the merits of Thy sacred passion—the whip, the thorn, the heavy cross, the piercing nail, the cruel spear which opened wide Thy Sacred Heart—to grant us the grace that we may take up Thy cross and follow Thee! Follow Thee along the pathways of honesty; follow Thee, if necessary, along the tortuous road to Calvary! There from Thy Sacred Heart may Thy precious blood continue to flow forth as from a fountain of new life, to bless, to cleanse, to strengthen and preserve every one of us.

" 'With malice toward none and charity toward all'—may we cease even righteous anger and say for those whom we judge to be responsible for our present misery, 'Father, forgive them, for they know not what they do.' "

I account for the huge following of this clerical agitator largely because he has taken the side of the forgotten man, woman and child in the frightful industrial disaster that has overtaken us. The average man, the "man in the street," hasn't many friends at court, in church, or state; and in the vivid attacks of this priest upon the powers that be politically, the system that has got a strangle-hold on the man farthest down, Mr. Common Citizen pricks up his ears, his heart beats faster, a new light shines in his eyes, and he feels that here is a voice that expresses his own inarticulate ideals, yearnings, dreams. Any man who thus speaks with forthrightness and castigating candor, be he politician, preacher or editor, is certain to be called a "demagog" and there are many to apply that bitter stigma to Father Coughlin, who doesn't seem to mind it in the least. In truth, I fancy he rather enjoys it, and it is tip-top publicity.

As an illustration of the nature and extent of the Catholic criticism of Father Coughlin the following paragraph from an article by the Rev. Edward F. Murphy which appeared in *The Acolyte* of February 4, 1933, entitled "Magnavox" makes lively reading. It should be stated that *The Acolyte* is published "To Serve the Priests."

> "There is a famous hour called Golden, dedicated to the meekest and sweetest of saints. Its purpose doubtless is to increase devotion to little Teresa of the Child Jesus; but it has degenerated into a mélange of economics, social querulousness, and political attacks, charlotte-russed with a few hymns and not a few Gospel references. As a result, the Little Flower unmistakably plays second fiddle to the extremely eloquent and able conductor of the hour himself, and has received vastly less publicity; in fact, her still, small voice is hardly heard in the proceedings at all. The stage has been quite stolen from her. But the sovereign People are pleased with this 'olla podrida' of personality, piety and protest; indeed, as they loll back and listen in, they are hugely delighted and regaled by these Sunday-night revelations on how cruelly treated they are and what a

great friend Washington isn't. Love for the things of heaven becomes, in consequence of these stirring talks, a preoccupation with the things of earth; which, to be sure, is excellent for the reverend broadcaster's popularity, but of parlous significance to souls."

Father Coughlin's besetting sin, as I see it, is a malignant sort of intolerance when he discusses a theme, such, say, as Prohibition. Here he throws fairness to the winds. He fails to take into consideration the fact that there are many high-minded intelligent Americans who still believe, with all its failures, that the Eighteenth Amendment is the best method yet devised for handling an age-old evil. At any rate this mighty-voiced, independent priest does not bring the same sense of fairness to the discussion of the Prohibition question that he does to other subjects. Take for instance that fact that he has not been fair to his debonair fellow churchman, Colonel Patrick H. Callahan, of Louisville, Kentucky, who is an ardent Dry and head of the Association of Catholics Favoring Prohibition. Colonel Callahan wrote him numerous times asking that he correct over the air an erroneous statement with regard to the position of the American Medical Association on Prohibition, but in vain. This is a pity, and it is poor strategy. Long ago Abraham Lincoln set an example for all of us who discuss controverted subjects in public. It is this: "State your opponent's case as fairly as he himself can state it, then proceed to demolish it—if you can." Father Coughlin might take this counsel of one of the wisest of men to heart. But I doubt that he does.

Father Coughlin's method of preparation is distinctly modern. He has a staff of secretaries, several of whom are expert in the field of economics. These do research work and check the facts to be used in the sermons or lectures. He employs four personal stenographers most of the time and works them hard. He dictates rapidly and is safeguarded from everything except emergency calls in his parish. He is not easy to see, makes few appointments and seldom responds to the telephone calls that come insistently from unknown admirers and critics for neither of which he has any time to waste; yet to those who are admitted to his home or office, he is a delightful companion, witty, jovial, wonderfully well informed and extremely fluent of speech.

Not even the President of the United States has such a correspondence. Before Father Coughlin began his series of discourses in which he excoriated the financiers upon whom he lays the blame for our monetary troubles, his letters averaged one hundred thousand a week. Since his attack on the bankers and speculators his mail has gone as high as four hundred thousand letters weekly. The Shrine, as his church is called, maintains a mail truck of its own, and the week following his speech which drew the heavy fire of the *Detroit Free Press,* it became necessary for this truck to make two trips a day to the post-office, returning with nineteen heavily loaded sacks, containing on an average four thousand letters to a sack.

No funds are solicited over the radio yet the money that comes by reason of Father Coughlin's broadcasts pays the enormous cost of his use of the air, supports his large office force, and provided the funds for the marble tower and shrine. In one week's mail, it is said on excellent authority, that thirty thousand dollars in one-dollar bills were received. He prints his sermons by the tons and distributes them widely without a penny of cost to those who request them by mail. He takes a long summer vacation, preferring the waterways if possible. The priest's constant companion, and possibly protector as well, is a Great Dane dog named Pal.

With the exception of the Crucifixion Tower, built at a cost of two hundred and seventy-eight thousand dollars, Father Coughlin's present church is extremely modest, a frame structure seating only a few hundred. But he has announced plans for a great new edifice to cost one million dollars, and the contract for the building has already been let. Among the unusual features planned for the new Shrine will be an open altar in the center of the building. The church is to seat over twenty-five hundred people. To begin such an enterprise in times of depression is certainly a project of faith. However, Father Coughlin has wealthy friends among his admirers as well as host upon host of humbler folk who will sacrifice to contribute their mite. In announcing his plans this irrepressible priest said: "We are planning to pay all the craftsmen who work on the building wages higher than the scale of the American Federation of Labor, and we will establish a minimum wage of fifty cents an hour for common labor. In this way eighty-two and one-half cents of every dollar expended for the building will go for labor. In most ecclesiastical building only seventy cents of every dollar goes for that purpose."

Father Coughlin is the most thoroughgoing publicist of my acquaintance among the clergy, not excepting the irrepressible Dr. William L. Stidger, now the preacher at the Church of All Nations, Boston, whose flair for publicity is extraordinary. Both of these men are promoters of the institutions which they represent, and of themselves, but they are much more than promoters. Father Coughlin handles his own publicity with the skill of an expert. He takes advantage of big events; he knows how to capitalize conventions, parades, politics—everything. When the American Legion Convention met in Detroit, he took half of an entire page in one of the daily newspapers, and in this space there appeared a large picture of the crucifixion tower, beautifully done, and to one side of the drawing, the following announcement prominently printed:

> "Reverend Charles E. Coughlin of the Shrine of the Little Flower invites you to the Field Mass held for the American Legion Veterans on Sunday, September 20th, at 10:30, 11:30, and 12:30 a.m.
>
> "He wishes to take this occasion to congratulate the Legionnaires on having received their so-called 'soldiers' bonus.'"

Unconventional as it may sound and unpleasant as it may be to this Savonarola of the air, I am moved to call Father Coughlin the Billy Sunday of Catholicism, but a Billy Sunday plus a frontal attack on social and economic evils such as the picturesque evangelist never so much as dreamed of in all his varied and vivid career.

VANCE, James Isaac, clergyman, author; *b.* Arcadia, Tenn., Sept. 25, 1862; *s.* Charles Robertson and Margaret (Newland) V.; A.B., King Coll., Tenn., 1883, A.M., 1886; grad. Union Theol. Sem., Va., 1886; D.D., King Coll., 1896, Hampden Sidney Coll., 1896; LL.D., King Coll., 1913, Austin Coll., 1916; *m.* Mamie Stiles Currell, Yorkville, S. C., Dec. 22, 1886; children—Margaret, Currell, Agnes Wilkie, Ruth Armstrong, James Isaac (dec.), Charles Robertson. Ordained ministry Presbyn. Ch. in U. S., 1886; pastor Wytheville, Va., 1886-87; Alexandria, 1887-91; Norfolk, Va., 1891-94; First Ch., Nashville, Tenn., 1894-1900; North Ref. Ch., Newark, N. J., 1900-10; First Ch., Nashville, Dec. 1, 1910-. Platform speaker. Chmn. exec. com. foreign missions Presbyn. Ch. Served as moderator Presbyn. Ch. in U. S.; chmn. Protestant Relief in Europe. Trustee Southwestern Coll. *Author:* Young Man Four-Square, 1894; Church Portals, 1895; College of Apostles, 1896; Predestination (pamphlet), 1898; Royal Manhood, 1899; Rise of a Soul, 1902; Simplicity in Life, 1903; A Young Man's Make-up, 1904; The Eternal in Man, 1907; Tendency, 1910; Life's Terminals, 1917; The Life of Service, 1918; The Silver on the Iron Cross, 1919; The Breaking of Bread, 1921; Being a Preacher, 1923; God's Open, 1924; Forbid Him Not, 1925; Love Trails of the Long Ago, 1927; This Dreamer, 1928; The Field Is the World, 1930; Sermons in Argot, 1931; Worship God, 1932. Contbr. to mags. and reviews. *Home:* 118, 21st Av. S., Nashville, Tenn.; (summer) Blowing Rock, N. C.

VANCE, Joseph Anderson, clergyman; *b.* Sullivan Co., Tenn., Nov. 17, 1864; *s.* Charles Robertson and Margaret (Newland) V.; A.B., King Coll., Bristol, Tenn., 1885; B.D., Union Theol. Sem., Hampden Sidney, Va., 1888; D.D., Huron Coll., S. D., 1902, King Coll., 1904; LL.D., Austin Coll. Tex., 1917; *m.* Mary B. Forman, of Louisville, Ky., Jan. 15, 1890; children—Dorothy, Joseph A., Mary F. Ordained Presbyn. ministry, 1888; pastor Woodland Av. Ch. Louisville, 1888-91, Maryland Av. Ch., Baltimore, 1891-99, Hyde Park Ch., Chicago, 1899-1911, First Ch., Detroit, Sept. 1, 1911-. Dir. and mem. exec. com. Charity Organization Soc. while at Baltimore; ex. moderator Md. Presbytery and of Chicago Presbytery; ex-pres. Presbyn. Ministers' Assn. of Chicago; mem. Ch. Federation Council of Chicago; ex-pres. Detroit Federation of Chs.; pres. Nat. Bd. Missions of Presbyn. Ch. U. S. A. *Author:* Westminster Assembly and Its Confession for God, 1897; Home, 1900; Religion and Money, 1903; American Problems, 1904; The True and the False in Christian Science, 1904; Consider Christ Jesus, 1913; Why We Are Going to War, 1917; Christianity and Capital Punishment; America's Future Religion, 1927. *Home:* 45 Edmund Pl., Detroit, Mich.

CHAPTER XVI

THE BROTHERS VANCE—UNLIMITED

TENNESSEE is the state where celebrities come in couples, to wit: the two "Andys," Jackson and Johnson; the two Taylors, "Bob" and "Alf," and the two Vances, "Jim" and "Joe." Dr. James I. Vance has been pastor of First Presbyterian Church, Nashville, since 1910. Prior to this he was minister at Wytheville, Alexandria and Norfolk, Virginia. Dr. Joseph A. Vance, has led First Presbyterian Church, Detroit, Michigan, since 1911. Before coming to the Motor City, he served in Louisville, Kentucky, Baltimore, Maryland, and Hyde Park Church, Chicago. In the twenty years that this able preacher has been a Detroiter he has seen that city triple its population, pyramid its wealth and become the world center of the automobile industry. Brother James at Nashville is minister of a large congregation, conducts numerous preaching missions, writes many books. Brother Joseph at Detroit has an old and historic church, is prominent in civic as well as national religious activities. Both men retain remarkable pulpit vigor, are forthright personalities, born leaders of men.

Physically the brothers are large men, not fat but big of frame, broad-shouldered, and lean of flank. Their bodies have the ranginess that distinguishes men of the mountains, and they are the product of generations of rugged pioneering souls who endured hardship, blazed paths where highways never ran. The Nashville Vance is rounder of face and less angular of figure than the Detroiter. Both are built on the Abraham Lincoln order, and Joseph's features resemble the great Kentuckian's, the large mouth, full lips, deep-set eyes, and the contour of jaw that suggests firmness and mercy.

The long and crowded ministerial careers of these brothers is eloquent evidence of sound minds in sound bodies, to Anglicize a familiar Latinism.

James I. Vance is, by quite general consent, the premier preacher of the Presbyterian Southland. What Joseph Parker said of Alexander Whyte might be said with equal discrimination and sincerity of this preacher, "royal, fearless and tender." Seldom the reformer in the pulpit, and never the muck-raker, he boldly fights against the powers and principalities of evil. Upon moral issues no one needs to ask where he stands, yet he has never been charged with taking politics into the pulpit. James I. has a voice of splendid range and depth and keeps it under control. In a region where oratory is still highly rated, this preacher could scarcely be called an orator, yet he belongs in the list of exceptionally able speakers. His style is simple, never florid. He likes the short sentence. He articulates clearly. He has no pet words or phrases. He usually employs the conversational tone, but he can and does wax warm when the occasion warrants it. His favorite gesture is a movement of the right arm, hand extended with open palm; sometimes with arms extended, he clasps his hands in an impressive downward gesture, all his own.

He is liberal in his thinking, but not a liberal in theology. Faith in the deity of Jesus is, according to an intimate friend and brother pastor, his one and only test of orthodoxy. He loves his Presbyterian Church but is not a sectarian. The radiance of religion is not a lost art with James. No doleful sounds come from the Good News he preaches. He loves people and loves them to such an extent that some think he is not a good judge of human nature. He is imposed upon so often. Laughter is in this preacher's creed and he greatly enjoys a laugh at himself. Here is one of his stories:

"A stranger came forward and informed me that he had come a hundred miles on the train to hear me preach. 'I hope you feel repaid,' I said with a smile. 'Yes,' responded the visitor hesitatingly, 'I ride on a pass.'"

For recreation this Dr. Vance takes care of his own car, loves to putter around in his yard and garden. He is a member of a golf club but is seldom seen on the links. He spends his vacation at his summer home at Blowing Rock, North Carolina, where he loves to explore the mountain trails and ride horseback.

He is a good organizer. The annual budget of his congregation is ninety thousand dollars, the preponderant part of which goes for missions and education. He is away from home preaching and holding meetings a large part of the time. His church gives him the privilege of being absent one Sunday a month. The only criticism that one ever hears of this beloved preacher among his people is that he is away too much. When Dr. James I. spoke to a layman in his congregation about missing him from church, the layman came back with this: "Well, Doctor, I have been missing you too." To me it is little short of miraculous that such preachers as George W. Truett, of Dallas, and James I. Vance, of Nashville, can be away from their churches so much of the time and yet on the whole serve their parishioners so acceptably.

Dr. Joseph A. Vance is one of Detroit's most eminent preachers and publicists. He touches the city's life at many points. He has a good mind, vigorous and rugged; he possesses strong style as speaker and writer, marked by simplicity and clarity. I have heard him on many occasions and in various kinds of public addresses, and I have never known him to be unprepared, slipshod, dull or uninteresting. There's a freshness of thought, newness of illustration, and a spice of humor that keeps him well up to the top of effectiveness. Most public speakers, particularly preachers, as they grow older, incline to long drawn out discourses. Their terminal facilities are frightful. It's a pity, but it's true. Not so, Dr. Vance; he can preach a twenty-minute sermon to-day with plenty of punch and with real finish. His "quittin' sense" is commendably good. Maybe this is one reason why he wears so well in the pastorate.

Vance of Detroit is something of a controversialist, and when the occasion warrants, believe me, he is the old-time debater, asks no quarter, is a hard hitter, yet I think always fair. Some of his brother Presbyterians who have gone to the mat with him think him something of a dictator, at times a martinet, and possibly a trifle bossy, but even these hold the doctor in vast respect, and willingly pay tribute to the vigor of his mind, the wisdom of his counsel and the all-round ability of this able churchman. Here is a preacher who can not remain silent when a statement is made in his hearing reflecting upon what he feels to be vital in religion. He comes to life like an old-time fire horse at the tap of the bell, goes into action, does not mince words, gives a reason for the hope that is within him, and his opponent, whoever he may be, knows, when the thing is over, that he's been in a fight.

Joseph A. Vance does not prophesy smooth things. He is no talker for pink teas; he never plays rhetorical tiddledy-winks. He has a habit of getting beneath the surface of things and dealing with the hard inescapable facts of life. He believes in Capital Punishment and defends his belief with sturdy eloquence. He preaches much about sin in a day when that word is missing from thousands of sermons. He is a good exegete of the Scriptures. He is given to a great deal of expository preaching and does it exceptionally well. He is something of a theologian, and an exponent of the higher Calvinism; he can be tonically severe. In a minister's meeting when the topic bore on preachers and preaching, in the general discussion that followed I heard Dr. Vance say:

"The trouble with most of us preachers is that we do not impress the public as holy men. We are known as soap-box orators, good self-advertisers, excellent politicians, and good fellows generally, but not many people think of us as prophets, holy men of God."

This Detroit preacher is a wise counselor. Numerous people resort to him for advice, almost as many outside his church as within. His judgment is usually sound and practical. His statesmanship has been often in evidence in the activities of the Detroit Council of Churches in the creation of which he was a leader. He is minded to be skeptical of radical ideas and innovations, suspicious of short-cuts and panaceas, yet I should believe him to be the last man to hold to any outworn method simply because it is old. But he must be reasonably sure of a plan or an idea before he champions it. Once assured, it matters not how unusual or radical it appears, he gives every ounce of his influence in its behalf, and what blows he can strike when fully aroused!

Joseph scarcely looks his years, dresses well and favors double-breasted suits, browns or grays. He gives the appearance of good but not robust health. He is not often in the papers, but whatever he gives out for publication is timely, worth reading and pungently phrased. "Solid" is the word that best describes this Presbyterian minister and civic leader.

The Detroit Vance is administrator and executive as well as preacher. His church is splendidly organized, with a fairly large staff of assistants. I do not know a down-town congregation that is more ably directed and ministered to than the First Presbyterian Church of Detroit. Because of his administrative gifts, together with the soundness of his judgment, Dr. Vance has been called to head various important commissions in Presbyterianism. He is out of the city frequently, and nearly always in connection with denominational or inter-denominational activities; and he preaches often in pulpits other than his own. Brother Jim has been Moderator of the Presbyterian Church in the United States (Southern), and Brother Joe received a creditable vote for the Moderatorship of the Presbyterian Church of the United States of America (Northern). Curious, is it not, that these brothers in the flesh and the ministry, run neck and neck "the race that is set before them?"

Joseph A. Vance has not published anything like the number of books that have come from the pen of James I., but he has to his credit *America's Future Religion,* which appeared in 1927. The book is dedicated to "The Wranglers," that joyous preachers' club whose members are well represented in these pages. The doctor first preached these chapters as sermons in his own pulpit and they found a still wider audience over the radio. The tone of this book is optimistic. A robust faith is everywhere distinguishable. Sample this paragraph, the next to the last in the closing chapter of the volume:

> "America's religious life is not headed for the scrap heap. Efficiency in business is being more than matched in our nation with reality in religion. Some things are being discarded, and some things are being neglected; but who of us would really like to go back to the religious life of any century that lies behind us? The 'good old yesterdays' have given birth to a better today, and we have God's word for it that we are traveling toward a better tomorrow. The great question for every man to put to himself today is, Am I the kind of a Christian I ought to be? the kind that Christ was, and would have me be?"

And these:

> "The redemptive vitality of a Christianity that has the Bethlehem Manger and Calvary Cross and the Empty Tomb at its heart has never failed those who put their trust in it. At the very hour when men were talking about it as "a spent force" or an "outgrown superstition," it was getting a vantage-ground for larger conquest.
>
> "Let us not be afraid of a faith that can break an outgrown shell, and is not afraid to discard shibboleths that have become platitudes. Nor need we have any fears about the future of a religion that has met the spiritual needs of nineteen centuries. Let us rather set our ambi-

tions on the type of Christian that the nineteen centuries of Christian living should produce."

These brothers have great times together. Every two or three years they arrange an exchange of visits. As pulpit hosts of each other they excel and the congregations are treated to a brotherly exchange of amenities that outshines Alphonse and Gaston.

"What do you think of your brother Jim as a preacher?" I inquired of Vance of Detroit.

"To say what I think of James I. Vance as a preacher is not easy. It puts me in a strait between being over-appreciative or hypercritical; because he is not only my brother but my most intimate lifetime friend.

"His style is fascinatingly beyond me. He permeates his thought with spirituality. He preaches the Gospel and has put his preaching into many books, but he preaches out of life and for the life of the people and his day. His message runs hot from his own heart, and when put on a printed page still tugs at my heart and often thrills me. I can not say as much for mine, or for that of many preachers.

"From his forebears for many generations he has inherited ancestral piety with a vertebral morality. God gave us a rare religious parentage and a godly home where religion was both a creed and a life; where family worship was pervaded with the deep spiritual experience of closet prayer; where religious instruction was of more importance than material prosperity and where the one source of all authority was 'the word of God contained in the Scriptures of the Old and New Testaments.'"

"Tell me," I asked Dr. James I. Vance, "what is your opinion of your brother Joe as a preacher?"

"Gladly; I like the subject. Joe and my youngest brother, Dr. Charles R. Vance, a physician at Norfolk, Virginia, one of the best men I know, and I, are not only brothers, but friends, and never so happy as when we can be together—which we manage to do a few days each year.

"Joe is my favorite preacher. To me he is the greatest preacher of my acquaintance. He makes my spine chill. Some preachers put me to sleep. He deals sledge-hammer blows. When he hits the devil, it is a solar plexus. There is nothing namby-pamby about his sermons. It makes little difference to him whether his congregation likes what he says or not. He does not preach for approval, much less for applause, but for conviction. A hiss stirs him more than a cheer. He has strong convictions himself, and does not hesitate to express them. He is not easy to handle in an argument, for he hits straight from the shoulder, and he never sugar-coats what he says. But he would not hurt a kitten, for his heart is as tender as a woman's.

"But he does not let his heart run off with his head, and he can not be bulldozed with ballyhoo.

"The biggest difference between us is that he gets his fun out of golf and I get mine out of riding a horse; but we both would rather preach than play, and each of us thinks more of people than sermons.

"There is no monotony in our annual conclaves, for our fondness for each other is not a product of so tame a thing as congeniality. There is red-hot discussion, theological, political and social. Joe is something of a modernist, I am a progressive conservative, and Charles is an old-time fundamentalist, who always votes the straight Democratic ticket."

So it seems the Vance Brothers have a fairly good opinion of each other, and thousands who are no blood relations, will agree with their estimate.

The best preacher story I ever heard is one that both the Vances love to tell. It has for setting a family in Dr. J. I.'s church in Nashville. The story deserves a paragraph, and shall have it.

According to Vance of Detroit, the sister of the late Senator Joseph W. Bailey, who belongs to his brother Jim's church, was breaking in a new colored maid. It happened that Senator Joe made an unexpected visit to his sister that week and the new maid started to the door in answer to his ring. Happening to be up-stairs the lady of the house saw the handsome Texan approaching, raced down-stairs, gently pushed the colored girl aside at the door, opened it, threw her arms about her brother's neck, hugged him hard and kissed him twice. Then, remembering the colored girl standing by, she turned to her and explained; "I don't suppose you know who this is, Caroline?" "No, ma'am," replied the grinning girl, "I sho' don't; unless—unless it's yo' pastor." I've heard Brother Joe tell this story four times and I'm a candidate to hear it as many more times as he wills to tell it.

The Brothers Vance are the sort of preachers you can hear fifty-two Sundays in the year without losing either your temper or your religion.

HOUGH, Lynn Harold, educator, clergyman; *b.* Cadiz, O., Sept. 10, 1877; *s.* Franklin M. and Eunice R. (Giles) H.; A.B., Scio College, Ohio, 1898; B.D., Drew Theological Seminary, 1905; post-grad. work, New York U.; D.D., Mt. Union-Scio Coll., 1912; D.D., Garrett Bibl. Institute, 1918; Th.D., Drew Theol. Seminary, 1919; Litt. D., Allegheny College, 1922; LL.D., Albion Coll., 1923, University of Detroit, 1928; D.D., Wesleyan Univ., 1924; unmarried. Entered M. E. ministry, 1898; pastor Arcola, N. J., 1898-1904, 1st Church, Cranford, N. J., 1904-06, King's Park, N. Y., 1906-07, 3d Ch., L. I. City, N. Y., 1907-09, Summerfield Ch., Brooklyn, 1909-12, Mt. Vernon Pl. Church, Baltimore, 1912-14; prof. hist. theology, Garrett Bibl. Inst., 1914-19; pres. Northwestern U., 1919-20; pastor Central M. E. Ch., Detroit, Mich., 1920-28, American Presbyterian Ch., Montreal, 1928-30; prof. of homiletics and comprehensive scholarship, Theological Seminary, Drew University, since 1930. Pres. Detroit Council Chs. 1926-28; v.p. Religious Edn. Assn., 1926-28; mem. Soc. Bibl. Lit. and Exegesis, Chicago Soc. Bibl. Research, Nat. Voters' League (dir.), Soc. Midland Authors; president Religious Education Council of Canada, 1929-30. Scottish Rite Mason (33°, Knight Templar). *Clubs:* Cliff Dwellers, (Chicago); Authors' (London). *Author:* Athanasius, the Hero, 1906; The Lure of Books, 1911; The Theology of a Preacher, 1912; The Men of the Gospels, 1913; The Quest for Wonder, 1915; In the Valley of Decision, 1916; The Man of Power, 1916; The Little Old Lady, 1917; Living Book in a Living Age, 1918; The Significance of the Protestant Reformation, 1918; The Clean Sword, 1918; The Productive Beliefs (Cole lectures at Vanderbilt U.), 1919; Flying Over London, 1919; The Eyes of Faith, 1920; The Opinions of John Clearfield, 1921; Life and History, 1922; The Strategy of the Devotional Life, 1922; The Inevitable Book, 1922; A Little Book of Sermons, 1922; Twelve Merry Fishermen, 1923; Synthetic Christianity, (Merrick Lectures, Ohio Wesleyan U.), 1923; The Imperial Voice, 1924; The Lion in His Den, 1925; Evangelical Humanism (Fernley lecture, at Lincoln, Eng.), 1925; Adventures in the Minds of Men, 1927; Imperishable Dreams, 1929; The Artist and the Critic, (Samuel Harris lectures, Bangor Theol. Sem.), 1930; Personality and Science, (Ayer lectures, Colgate-Rochester Div. Sch.), 1930. Writer S. S. Lesson Exposition for New York Christian Advocate, 1909-; lectures on theol., lit. and philos. topics; sent to Great Britain to speak on the moral and spiritual aims of the war, by the Lindgren foundation of Northwestern U., 1918. Editor and contbr. to "Whither Christianity," 1929. Contbg. editoı Christian Century. *Home:* Drew Forest, Madison, N. J.

Chapter XVII

LYNN HAROLD HOUGH

Dr. Hough is, by the general consent of those who know him best, one of the most brilliant preachers of this generation. It has been my good fortune to have heard many of the great preachers of our day on both sides of the Atlantic, and I unhesitatingly rank Lynn Harold Hough as the most scintillating and interesting of the inner circle of famous preachers of the Word. Dr. Hough's reputation is equally eminent in England and America. He has preached in most of the influential pulpits of non-conformity in Great Britain, and lectured often in university courses. Always intellectually aware, he is peculiarly effective as a preacher to preachers.

Physically, Dr. Hough is slight in build, and of complexion a decided brunet. His dark eyes are brilliant and flash fire. He speaks at a high nervous tension, using the explosive tone almost constantly. His style is nervous; his mannerisms, particularly the use of his hands, eccentric. Frequently he puts his thumbs in the armholes of his vest, or, as they say across the sea, waistcoat. He clutches the lapels of his coat and jerks them roughly. He teeters and sways on his feet. The content of his speech is always saturated with literary and historical lore. His vocabulary is astonishingly large and varied. Names, dates, quotations, episodes, tumble from his tongue in swift succession, sometimes fairly bewildering his auditors by the prodigality of allusion, metaphor and simile. "The element of surprise" is used by this preacher with fine effect. You never know what is coming next, though you may think you do. He speaks rapidly and is oratorically volcanic.

The doctor is a coiner of dazzling phrases that are not

merely ornamental but crowded with meaning, eloquent with conviction, meaty with fact and argument. He favors the terse sentence, but for the sake of variety occasionally employs Johnsonese and his periods at times roll and reverberate after the fashion of Daniel Webster and Rufus Choate. He is seldom, even when weary, commonplace or dull, and never platitudinous. He arouses your interest from his first sentence and holds it unflaggingly to the end. He seems never at a loss for the right word, the telling incident, the dazzling paradox, the clever repartee, the apt quatrain.

Dr. Hough loves to use unusual words. He is the first speaker, to my knowledge, to use the word "seminal" in such connections as "seminal-minded" and similar phrases. He may be over-fond of a few words—what speaker is not? "Urbane" is one of his prime favorites, also "wistful," and he loves "penetrating" with a very great love. He makes frequent and effective use of "poignant," and his syntax is often so unusual as to startle, but it is invariably correct. He is a Browning scholar and "The Ring and the Book" is so familiar to him that I dare say he could reproduce from memory entire sections of that difficult and lengthy poem.

As a specimen of the Hough style, listen to this, taken from his address on "Adventure of Preaching":

> "One of the things that I would like to do to-night would be to make every one of us discontented with any preaching which does not have the sheer heave of the mighty biological adventure from the day the first germ cell felt the first outreach towards fuller life to that mighty consummation of which it was said that Jesus is the very crown of the evolutionary progress. I would like all of us to feel that preaching somehow is echoing the marvel and wonder of that adventure in every moment of its own expression in the preacher's mind."

Dr. Hough is always preparing, constantly reading, writing, traveling, observing. He numbers among his friends famed preachers, publicists, editors, statesmen, orators. He is an ardent admirer of Woodrow Wilson and has a lecture on that world figure which is at once a thing of beauty and an assessment of Mr. Wilson's character from the beginning of his career as a college professor until he was "the pillar of a people's hope, the center of a world's desire"—a truly marvelous piece of oratory. Dr. Hough is a world student, a Christian internationalist, a competent critic of modern literature and a theologian of parts. He is at home almost anywhere, but chiefly, perhaps, with the intellectuals. He is impatient with the partizan and narrow nationalists, is anything but a denominationalist. His critics deem him over-intellectual and pronounce him "aloof" from the masses, but they do not know the heart of the man when they thus censure him.

Dr. Hough's eight years' ministry in Detroit was pitched upon a high level and of a city-wide interest. Just as the presence of royalty is indicated by the colors flying from the castle or palace, Central M. E. Church at Grand Circus Park flamed with life when its pastor was at home and in the pulpit. The midweek meetings had record-making attendance; the Sunday services enjoyed capacity crowds in the morning and well-filled church in the evening. Wherever Dr. Hough appeared as a speaker, before luncheon clubs, literary societies, and fraternal groups, the stage was set, the atmosphere was right, the setting perfect.

It is a curious coincidence that Dr. Hough's ministry each fall was off to a good start due to some unusual happening, widely exploited by the newspapers. Thus one season a country preacher, an old-timer, brought heresy charges against the Detroit celebrity and lodged them with the proper committee at the district conference. The story broke just as Dr. Hough landed in New York from a vacation in Europe. The New York correspondent of a Detroit evening paper interviewed Dr. Hough and the brotherly spirit in which he met the heresy charge, the gracious words he spoke in behalf of the old minister, made a capital story, and the result—Dr. Hough opened up his first Sunday services to audiences that overflowed into the street.

At another season, an article by Dr. Hough appeared in *Plain Talk* in which he took the position and argued it ably that the Catholics deserved a president of their faith in the White House. Inasmuch as Governor Smith's candidacy was then in the offing, this article created a small sensation among the Methodists and some of them were nonplussed, not to say shocked. The newspapers gave liberal space, and published extracts from the article. That edition of *Plain Talk* was soon exhausted and all the while crowds thronged Central Methodist Church and the name of its pastor was on myriad tongues.

Yet these episodes were mild compared with the furor that broke when Hough in a speech before the City Forum, subject "Patriotism," chastised blisteringly the Daughters of the American Revolution for having blacklisted such notable characters as Jane Addams, Rabbi Wise and others. He referred perhaps ungallantly, to this proud aristocratic organization as "Daughters of the Ku Klux." This was the last straw. Things began to happen fast. The morning newspaper bitterly assailed Dr. Hough. A G.A.R. post somewhere in Michigan "resolved" to petition the office bearers of Central M. E. Church to ask for his resignation. Various patriotic societies passed resolutions of censure. Yet at the identical time the front pages of the daily press were carrying William Allen White's criticism of the Daughters, and the statement of Mrs. Helen Bailey Tufts who was resigning from the D.A.R. because of the policy which Mr. White and Dr. Hough attacked. Amid this storm of controversy, Hough preserved a calm cool silence, went about his business circumspectly and when he was reviled, reviled not again.

One other episode is worth chronicling. The doctor had received a flattering call to become minister of the American church at Montreal. While he was considering this invitation, he counseled naturally with the leading men in his church and others outside. One day he sat in conference with one of the most influential of Detroit's big business men. This man is a member and an official of Central M. E. Church, a charming gentleman, somewhat conservative and sharing the fears of his group regarding radicalism. To this man, his loyal friend, who had just urged him to remain, Dr. Hough said, in substance, this:

"I believe my work in Detroit is done. I have fought on a number of battle fronts for causes that needed defenders. I have made some enemies. That was to be expected, but I doubt the advisability of prolonging my pastorate here, and for this reason: I predict that within a few years Detroit will experience a frightful upheaval in industrial circles. Labor and Capital will fight it out to the bitter end. If I were in the city at the time, my voice would be lifted for justice. It migh embarrass some of my splendid friends who are prominent employers to have me on hand at such a time. I think I had better go to Montreal."

It is to the credit of this highly placed business man that he answered: "In case you are right in your prophecy, and God forbid, may it not be, Dr. Hough, that we shall greatly need your voice, your courage, your judgment?"

Nevertheless Dr. Hough sent in his resignation and closed his ministry in a whirl of social affairs, speaking engagements, farewell dinners, that carried him swiftly to the last Sunday with its vast audiences and tearful farewells. His going from the Fourth City was like the passing of a blazing meteor across the night skies, a flash, a flame, and—things as they were. I say it was like that, and it was more, it was the departure of a prophet-preacher of rare brilliance and lofty courage, leaving "a lonesome place against the sky."

Dr. Hough is an effective public speaker almost any way you take him. He has traveled so widely, read so prodigiously, companied with so many fine minds and radiant personalities, that he has at hand an inexhaustible store of illustrative miscellany. I remember hearing him along about 1922 or '23 at some kind of peace meeting, an Armistice Day address possibly, when in the midst of a service investitured with flags and banners, and with hundreds of men in khaki present, he said:

"I think I will tell you how I made peace with Germany after the war. It happened in this way. I had gone to Hamburg with a dear friend of mine, an editor, whose name many of you would recognize, whose son was killed in the war. As we drove about Hamburg looking at the flowers, this English editor said, 'They love beauty.' And then he picked out of his pocket a picture of the boy killed in the war, and he said, 'You know, we have got to make the world a good world for all of us; these people here and ourselves. That is the only way to justify the sacrifice of our fine lads.' I said, 'It is worth coming across the Atlantic to hear you say that.' And then I was sitting in a railroad station and near me was a German mother with a little baby, and this little baby came and put one hand on one of my knees and one on the other knee, and I looked down into the face of that German baby and then and there made peace with Germany."

Now this is an eloquent paragraph even when transferred from the platform to the printed page, but it is not quite possible to convey in type the expression on the speaker's face, the sudden softening of his voice, and the dramatic climax that swept the audience. It was a peace sermon in itself. The gospel of reconciliation was never more adroitly and powerfully proclaimed.

The cleverness of Dr. Hough to adapt himself to almost any platform exigency was never better illustrated than in a symposium of four addresses which was held in Detroit January, 1933, for the benefit of the unemployed. The speakers were Clarence Darrow, whose subject was "Why I Am an Agnostic," Judge John P. McGoorty, who spoke on "Why I Am a Catholic," Rabbi Leo M. Franklin on "Why I Am a Jew," and Dr. Hough on "Why I Am a Protestant." A huge audience was present. The order of the addresses was decided by drawing lots and Dr. Hough drew the first speech. He spoke with that sparkling abandon for which he is noted and gave the following reasons for being a Protestant: 1. Because I am a Jew; and he showed the vast debt of Protestantism to Judaism. 2. Because I am a Catholic; and he paid tribute to the Catholic Church for many priceless gifts. 3. Because I am an Agnostic; showing that Protestantism has always wanted to know why and how, and when, and so in the end becomes skeptical of skepticism; and 4. Because I believe in the Sacredness of Personality. It was a daring achievement and evoked both praise and criticism, the latter on the ground that it was "too clever."

A friend and ardent admirer of Dr. Hough once said this about his hero: "If something happened to Dr. Hough to send him into the valley of the shadow, some deep and awful sorrow, he would emerge the greatest preacher who stands in a pulpit the world over." This same thing has been said of other preachers, also of prima donnas, painters and poets. But we need not wish such experiences for ourselves or for others—they come somewhere along the way, come crashing upon us unannounced and often from cloudless skies.

Dr. Hough is only a little past fifty and a bachelor. He has conquered many worlds—literature, history, theology, philosophy—and has written many books. He has been the president of a great university and pastor of conspicuous churches. He resigned the Montreal pulpit to become a member of the faculty of Drew Theological Seminary, where he is Professor of Homiletics and Comprehensive Scholarship. There too he is the morning preacher for the Methodist Church of Madison, New Jersey, three Sundays a month. He lectures widely throughout the states, on preaching, literature, and related subjects, and always he is busy with a book in the making. It is the opinion of those who know him intimately that Dr. Hough will some day occupy a pulpit throne in London, where he is at home whether in Fleet Street and those quaint shops where the literary-minded gather and company with the mighty spirits of the past, or mingling with his contemporaries of the pulpit, classroom or political realm—an arresting figure always.

MACARTNEY, Clarence Edward Noble, clergyman; *b.* Northwood, O., Sept. 18, 1879; *s.* J. L. (D.D.) and Catherine (Robertson) M.; B.A., U. of Wis., 1901; M.A., Princeton, 1904; grad. Princeton Theol. Sem., 1905; D.D., Geneva Coll., 1914; unmarried. Ordained Presbyn. ministry, 1905; pastor 1st Church, Paterson, N. J., 1905-14, Arch St. Ch., Phila., 1914-27; First Church, Pittsburgh, since 1927. Dir. Westminster Theological Seminary; moderator Presbyn. Church in U. S. A., 1924-25. *Author:* The First Presbyterian Church, Paterson, N. J. (hist. sketch), 1913; The Minister's Son, 1917; Parables of the Old Testament, 1916; Twelve Great Questions about Christ, 1923; Lincoln and His Generals, 1925; Putting On Immortality, 1926; Highways and Byways of the Civil War, 1926; Of Them He Chose Twelve, 1927; Christianity and Common Sense, 1927; Wrestlers with God, 1930; Things Most Surely Believed, 1931; Lincoln and His Cabinet, 1931; The Way of a Man with a Maid, 1931. Compiler: Great Sermons of the World, 1927; Paul the Man, 1928; Sons of Thunder, 1929. Contbr. lit. and hist. articles to mags. *Address:* First Presbyn. Church, Pittsburgh, Pa.

Chapter XVIII

CLARENCE EDWARD MACARTNEY

Dr. Matthews, of Seattle, and Dr. Clarence Edward Macartney, of Pittsburgh, have both been Moderators of the General Assembly of the Presbyterian Church in the United States of America; and both are leading militant fundamentalists but here the parallel halts abruptly. They bear no physical resemblance, and their mental processes and pulpit style are wholly unlike. They have fought side by side in those theological battles which used to characterize the meetings of General Assembly and contributed piquancy and dramatic interest to them. They are of the identical school doctrinally but Matthews is a southerner by birth and upbringing while Macartney is an Ohioan, born in Northwood in 1879, and brought up in Pennsylvania.

Dr. Macartney began his ministry at Paterson, New Jersey, where he remained nine years. Then he accepted an invitation to the Arch Street Church, Philadelphia, where he remained thirteen years. Since 1927 he has been minister of the old, wealthy and tremendously influential First Church, Pittsburgh. He has been an indefatigable author and has published sixteen books besides myriad pamphlets and sermons. He has an historical bent and three of his volumes deal with the Civil War period and Abraham Lincoln. His sermons and other writings mirror the reader of many books and the world traveler who loves to pilgrimage to the famous shrines and muse amid the memorials and monuments of the great old days.

Macartney is a natural born preacher who dearly loves to preach and is never far removed from the mighty business of unfolding the Scriptures and appealing to his hearers to heed the leading of God's Spirit. The titles of his books are suggestive of his interests and emphasis, *Twelve Great Questions about Christ, Putting on Immortality, Christianity and Common Sense, Wrestlers with God, Things Most Surely Believed, Paul the Man, Sons of Thunder, The Way of a Man with a Maid—Twelve Sermons on Right and Wrong Relations between Men and Women.*

His latest volume, *Sermons from Life,* contains twenty-three chapters and is not doctrinal, but pastoral, intimate, and suggests the confessional. The discourses are based on the author's numerous contacts with the men and women who come to him for advice and help. Some of the sermons were inspired by chance remarks he happened to overhear on the city streets and in throngs in the midst of which he chanced to be. They are strongly evangelistic in tone, searching and personal, illuminated by incidents fresh from life. The titles are unusual and pique the curiosity. Thus he preaches on "I Can't Let Her Go" from the text in I Corinthians 10: 13, "God is faithful, who will not suffer you to be tempted above that ye are able." The subject grew out of an interview and words spoken probably in Dr. Macartney's study, by a man who had formed an illicit relationship with an attractive woman. Since the introductory paragraphs tell the story and indicate the tenor of the discourse, I include them here.

> "'I can't let her go!' It was his answer to my suggestion and advice, which he had sought. The words were spoken, not defiantly or impetuously, but slowly, quietly and sadly. 'I can't let her go.' It was not so much the words that impressed me, as the way he uttered them. It was the expression in his face, the accent of his voice.
>
> "It was one of those tangled webs which human love and human sin are always weaving. He had conceived an infatuation and established a relationship which was wrong, contrary to the laws of man and forbidden by the laws of God. It could have no other eventuation

than guilt and misery. Indeed, the misery was already apparent. That was why I told him that there was but one thing for him to do: break off the relationship and abandon the companionship. To this proposal he made the answer of our subject, 'I can't let her go.'

"Let none speak contemptuously of his weakness. Who art thou that judgest thy brother? Consider thyself lest thou also be tempted. Wait until you are caught in a swirling and rushing tide of a similar affection. You, whose attachments and choices have always moved along conventional and legitimate desires and attitudes—wait until you, too, have been lost in this tangled wilderness, where what you want and desire and love, and what you ought, are set over one against the other and can not be reconciled, before you point the finger of scorn at this man.

"This thing had befallen the man in middle life, that period of life in which so many go down before the assault of temptation. Perhaps, if he had faced the issues before, or had sought advice before he had gone so far in his course, it might have been different. But he had not done that. There was no use, therefore, in going over the past with him. What he had written, he had written. The question was what to do now. He had gone far; but there was still something that could be done, much that could be avoided. The fact that he was troubled in conscience and sought advice in his procedure was evidence that he had not altogether acquiesced in the course along which he had been moving. While there is fight, there is hope.

"He said it so deliberately and quietly, and with such an air of dismissing the subject, that I almost began to feel that what he said was true, that it was impossible for him to break off this relationship and that his temptation was too strong for him. But judgment corrected at once the indulgence of sympathy, and I told him that with the help of God he could, if he would, do what he ought to do, and that to a moral purpose there is nothing impossible. Where there is a will, there is a way. It would mean a sacrifice, of course; it would mean pain and loneliness. The question was, Could he, or rather, Would he, make the sacrifice?

"What I said to him, and what I now say to you to-night, is summed up in the words of our text, where men of like passions with us are warned against the power of temptation. 'Wherefore let him that thinketh he standeth take heed lest he fall. There hath no temptation taken you but such as is common to man: but God is faithful, who will not suffer you to be tempted above that ye are able; but will with the temptation also make a way to escape, that ye may be able to bear it.'"

Following these introductory paragraphs Dr. Macartney develops his theme under three heads, to wit: I. Sin and Yielding to Temptation Always Brings Sorrow, Pain and Misery. II. The Power, Danger, Subtlety and Universality of Temptation, and III. The Limits of Temptation and Sin.

Now this is powerful preaching, as powerful as a two-edged sword. It is the kind of preaching which never goes out of fashion. It is the kind of preaching that has made the pulpit an invincible power for righteousness, and saved poor lost broken humanity time and time again.

For a radically different kind of sermon take his discourse on "Predestination." This is not a theme heard often to-day, not even in pulpits Presbyterian. Dr. Macartney preaches on that subject however and at an evening service which is supposedly the period for discussion of popular themes. Moreover the Doctor makes his subject interesting and while the Biblical and credal appeal is insistent the treatment is practical and related to the present. The text is Acts 2:23: "Him, being delivered by the determinate counsel and foreknowledge of God, ye have taken, and by wicked hands have crucified and slain." The printed sermon contains twenty paragraphs of which the first, second and sixteenth, are here quoted:

"Contrary to the opinion of those who held that Abraham Lincoln was fortunate in his death, Horace Greeley thought him most inept for the leadership of a people involved in a great struggle for self-preservation, but that few men were better fitted to guide a nation's destinies in time of peace. Greeley says: 'I sat just behind him as he read his inaugural on a bright, warm, still March day, expecting to hear its delivery arrested by the crack of a rifle aimed at his heart. But it pleased God to postpone the deed, though there were forty times the reason for shooting him in 1860 that there were in 1865, and at least forty times as many intent on killing him or having him killed. No shot was then fired, however, for his hour had not yet come.' In that sentence, 'His hour had not yet come,' Horace Greeley gives us his philosophy of history. Lincoln was not assassinated in 1861 because his hour had not yet come.

"The Westminster Confession of Faith, at the end of the chapter on Predestination, says the doctrine of this high mystery is to be 'handled with special prudence and care, that men attending the will of God revealed in His word, and yielding obedience thereunto, may be assured of their eternal election. So shall this doctrine afford matter of praise, reverence and admiration of God, and of humility, diligence, and abundant consolation to all that sincerely obey the Gospel.' Never out of curiosity, but always with the purpose of strengthening faith and persuading men to believe, this truth of the Bible is to be preached. In that spirit and with that high purpose, we speak of it to-night.

* * * * *

"The misfortunes and adversities of life, so called, assume a different color when we look at them through this glass. It is sad to hear people trying to live over their lives again and saying to themselves: 'If I had taken a different turning of the road,' 'If I had chosen a different profession,' 'If I had married another person.' All this is weak and un-Christian. The web of destiny we have woven, in a sense, with our own hands, and yet God had His part in it. It is God's part in it, and not our part, that gives us faith and hope. In a wonderful letter, written to a bereaved friend, instead of repeating the ordinary platitudes of consolation, Blaise Pascal comforted his friend with the doctrine of predestination, saying: 'If we regard this event, not as an effect of chance, not as a fatal necessity of nature, but as a result inevitable, just, holy, of a decree of His Providence, conceived from all eternity, to be executed in such a year, day, hour, and such a place and manner, we shall adore in humble silence the impenetrable loftiness of His secrets; we shall venerate the sanctity of His decrees; we shall bless the acts of His providence; and uniting our will with that of God Himself, we shall wish with Him, in Him, and for Him, the thing that He has willed in us and for us for all eternity.'"

Whether one is ready to accept the reasoning of this sermon or not, it could not be termed truthfully dry-as-dust preaching; and buttressed by a sturdy figure, a strong and pleasing voice, spoken, too, with the accents of conviction, the discourse drives home. Old Dr. Sam Johnson, to be sure, would answer the age-old dispute by growling: "Sir, we know we are free, and that's the end of it!" Dr. Macartney wouldn't agree with the great old Tory; neither would John Calvin, nor Woodrow Wilson; not that it matters much perhaps, yet such differences contribute to the zest of life.

I urged Dr. Macartney to tell me of his habits of study and sermon-making. He talked freely and to the point.

"My texts and themes are suggested as a rule by the

regular reading of the Scriptures. When a theme or a passage strikes me, I file it away in a pocket, and from time to time make notations and comments. I carefully outline in longhand my sermons, and after several drafts, dictate them. All the sermons are fully written.

"My mornings are devoted to study, and any other hours at other times of the day or night which I can employ. Many ministers waste their time through the want of a definite plan, and the will power to adhere to such a plan.

"I visit almost every afternoon and evening. I have two assistants who are constantly in the field; but I go when and where I can."

"Do you have any favorite sermons—ones you especially enjoy preaching? Do you indulge in any kind of sport? Have you a hobby?"

"I have no favorite sermon, such as you refer to; and the one I like to preach the best is generally the one I have prepared last. However, I do preach a sermon on the same text every autumn. The text is II Timothy 4:21, 'Come Before Winter.' It is a sermon on opportunity, the proposition being that just as Timothy must go to Paul at Rome before winter, or wait until the spring, because of ancient navigation conditions, so there are things that must be done now or never. If Timothy waited until spring, he waited too long, for Paul was executed before that time. Before winter, or never! It makes a warm and stirring appeal, and never fails to bring an interesting collection of letters. There is evidence, too, that the preaching of the sermon has moved not a few to do at once what ought to be done. The climax of the sermon, of course, is the invitation to repentance toward God and faith in Christ now—to-day.

"I never confess to having a hobby, as it has always to me savored of intellectual weakness. However, as you know, since you say you have my books, I have done a great deal of traveling, studying and writing, in the field of the Civil War. Not quite so far from the field of my ministerial work is a long-time interest in Saint Paul. I have made four journeys in the footsteps of Saint Paul, and there is still some land to be possessed.

"The most serious weakness of the modern pulpit in my judgment is the fact that it is non-Scriptural, ignores Redemption and the Atonement, and does not preach Sin and Repentance."

The nub of Macartney's theology is in the last quotation, and also his attitude. He is ready to debate his positions, stoutly defend them, and if possible, commit his communion to the tenets of fundamentalism. He has been through many heated sessions with his brethren and his Moderatorship rode through a sea of storms, he and William J. Bryan standing shoulder to shoulder in those turbulent days.

It was at the Baltimore meeting of the General Assembly that there occurred a dramatic and amusing incident which lessened the tensity of a heated session and enabled the Assembly to close in the spirit of brotherhood. The chief figures in the incident were Dr. Clarence Macartney and his preacher brother, Albert Joseph, now of Washington, D. C. Brother Clarence had just made a speech, able but adamant and uncompromising, and had taken his seat. The air was surcharged with the controversial. Then Brother Albert took the floor and began, "Mr. Moderator, fathers, and brethren, and Brother Clarence." That broke the tension and evoked applause. He continued, "Clarence is all right, friends. The only trouble is he is not married. If that old bachelor would get married he would not have much time to look after other people's theology. (Laughter and applause.) When Clarence and I were boys, brought up in an old Pennsylvania home, Mother had us say our prayers at her knee. Then she took Clarence in her arms and sang him to sleep, singing 'Rock of Ages, Cleft for Me!', then sang for me 'There is a Fountain Filled with Blood.' We did not know what the words meant then, but we knew that Mother loved us and that Christ died for us. If Mother should come back to us now there would still be room for Clarence and myself at her knees, and I believe there is room for him and me, and for all of us at the altar of this Mother Church of ours."

The spirit of this episode, the commingling of humor and pathos, the good sense of it, and the love of it, melted the Assembly. All the ice went out, and suffused with a glow of brotherliness and tolerance the session came to a truly climactic close. Brother Clarence's eyes were wet, and his hand clasped many another hand that night in fraternal grip. For Clarence Edward Macartney is a sensitive human being as well as a fighting fundamentalist.

FISHER, Frederick Bohn, clergyman; *b.* Greencastle, Pa., Feb. 14, 1882; *s.* James Edward and Josephine (Bohn-Shirey) F.; B. Sc., Asbury Coll., 1902, B.A., 1903, D.D., 1916; Boston U. and Harvard, 1906-09, 1920; S.T.B., Boston U., Ph.D., 1909; D.D., De Pauw U., 1920; LL.D., Wesleyan, 1924; *m.* Edith Jackson, of Muncie, Ind., Feb. 4, 1903 (died June 5, 1921); *m.* 2nd, Welthy Honsinger, of New York, June 18, 1924. Deacon M. E. Ch., 1903; pastor, Kokomo, Ind., 1903; missionary in India, 1904-06; student pastor, N. Cohasset, Mass., 1907; First Ch., Boston, 1908-10; sec. Foreign Missions, M. E. Ch., and Laymen's Missionary Movement, 1910-20; bishop M. E. Ch., official residence at Calcutta, India, 1920-30; pastor First M. E. Ch., Ann Arbor, Mich., since 1930. Del. to World Missionary Conf., Edinburgh, Scotland, 1910; missionary tour of India, Japan and China, 1917-18; sec. industrial relations dept. Interchurch World Movement, 1919. Fellow Am. Geog. Soc., Royal Geog. Soc. Mason (K.T., 32°), K.P. *Clubs:* Rotary, Kiwanis (hon.). *Author:* The Way to Win, 1915; Gifts from the Desert, 1916; India's Silent Revolution (with Gertrude Marvin Williams), 1919; Garments of Power, 1920; Which Road Shall We Take? 1923; Indians in South Africa, 1924; Creative Personality, 1929; Building the Indian Church (with Walter Brooks Foley), 1929; Personology, 1930. *Home:* 1430 Cambridge Rd., Ann Arbor, Mich.

Chapter XIX

FREDERICK B. FISHER

Rarely does a preacher who has attained a bishopric resign of his own accord that high office. Yet that is precisely what Dr. Frederick B. Fisher did, much to the chagrin, if not the surprise, of his friends and associates. He was missionary bishop to India, elected by the Quadrennial Conference of the Methodist Episcopal Church in 1920. Going to India was the culmination of an ambition he had cherished for years; for at the age of twenty, at the World's Student Volunteer Convention in Toronto, Canada, young Fisher heard Bishop James M. Thoburn, of India, hung upon his words, visited him in the home where he was staying and before he left, said to the bishop, "I have decided to go to India as soon as I finish college." And to India he went.

Thirty-eight years is rather young to be chosen bishop and successor to the great Thoburn, but Fred Fisher was ready for the big job. He had had a three-years pastorate in Boston, and this was followed by seven years as an associate secretary of the Methodist Board of Foreign Missions, and a secretarial relationship to the Laymen's Missionary Movement. He went to India with ideas, plans, high purposes, and he was not long in putting these into practise. The truth is this man Fisher had India in his soul before he ever saw India with physical eyes. Equipped with almost perfect health, an iron constitution, and an indomitable will, this youthful bishop of India moved swiftly and with flaming enthusiasm across that mysterious country whose people brood over things spiritual and fight poverty from the first to their dying breath.

It is one thing to resign from high office when the tides are against you; it is another thing to quit a lofty position when your success is notable. Thus it came about with his work flourishing, yet unenamored by the prestige of his office, anxious of mind and troubled of heart, Bishop Fisher decided to resign his office of bishop and return to the pastorate. It were better to let this preacher state his own case instead of attempting to explain for him this unprecedented action. I quote from his article in *The Christian Century* entitled "A Bishop Seeks Sane Freedom."

> "At my age, had I remained in the episcopal office until normal retirement, I would have had twenty-six more years of power. It was simply unthinkable. Adaptation or release became imperative. I could not afford to drift, nor to fight. If freedom could not come by remaining within the organism and becoming increasingly loyal to it, then the only honorable and Christian thing to do was to withdraw from it.
>
> "Two years ago I wrote an article for Zion's Herald entitled, 'To Be Or Not To Be a Bishop.' Those who recall that revealment should not be surprised at the present outcome. My decision has not been sudden. It is the result of a growing and deepening conviction that our Methodist episcopacy is too much burdened with administration and too little harnessed to definite spiritual functions.
>
> "In the old days of general superintendency, our type of episcopacy evidently found full spiritual expression. We have now turned toward diocesan responsibility and authority without diocesan amenability or election. We are compelled by our constitution to exercise certain executive tasks, but our spiritual contacts are so indirect that they are made concrete among the people only by special invitation and arrangement. This develops criticism for semi-secular executive acts, without engendering that love, fellowship and sacredness of function which is the inevitable accompaniment of the more spiritual episcopal and pastoral forms.

"The invitation to the pastorate of the Ann Arbor church met the need of our souls. Other opportunities, as is doubtless the case with all bishops, had come to us but they lacked the magnetic pull. This call fully satisfied both Mrs. Fisher and me. The broad liberty which Dr. Stalker had enjoyed in this pulpit for twenty-five years; the great university faculty and student body of ten thousand, of whom nearly four hundred are Asiatics; the strong community congregation and officiary—all these gave us a spiritual and intellectual challenge that transcended title, position, and power. The new task, dependent as it is upon sheer spiritual resource, has called us to humble prayer. In youth it was the Christian ministry, not any far off expected position, that challenged my soul. Just as I felt a quarter of a century ago the call to cross the world to help carry the Christian message to another race, so now I feel the same thrilling call to bring back to the present youth of my own country the discoveries, lessons, and experiences of joyous international service."

Dr. Fisher's choice of field is commendable; to one who has the ability and an understanding of the student type, a pulpit in a great university center is an opportunity big with possibilities. His ministry at Ann Arbor began with almost sensational sized crowds and has continued at a high level of interest. It is a forceful combination—a church that knows how to capitalize a celebrity of marked preaching gifts, wide range of reading, amazing experiences of travel, an enthusiasm that maintains an incandescent glow. Dr. Fisher's morning sermons are broadcast and the promotional committee of his church sees to it that the home of every Methodist student at Ann Arbor in the state, receives a neatly printed announcement that Dr. Frederick Fisher is on the air every Sunday morning at eleven o'clock and can be heard in person by their sons and daughters at Ann Arbor—provided the youngsters can get a seat.

Dr. Fisher is an intimate friend of Mahatma Gandhi and has done much to interpret and popularize this powerful little man whose fame fills the world. To Fisher, Gandhi is a saint. His lecture on Gandhi consumes an hour or better and is full of thrills. The speaker puts a spell upon all who hear this lecture—the spell of India. You are transported by a verbal magic carpet to Calcutta, Bombay, Madras, Delhi. You behold a young Hindu, English-trained, slowly emerging into a spiritual power unsuspected in so frail a body and so quaint an asceticism, expanding until the slight figure takes on titanic proportions. You glimpse a new India, struggling toward political self-realization, Gandhi-ized into life, a colorful panorama, which leaves an indelible impression on the minds of auditors of almost every class and condition.

The former bishop does not claim that Gandhi is a Christian; he does affirm that it is through Christ and His Gospel that this pertinacious religionist and sublimated politician has come into his far-flung fame and power. He believes that Gandhi practises what Jesus taught, while multitudes of conventional Christians call Jesus, "Lord, Lord" and do not do the things He taught. He has confidence in Gandhi and thinks his greatest days are yet to come. It is amusing to recall in this connection that Dr. Fisher telephoned to Gandhi from Wisconsin when Gandhi was in London in 1931, urging him to come to America. That may or may not have been wise but this impulsive Methodist preacher sincerely thought it was and invested a tidy sum of money in the trans-Atlantic call. When some one told Gandhi that it cost Dr. Fisher two hundred dollars to telephone him, the abstemious little Mahatma remarked that he supposed a preacher would have more sense than to waste money in such a manner. He probably said this with a grin.

There are other good stories about Dr. Fisher and Gandhi in circulation, and the best of the lot is the following: Some one asked Gandhi how he happened to use Monday as a day of silence in preference to another day of the week. The

Mahatma explained it this way: "Bishop Fred Fisher first came to visit me on a Monday. He talked all day. I couldn't even get a word in anywhere. All I could do was listen. I kept my mouth shut and let the Bishop talk. The rest did me so much good that I have ever since kept Monday as a day of silence."

No estimate of Frederick Fisher's ministry would be adequate without some reference to his gifted and charming wife. Before her marriage to Dr. Fisher she was Miss Welthy Honsinger, and a missionary to the interior of China. Not only is Mrs. Fisher a most personable lady, but she has an exceptionally fine mind and her public speaking ability is of the highest order. She is above the average height, fairly slender, while her husband is short of stature and stout of figure. To meet these delightful people in their Ann Arbor home, surrounded by tokens and relics of India, pictures, porcelains, books, souvenirs, gathered from all parts of the Orient, is an event long to be cherished. They are a democratic couple, easily approached, hospitable and Christian in the noblest sense of that noble title.

It is good to see Dr. Fisher through his wife's eyes. Most wives of distinguished men are the best interpreters of their husbands, though not many are adequately gifted in tongue or pen to tell the world. Mrs. Fisher says that her husband holds money to be the cheapest thing in the world. He never writes a check or pays a bill. His wife sees to these. When Dr. Fisher starts on a journey it is his "better two-thirds" who sees to it that he has cash enough for the trip. In his first charge which was in Kokomo, Indiana, his salary was three hundred dollars per year, and when he announced to his office bearers his subscription would be thirty-five dollars the year, they were so surprised and flabbergasted that they straightway raised his stipend to one thousand dollars annually. It was from Mrs. Fisher that I learned her husband gives two-tenths of his income to the church, and fifty-five per cent. to all causes. It was from her too that I had a graphic description of his habits of study. He rises at four o'clock in the morning—that was also the rising hour of George Washington, Thomas Jefferson, Alexander Campbell, and I know not how many other celebrities.—He reads till six, pauses for a light breakfast and is back to his books again. He seldom goes to bed until midnight. He reads everywhere, on trains, in his berth in sleeping cars, in waiting-rooms of railway stations, on street corners while waiting for a car or bus. He writes all over the margins and fly-leaves of his books, with one exception—he does not mark up his Bibles. He rarely uses library books or borrowed books. A book to mean anything to him must be his own or his wife's. His book bill is larger than his grocery bill. He loves most to preach, and nothing so bored him as the necessary business routine of his bishop's office, which he felt took him away from his beloved preaching, to figures of finance, and statistical tables.

Dr. Fisher seldom writes a sermon out in full, but makes very ample notes not with a pen but with a lead pencil. A *pencil* instead of a pen! I should like to know how many of these famous parsons can manage a fountain-pen. My own experience with a fountain-pen has been disastrous. In the past twenty-five years I have owned nearly that many pens, gifts from members of my family and friends, and my own purchase. I lose them, leave them at hotel desks, go back to find them gone, have difficulty in keeping them fit. Most of the time they are inkless when I need them most, or, on the other hand, they are fluent to the point of embarrassment. But Dr. Fisher uses a pencil. He is wise. However, his secretary takes his sermon in shorthand and he gets a very full transcription of it after the delivery. Shannon, of Chicago, writes out his sermons after delivery also, and it will be remembered that Robertson, of Brighton, followed the same practise in the heyday of his famed ministry. Dr. Fisher loves most to preach from New Testament texts and has preached more sermons on the Sermon on the Mount than any other portion of the Bible.

The budget in Dr. Fisher's church is looked after by capable laymen. Dr. Fisher has no official relationship to the budget committee. He does not preside in official board meetings. I was interested to learn that although he preaches on "Stewardship," he does so without mentioning that word. I am glad to know this, for if there is any other word on the tongues of preachers and in the columns of religious journals that is more overworked I do not know what it is, unless it is the word "fellowship," but the latter word has a clear-cut meaning, and a wealth of background, while the word "stewardship" connotes very little to the average church attendant, has a hollow ring. Personally I much prefer "trusteeship," which at least is modern enough to be understood and not mouthed and misused constantly. But Dr. Fisher preaches on giving, on money and property obligations. Who could conceive of a Methodist preacher who never spoke on the financial obligations of a child of God? Great old John Wesley himself preached by word and deed on divine ownership and human trusteeship.

I think it likely that within another decade Frederick Fisher will be recognized as belonging to the elect company of mighty American preachers. Despite all that he has accomplished he is just beginning. He is still growing. Alluding to the years he had been in the ministry this Ann Arbor preacher confided to a friend, "Twenty-six years, and I have only got to first base. Ten years from now I will talk to you about second base. Ten years after that I'll talk to you about getting to the third base; and ten years after that I'll talk about the home base. Will you be here? All right."

"Tell me about your plans at Ann Arbor, Dr. Fisher," I urged. "What is your method of sermonizing? Do you make many pastoral calls? Do you follow a close schedule day after day?"

"I plan my sermons long in advance. By the first of October, every sermon topic for morning and evening has been selected up through Christmas and the New Year.

Then by the second Sunday in January, the entire schedule up through June has been completed," Dr. Fisher replied. "I do not do a great deal of pastoral service, because we have a very efficient associate minister, and also a director of the Wesley Foundation. These two men do most of the pastoral service, and they give me occasional tips concerning the places I ought to go. Yes, I have my own rules for ministerial conduct, four in number. Who can say whether I always live up to them? But this is the discipline that I lay before my own life.

"1. Nobody can offend me.

"2. I can not be discouraged. That is, I will keep my ideals dominant.

"3. I will let other people think, finding stimulation in differences rather than fighting opposition.

"4. I will make Jesus Christ my example and test every sense of victory or defeat by trying to decide how he would have met a similar situation."

Something has already been said about Dr. Fisher's sturdy frame. A mutual friend declares that he has the "constitution of a horse. He can preach and lecture every day in the week, travel thousands of miles, and appear as fresh on Sunday in his own pulpit as if he had been resting all week." This friend also loves to tell of a time when he took the Bishop to Jackson (a city about thirty miles from Ann Arbor) where Dr. Fisher addressed a gathering of schoolteachers at two in the afternoon. A little after three he started for Indianapolis, and stepped on the platform at eight o'clock to address thirty-five hundred people on Gandhi. His eyes were clear, his voice was strong and resonant. He put an immense amount of vitality into the delivery, and spoke an hour without the slightest indication of fatigue. That's Fisher!

At this period Dr. Fisher's sermons and addresses as well as conversation contain many references to India and Gandhi. I overheard some Ann Arborite remark, "Fisher is great, but we have India and Gandhi for breakfast, dinner and supper, you know." It was a superficial criticism yet not without point. No public speaker, not even a genius, can make a hobby of any subject, however pertinent and interesting that subject may be, without entailing a risk; and this reminds me of the old story of a minister who took up a new pastorate after having been located for twenty years at a town called Jonesville. He had a great deal to say about that town both in public and private. He praised its citizens, he illustrated many points with allusions to certain things that had occurred at Jonesville, and all of them reflecting credit on that place. He kept this up for a year or more. One night at the mid-week prayer-meeting, the topic was "The Heavenly Home." Several talks were made on the subject by people who were sure they would some day get to heaven. Then a timid woman arose and confessed that she sometimes doubted whether she would ever get to heaven, but she hoped by the grace of God that she would at least get as far as Jonesville.—Maybe it never happened, but well it might.

For my part I would go a long way to hear Dr. Fisher on Gandhi, and there are many like me. Moreover, our day needs to know of the man who has turned the world upside down. I venture a prediction—with the passing years this flaming evangel will have less and less to say of India and her saint, not because he will have changed his high opinion of that great little man, or has ceased to be challenged by "India, sad India," but because the roots of his present ministry will have gone down farther into the soil of the homeland, and he will carry upon his heart the burdens of the people around and about him. It is always so with great souls the world around.

No assessment of Frederick B. Fisher would be complete that failed to chronicle the fact that he it was who inspired Stanley Jones to go to India. What an achievement! For that Spirit-filled personality, author of *The Christ of the*

Indian Road, next to Gandhi himself, is the most illustrious religious leader in a country where seekers after God abound. And there are those who would name Stanley Jones first, since he is confessedly Christian and by his work and writings has made the name of Christ luminous and honored in circles where before he began his ministry that name was unknown or if known not signally honored.

It is helpful to listen to the critical comments of Dr. Fisher by his fellow-ministers, Methodists included. They concede his ability, some claiming that the secret of it is the fire of his delivery, his natural flair for oratory and immense physical vigor. Others say it is his press-agents who have succeeded in giving him reams of valuable newspaper publicity. Still others cite his background of twenty years in India and the fact that he resigned a bishopric with as apparent unconcern as one declines a rich pastry at the family meal. A few point out his sincerity and friendliness, together with his daring statements which cut across so many conventional and standardized positions. These they aver account for his success. Again, some say it is not his fine speaking ability, his varied experiences in the Far East, nor the sounding-board of wide publicity, though they have undoubtedly helped, but the mainspring of his power is his passionate devotion to the person of Christ, his singular selflessness and persistent purpose to exalt the ideals and embody in his own life the spirit of the Master, that gives verve and appeal to his preaching.

And "lastly"—blessed preacher word—I said to a townsman and fellow-pastor of Dr. Fisher, "Tell me the finest thing you know about Fred Fisher as a preacher." Face aglow, he replied: "I'll do it. It is the way in which, at the close of a prayer, Fisher looks toward heaven and says with great emphasis 'For JESUS' sake, Amen.' I was proud of him at Commencement exercises in Ferry Field. There amid all the professors in their gowns and hoods, and with the graduates in front of him, he prayed a very earnest prayer in a voice that was heard everywhere, and at the close, with his chin in the air, he exclaimed, 'All this we ask for JESUS' sake, Amen.' He's not ashamed to own his Lord."

That too is Fisher!

MILLER, Raphael Harwood, clergyman: *b.* Syracuse, N. Y., Oct. 27, 1874; *s.* John L. and Mary (Hollenbeck) M.; B.A., Hiram Coll., 1896; grad. Auburn Theol. Sem., 1904; D.D., Drake U., 1917; *m.* Nellie G. Burrows, of Rochester, N. Y., Oct. 12, 1898. Ordained ministry Disciples of Christ, 1902; pastor, Richmond Av. Ch., Buffalo, N. Y., 1903-14; sec. Men and Millions Movement, Cincinnati, 1914-19; pastor Independence Boul. Christian Ch., Kansas City, Mo., since 1919. Has visited colls. and univs. throughout U. S. as student preacher, recruiting for ministry and missionary service. Mem. bd. of mgrs. United Christian Missionary Soc. *Address:* Independence Boul. Christian Church, Kansas City, Mo.

Chapter XX

RAPHAEL H. MILLER

"Tall, very tall; thin, very thin," is the way a fellow-townsman described Dr. Raphael H. Miller, the pastor of Independence Boulevard Christian Church, Kansas City, Missouri, and the description is good as far as it goes. Dr. Miller is six feet one inch in height and weighs about one hundred and fifty pounds, with the waist-line of a débutante, and not a suspicion of a double chin, though he was born in 1874. His one-time dark hair is generously streaked with gray; his face is thin, neck long and also thin, arms Lincolnesque, and his smiling eyes gleam through professorial glasses. Most tall men begin to droop the shoulders as they cross the fifties, but not this tall man. His bodily movements are alert, elastic, youthful. Attired in a swallow-tail coat and derby hat, his supple slenderness suggests a rampant exclamation point.

Somebody has likened Dr. Miller physically to the late Senator John J. Ingalls, of Kansas, and the comparison is appropriate. The Kansas Citian is as tall and almost but not quite as thin as the famed senator from the Sunflower state. They used to tell in Washington this story about Ingalls:

He was in a doctor's office when a newsboy with a bundle of papers came in and the physician just for fun opened a cabinet and disclosed a skeleton and rattled the bones. The boy took one look and fled pell-mell from the office. Senator Ingalls, who wished to purchase a paper, stuck his head out of a window and called to the boy who, running across the street, stopped, looked up, saw the lean figure and yelled; "I'm not coming back. I know you, even if you have put your clothes on."

In 1914 Dr. Miller left his busy pastorate of a decade at Richmond Avenue Christian Church in Buffalo, New York, to become the flaming evangel of the Men and Millions Movement—that enterprise which stirred the communion known as Disciples of Christ from center to circumference, resulting in the raising of six million dollars and enlisting one thousand men and women in the ministry and mission fields. Dr. Abram E. Cory, beloved among the Disciples as "Abe," was the promotional generalissimo who directed this remarkable movement; "Rafe" Miller was the prophet whose voice rang out like a silver trumpet rallying the recruits to the standard of the Cross. Gathered about these key men were half a dozen picked specialists in Christian work. This team conducted rallies and "set up" meetings throughout the nation and everywhere they went they left a new conception of Christian trusteeship. Dr. Cory used to say, "The leaders of this movement are just average men caught up by a mighty vision, but one of the group, Rafe Miller, is not an average man; he is the only genius among us." This fine statement is, however, a half-truth, for in his own way, Dr. Cory is as much a genius as Miller in his.

Who of us that heard these crusaders on their memorable circuit can forget Dr. Miller in a famous passage of an address delivered from coast to coast in which he lauded Dr. Albert L. Shelton, missionary to Tibet who gave his life in martyrdom out there on the roof of the world? The passage delivered with fire and passion came at the close of a speech that abounded in thrills of burning eloquence:

"Or go with stalwart Christ-driven Shelton out to Tibet—the loneliest mission station in the world—out on those lofty highlands inhabited by forgotten men.

"He rides the peaks of the uplands with the restless and insatiable spirit of Christian adventure and for him the stars are nearer neighbors than the friends he left behind when he answered the call of Jesus.

"He seeks the lost through inaccessible fastnesses of

devil-haunted mountains. He holds lonely communion with the Good Shepherd up there where the stars trail their golden fleeces over those heaven bedewed meadows where God pastures His celestial flocks."

In public speech Miller is a strong combination of intellectual and emotional appeal. His thinking is clear, logical, direct; he speaks with rapidity and a kind of verbal sword thrust, very effective. Many pulpit and platform men of ability have their moments of dulness or commonplace utterance; Miller, however, maintains a high level of logical eloquence, a rushing tide of impeccable English, with now and then a telling illustration or a short pungent quotation, not thrown in, but woven closely into the texture of the sermon or address, and withal there is spontaneity, freshness, charm, vivacity.

Theologically this preacher is moderately conservative, but not a reactionary or an obscurantist. His preaching is an excellent example of the higher dogmatism which is positive without being oracular; authoritative without the cock-sure quality which is so offensive to sensitive hearers. He is not a fundamentalist but he believes in the fundamentals of the faith with a conviction that is heartening. He is not a modernist but he possesses a modern mind, which he dearly loves to match with the jaded high-brow culturists who specialize in knocking the churches. He is, in the better meaning of a much abused term, a "Bible preacher."

One of Dr. Miller's recent sermons is entitled "Symbols and Men." It is based on I Samuel 7:3: "And Samuel spake unto all Israel, saying, If ye do return unto the Lord with all your hearts, then put away the strange gods and Ashtaroth from among you, and prepare your hearts unto the Lord, and serve him only: and he will deliver you out of the hand of the Philistines." The sermon is a strong appeal for reality in religion and solemn and penetrating assault upon that type of devotion which makes a fetish out of symbols and fails to realize the substance of sacrificial living. He introduces his subject by referring to the misuse of the Ark of the Covenant by the Israelitish people. "They took," he says, "the Ark of the Covenant from behind the curtains of the tabernacle and sent it forth into the battle, hoping that God would at least preserve his Ark no matter though His people had forgotten Him. But Israel went down to a terrible defeat, and the Ark was captured and insulted by the enemy and it was a long time before it came back." He continues:

"Another word I want to speak. What they sought for when they sent that Ark out there into the midst of the enemy where they were afraid to go themselves because their hearts were unhinged by their infidelities and their lives were weak through their dissipations at the altars of false gods, what they hoped was, that the Ark would scare the Philistines as a symbol of power. But the Philistines were not afraid of a symbol. The devil is not afraid of a symbol. The uprising hordes of barbarism from the lower orders and levels of our society in these modern days—these have no fear of symbols. The racketeer of America, the lawbreaker, the anarchist in society and against all ordered government, he has no respect for flags; he has no fear of symbols; he cares nothing for Declarations and Constitutions. There is nothing in the world that can hold him back but the ordered ranks of a disciplined people whose hearts are set toward God.

"I have traveled in many lands. There I have looked for the symbols of nationalities and the symbols of societies and the symbols of peoples and I have found them on every hand; but there is nothing that has so wrenched my heart as the symbol of the Crucified. I have seen Him by the wayside shrines in Europe. I have seen Him along those ways where our boys marched as they trampled the muddy mire beneath their feet and went down before the very face of that Crucified, in the red burial of battle, I have seen Him over the altars of cathedrals. I have seen Him in halls of legislatures and in the courtrooms of the great, and He is always crucified, hanging there pitiful and pitying—His visage scarred more than any man's—His head hanging helplessly upon His breast—a symbol—a symbol of sacrifice. And we have the vast and futile superstition that if only we can lift Him above our churches and set Him in our streets and get Him up there somewhere where the world can see Him then all is well—that if we can only get the symbol out against the enemy, the enemy will turn and flee.

"No treaty, no constitution, no legislative enactment for the healing of our wounds or the leading of our people will be worth anything that is not backed by men of good will and men who know Christ and have Christ's spirit toward men. There is no way of giving anybody power by sending them out alone with the symbols of democracy and the symbols of faith, and the symbols of life until that power is also not only concentrated but distributed and until power reaches down into the hearts of men and women in this modern world and this America of ours and we learn ourselves, how to exercise power that is ours, not by doing as we please, but by doing as God pleases under the power of lives that are brought subject to His law.

"How I am asking God today to help me to lay aside all my prejudices and all my symbols and my little creeds and my little prescriptions and my little wishes and bring my own life under those disciplines, under those ideals, under those motives, so that if all men would live the kind of a life that I shall try to live in prayer and humility under God, this world can be saved. For we have reached a point now where it can't be saved any other way. The President can't save us, preachers can't save us, nobody can save us until we bring ourselves as Samuel said to obedience to God. Then He will bless us. Oh, bring Him down, my friends, from that place where He hangs crucified, and set Him where the last pages of this Bible put Him, on a throne, crown Him with many crowns, King of kings and Lord of lords, before whom that mighty throng of those whose robes have been washed in His blood bring 'blessing and glory, and wisdom and thanksgiving, and honor, and power, and might,' to lay them at His bleeding and glorified feet."

This is distinctive sermonizing. It is aimed at a verdict. It is ageless preaching, the kind that is suited to every period and to all sorts and conditions of men. Preaching on "The Wistful Prodigal," Dr. Miller says:

"A radiant memory is a safer monitor than doubtful companionship. Keeping up with son in all the careless and passionate indulgences of untempered youth does not make a fatherhood whose image shall some day stir a great wistfulness in the heart of a boy who has come to feel in want for something more real than pleasures and husks.

"The silly, game loving, thrill obsessed, cigarette smoking 'modern' mothers who 'have a right' to do what their daughters do are not getting ready for the day when the light of heaven in a mother's eyes and the tender beauty of a mother's face will turn back some careless girl to her better self and to God.

* * * * *

"The Prodigal is wistful not for what he has wasted but for what his father has kept."

In making a sermon, Dr. Miller spares no pains, is methodical and plans his preaching far ahead. Yet he claims not to have "a fixed program" in preparing to preach. He tries early in the week to decide on the topic for the Sunday morning sermon and having decided, he mulls over the subject as he makes his calls, and between periods of dictation as he clears up his correspondence. Like Phillips Brooks, Miller is an inveterate keeper of note-books in which he jots down texts, subjects and suggestions for sermons. He has accumulated a small library of these little books, indexed for ready use. He takes extensive notes into the pulpit but is not a slave to them. When asked to what extent his reading bore upon his sermons he replied:

"I find that my recent reading determines in a large measure both my theme and its development. I read two or three what I call heavy books each week—books that cover the field of religion. This aside from general reading. I do a great deal of my reading at night and in bed though the real concentration for sermon preparation is done in my study.

"I have, throughout my entire ministry, been a reader of current books. I try to keep abreast with the best that is written. The manager of one of our large book stores has an arrangement with me by which he sends the books which he knows will meet my requirements just as soon as they come from the publishing houses. I mark and annotate my books liberally so that passages can be referred to readily in time of need. I read very little fiction, but enjoy poetry and history."

I was eager to know Dr. Miller's opinion of the kind of preaching needed now, and sought to draw him out:

"I am at a loss to give a very satisfactory answer to your question, what kind of preaching does this day demand," he mused. "Each man is likely to judge according to the type of preaching which he enjoys and which he finds most effective. I would say that sincerity and conviction are indispensable. Also there should be some note of confidence in the message and in the people and the bringing back of the radiance of Christian faith. There is a demand for practical preaching that is direct and pointed and with personal appeal out of personal experience. The man who preaches effectively must bring to the gospel message an experience of gospel in his own life and through his own life in service. It must be a spiritual message but with very definite application to the individual and society. I would say that there is refreshing response to Scriptural preaching. By this, I do not necessarily mean expository preaching. But people do respond to the words of the Scripture and especially the words of Christ and there is a need to refamiliarize the people with the great passages of the Bible.

"And there is need for passionate preaching. Not that it should stir the superficial emotions but that it hits down to the red centers of thought and feeling and action. The pulpit must burn like the desert bush that was burned but not consumed if we are to expect people to turn aside to see what this means.

"As I see it the weakness of our modern pulpit is its casualness, that there is more of the note of information than of redemption. I think there is a straining to be modern in a rather technical sense and the making of the business of preaching a ritual rather than a sacrifice.

"Every sermon should be an event in the life of the minister and therefore in the life of the congregation. The average minister is called upon to speak too many times in the course of a week and thereby loses something of the momentousness of preaching.

"I think also that we strain to be up-to-date and fail to strike the note of the changeless and the Eternal, though in my opinion there is as much good preaching in the world to-day as there has ever been and in view of the fact that there is very attractive competition to the pulpit in the radio and the movie, much can be said in commendation of the splendid and potent effectiveness of the modern pulpit."

Questioned as to pastoral visitation, Dr. Miller disclosed the fact that his record in this field is unusual for one who has a preaching reputation of eminence.

"As to pastoral calling, I would say that I do more than

the average among my fellow-pastors in the matter of calling. I spend at least three half-days in visitation and make from seventy-five to one hundred calls a month, but as you know this is a very large congregation and visitation upon the sick requires a great deal of my time and I have no pastoral assistant. However the Women's Council of this church is thoroughly organized for visiting and the congregation is divided into sections and in each of these sections there are women appointed to assist me in making calls so that we are able each month to make a very sizable report in the matter of pastoral visitation.

"I have no hobby," he concluded. "My chief enjoyment is in my work. I do not fish or hunt or play golf. I find my recreation in walking but not much of that. I enjoy travel and, as you know, have done a great deal of it."

Reference has already been made to the work of Dr. Miller and Dr. A. E. Cory as the dynamic leaders of the Men and Millions Movement. There was a team—Rafe and Abe! The two men are utterly unlike in appearance, methods, everything, except the missionary passion. Miller is meticulous as to attire. Cory is careless as to clothes. Cory who lived for years in China has something of the Oriental about him. Miller, educated on the Western Reserve, possesses something of the down-East manner. Miller takes the shortest road to any given point and travels fast. Cory chooses the most circuitous and loafs en route. The point is both arrive! And now for a story of the twain.

The plan followed by the Men and Millions "team" in localities, urban and rural, was to hold a "set-up" meeting at some central point, a county-seat town, or in a city where the Disciples are strong. At such meetings which were largely attended, the leaders presented their cause in a series of remarkable speeches, informative and inspirational. This meeting would be followed within the next few days by a solicitation among the people, pledges being taken from five hundred dollars up, payable in five years. In a certain Missouri town the set-up meeting was held with marked success and for the next ten days solicitation flourished and additional meetings were held in the smaller places. At one of the latter which happened to be near by the cemetery where the notorious James boys are buried, Rafe and Abe had a marvelous time. The church was packed, the people enthusiastic. When Cory and Miller returned to the headquarters in the county-seat town they reported their convictions that the community visited would respond with unprecedented gifts. The pastor of the church in the county-seat, who had been there a long time, advised them not to be too optimistic. Bluntly he told them they were in for disappointment. But Rafe and Abe laughed it off and said something about "bringing home the bacon."

They were gone for three days and when they put in their appearance late on the evening of the third day they were a dejected-looking couple, weary and dragging their feet. They met their confrères around the supper table, and explained their plight. Addressing the local pastor, Cory said: "You were right. That was the stingiest, meanest crowd we have come across in all these years of canvassing. They came out to the meeting and sang like sixty, but that was all. We put in two full days seeing the well-to-do farmers of that community but it was no use. We gave it up and then Rafe and I made a special trip to the grave of Jesse James, where we held a brief service and cheerfully approved the only method that could make those fellows shell out. Ordinarily I am opposed to violence, but, brother, there are exceptions!"

This is a capital story 'most anyway one takes it, but I insert it here not solely because of its humor but also to indicate the intimate friendship which exists between the men. Having this in mind I requested Dr. Cory to analyze Dr. Miller for me, to picture him as a close friend sees him. This he did and in staccato fashion. Said he:

"Rafe Miller has strong likes and dislikes, both personal, religious and general. He is direct in all of his approaches. He is strongly orthodox, positive, versus the liberal position.

He arrives at this position by intellectual processes which he deems consistent and defensible both from the Scriptural and scientific standpoint. He has no half-way position. When he is interested in a specific position he becomes a fanatic.

"Rafe is known as a prophet and a great preacher, but I consider him as great a priest as he is a preacher. He is effective in the sick-room, in trouble, in advice and in general counsel. He knows organization but keeps it under control. He is Christ-centered in his preaching rather than God-centered. He has mystical tendencies but his analytical mind keeps him from the best that is in mysticism. He is a hard and untiring worker, never spares himself, allows both church and general work to absorb too much of his vitality.

"Rafe is one of the most widely read men I have ever known. He is a good observer and makes wide use of his experiences. He is very widely traveled in Europe from the time of his childhood, and returns frequently. He loves his home, his family and his church. They come first in his thought and program. Other things are secondary. His love of young people and love of the young people for him is remarkable. His vocabulary is unsurpassed.

"In spite of Rafe's likes and dislikes he fits particularly well into small social gatherings and will draw a whole group to him. It can not be said that he makes fun of people, but peculiarities and eccentricities attract him, and he derives great humor from them. He is one of the most sociable beings I have ever known. Rafe has a great capacity for friendship. He would die for his friends. He enjoys the fellowship of his friends, is keen in repartee, loves to hear a good joke, and loves equally well to repeat it. His character is complex and possibly paradoxical."

That Dr. Miller can achieve warm and enthusiastic friendships is clearly evidenced by the Jonathan-and-David-like comradeship between himself and Dr. Cory, as well as the affectionate regard in which his congregation holds him. Yet to many Miller is not quite the type of man who radiates friendliness. Few so appraise him on first acquaintance. There is a restraint and reticence about him that holds his admirers at a distance. He gives the impression on meeting him of taking your measure before he lets you have his. Intellectuals are seldom easy of approach. Woodrow Wilson once said of himself that he would like to be loved but was not sure that he knew how to make people love him. I imagine that Dr. Miller might say the same, in so far as the masses are concerned. In his earlier ministry he gained a reputation for caustic and sarcastic speech which while brilliant and arresting hurt needlessly some of his more sensitive hearers. The years have mellowed the man and taken away much of the sharpness of his tongue. He is tenderer, more considerate of the feelings of others, and uses not nearly so often the dangerous weapon of sarcasm.

There is a story of a preacher who, in the midst of a prayer not distinguished for anything up to the moment, stopped in the full tide of unglittering generalities and exclaimed; "O Lord, send us brains!" Rafe Miller is part of the Lord's answer to that and similar prayers. And his tarrying a while in the thirteenth of First Corinthians has helped his heart.

For thirteen years, Dr. Miller has ministered to the Independence Boulevard Christian Church, one of Kansas City's most influential congregations, the church where R. A. Long, philanthropic lumberman, holds membership. Mr. Long is an active churchman, gave a million dollars to the Men and Millions Movement, and made possible the million-dollar National City Christian Church, Washington, D. C. Fruitful as Dr. Miller's ministry has been and now is, I look for richer accomplishments in the years to come. He has not yet reached the crest of the ministerial wave; he has not yet loosed and "let himself go." There has been much speculation among the Disciples as to the preacher who will go to the conspicuous pulpit of the new National City Church, Washington, D. C. I venture a prediction: Here is the man destined for that mighty preaching place. Given freedom of pulpit and executive activity, without which no minister however gifted can be himself or God's anointed, and Raphael Harwood Miller is the man to glorify that Washington pulpit and make it vocal with prophetic utterance.

EMERSON, Chester Burge, clergyman; *b.* Haverhill, Mass., July 28, 1882; *s.* John A. and Abbie Jane E.; grad. high sch. Farmington, N. H., 1900; A.B., Bowdoin, 1904, D.D., 1919; B.D., Union Theol. Sem., 1909; unmarried. Ordained Congl. ministry, 1909; pastor First Parish, Saco, Me., 1909-13. North Woodward Ch., Detroit, Mich., since 1913. Served under Y.M.C.A. in France, 1917-18; chaplain Gen. Hosp. No. 36, R.C. Corporate mem. A.B.C.F.M.; mem. exec. com. State Bd. Congl. Chs.; pres. bd. trustees. Mich. Conf. since 1919; moderator State Conf., 1925; mem. exec. com. Commn. on Missions of Nat. Council Congl. Chs. Overseer Bowdoin Coll.; mem. bd. dirs. Chicago Theol. Sem.; trustee Hampton Inst., Olivet Coll. Mem. Arts and Crafts Soc., Founders Soc. of Arts, Mus. of Detroit, Detroit Symphony Orchestra (dir.), Fine Arts Soc., Alpha Delta Phi, Republican, Mason (32°, K.T., Shriner, also 33° from Grand Council of Greece, Athens). *Clubs:* Detroit, Detroit Athletic, Alpha Delta Phi (New York). *Home:* 820 Blaine, Av., Detroit, Mich.

Chapter XXI

CHESTER B. EMERSON

It is a long leap from one of the best of Congregational pulpits to the deanship of an Episcopal cathedral, but that is the immense stride taken by Dr. Chester B. Emerson, who after nearly two decades of successful ministry in North Congregational Church, Detroit, resigned to go to Trinity Cathedral, Cleveland, Ohio, as acting dean. Such an event is, I think, unprecedented in American church history. It is an experiment too that is being closely studied by churchmen of all denominations, some sympathetically, others critically.

In England the pilgrimage of Reginald John Campbell from Congregationalism to the Anglican Church was the occasion of international comment. In this country, the reordination of Joseph Fort Newton in the ministry of the Episcopal Church after having held conspicuous pastoral relationships with the Baptists, Congregationalists and Universalists, attracted wide attention, and was the subject of many a spirited clerical discussion. It was also Associated Press news when Emerson of Detroit announced his purpose to become an Episcopal clergyman.

Dr. Emerson's place in the life of Detroit was so influential, and his relationship with his denomination so pleasant and important, that the announcement of his acceptance of the invitation to Trinity Cathedral created something of a sensation. But it was not a sudden decision, reached without due consideration; rather it developed from an interesting background in which there commingled a devoted friendship of many years' standing and an inherent love for the stately ritual of the Episcopal Church. For many years Dr. Emerson and the Right Reverend Warren Lincoln

Rogers, now Bishop of Ohio, have been bosom friends, boon companions and fellow-world-travelers. During the time when Bishop Rogers served as Dean of St. Paul's Cathedral, Detroit, he and Dr. Emerson were inseparable. Given these facts, and Emerson's action seems quite logical.

Emerson is a New Englander of a rich cultural lineage, an intellectual Brahman. The celebrated Concord poet and philosopher of the same name is a kinsman. Once when a friend sent Dr. C. B. Emerson a new biography of his illustrious relative, he dropped the donor a note of thanks in which he said: "The Emersons have always been a funny lot," alluding, I suppose, to their eccentricities. This interesting preacher rarely refers to Ralph Waldo; certainly he has never capitalized the relationship, but once upon a time I ran into him just after an admirer had put in his hands a priceless letter of the poet-philosopher, beautifully written and marvelously preserved. Chester B.'s eyes were shining and he beamed with joy. Well, who wouldn't? Autographed letters of Ralph Waldo Emerson are not picked up every day.

Dr. Emerson is a graduate of Bowdoin and Union Theological Seminary. He took high honors at both institutions, and his first parish of four years was at Saco, Maine, to which place he sometimes pilgrimages, to the joy of his old-time parishioners. His ministry in the "Fourth City" was unusually prosperous, happy and many-sided. He succeeded in carrying both heavy parish duties and wide-spread civic, social and fraternal responsibilities likewise. In addition to these he has served his denomination in numerous ways, both locally and nationally. Dr. Emerson is a high-up Mason, much beloved by his Masonic brethren, who have loaded him with honors. He is one of the few ministers I have known who can appear in gorgeous chapeau, plumes, splendid shining sword, myriad insignias and preserve his equilibrium. As Supreme Chaplain of Knight Templars, he was the preacher at their conclave in Minneapolis in May, 1931. His audience numbered fifteen thousand and a mutual friend who has heard Emerson preach many times, said on this occasion he reached new heights of eloquence, making a forthright and impressive appeal for the supremacy of the spiritual.

"Chet" Emerson, as his friends love to call him, is a patron of art and music. He was active on the board of directors of the Detroit Symphony Orchestra and the Detroit Civic Theater. He holds membership in various literary clubs and appears before them as lecturer annually. He is something of a connoisseur of art and music. His bachelor residence at the Deanery is most artistically furnished; excellent pictures, a baby grand piano, and bric-à-brac gathered from various parts of America and the Old World. Yet it would be a mistake to conclude that this minister is a dilettante; he is much more than that. Humanity interests him more than books or pictures. I have come across more than one young man who turned to Emerson in the midst of tribulation and despair and found him a very present help in time of trouble.

The lips of Dr. Emerson are thin and aristocratic, as is also his nose. He wears glasses similar to the style favored by Woodrow Wilson, and his New England accent is strong, especially his habitual use of the broad *a.* As a preacher, he is ready of speech, employing mostly, but not altogether, the topical type of sermon. The social gospel bulks large in his thinking; he is by no means satisfied with things as they are. I have heard him in the Wranglers Club read a paper or two of radical ideas, productive of much discussion, though not so basically radical, perhaps, as the papers of Dr. Reinhold Niebuhr before this preachers' club. I remember hearing Emerson say once that he sometimes saw "red," but that actually he didn't have enough courage to be "pink," and that he supposed his rightful color was, well, say, "heliotrope." This was whimsically said, but candor is one of this preacher's virtues. He is seldom evasive or inclined to "make believe." The longer you know the man the more you appreciate the truth of this statement.

Emerson's method of sermonic preparation is simple. He does not write out the sermons in full. That kind of preparation is distasteful to him. He shuts himself up in his study at the church, or more often secludes himself in his library at his residence. There he reads, and dreams, and walks the floor, and then reads, and dreams, and walks some more. Sometimes the sermon comes readily; other times he wrestles desperately before the sermon takes form. He makes a few notes or outlines, slender itineraries of his thoughts, usually divisional headings; these he takes into the pulpit but seldom refers to them. His language seems to be extemporaneous and yet it has precision; the diction is excellent. Frequently his sentences and paragraphs are rhetorically flawless and beautiful of figure and fancy. His fluency is pronounced and he is dramatic at times, making splendid use of his actor's voice.

This preacher is especially gifted in public prayer. He is poetical both in preaching and leading in prayer, but more so in the latter. His prayers are couched in noble and dignified phrasings, yet distinguished by simplicity. He writes prayers much more readily than sermons. Every week his church bulletin carried a prayer written by the pastor. I have examined a sheaf of these bulletins with interest and profit. The prayers cover a wide range, yet there is little if any repetition, certainly no pet phrases. The prayer that follows was taken at random from a bulletin of North Congregational Church.

> "We know not, Our Father, what a day may bring forth, but we may know what manner of man will meet the occasion. Changes may come that re-order our lives in a moment—an illness whose intimation is a deadly pain; an accident that hangs a heavy cloud of unshed tears forever over our lives; a loss that sweeps away the security of the years—countless changes that disturb our peace, scatter our prosperity to the winds, and leave us stark to circumstances as a tree after an autumn gale.

And yet that tree may stand bent but unbroken, stricken but unashamed, shorn but weaving within itself a glorious spring garment, daring the winds, defiant of the seasons because its roots are deeply gripped in realities and its limbs are grown lusty with the struggle. So may our souls be rooted in Thy providence, holding to Thy help with all our might of mind and soul. So may we stand fearless before the world in the confidence that Thou art mindful of us and will not fail us if we put our trust in Thee. Amen!"

Loafing with Emerson one day, I wanted to know how he managed his pulpit preparation in the midst of so varied and heavy a program. "You are speaking constantly, yet you are never guilty of slipshod, careless, public speech. How do you manage it?"

"I keep probably a dozen things going in my mind, subjects, texts, illustrations. I never preach without a text. My texts are suggested by biography, experience, poetry. Sometimes a whole year goes by before I preach on a text that I have been mulling over a long time. I carry in my pockets pages from note-books on which I scribble almost every day subjects I expect to preach on some time. Look at this:" He took out of a side coat pocket a crumbled sheet and handed it to me. It was a list of topics that he had been carrying for days, transferring the sheet from suit to suit when he changed his apparel. I examined it with interest. It was a list of sermon subjects, some of them in ink, others in pencil: "The Human God," "In the Image of God," "On Being Human," "As a Man Thinketh," "The Almost Man," "The Reasonableness of Prayer," "The Heroism of the Gospel," "All Things Work Together for Good," "The Living God," "What God Asks of Man," "The Old Symbol of Awakening," "The Solitary Soul," "Conquer Your Fears," "Moving Toward Unity," "What Would You Have Youth Learn," "The Universal Bane" (War), "The Windy Ways of Time," "Clutch Your Certainties," "Hidden Sackcloth."

A pretty good list I would say, made up at odd minutes on street-cars, in automobiles and the like.

"Do you ever write a sermon out in full?"

"Only enough to keep my style tight," Emerson replied. "Writing is laborious to me. I make outlines of my sermons, think them through, carry them into the pulpit and rarely glance at them. Occasionally I write out a sermon in full and read it—but only for the discipline it affords me."

Emerson is unmarried, and is, of course, the recipient of endless gibes, the butt of many a joke, because of his bachelorhood. Naturally he gets tired of this sort of horseplay, and occasionally flashes a phrase of feigned or actual resentment. It was at a big banquet in Detroit with General Pershing as guest of honor, that the most famous incident of this sort happened. Emerson was on for an address and the toastmaster in introducing him remarked that he was unmarried, wondered why, and ventured a story that was more or less appropriate. Dr. Emerson was seated next to a charming society matron; he arose, not a little nettled by what the toastmaster had said. "Some people would think I am a woman-hater," he began. "As a matter of fact, I am anything but that. I am fond of women. Why! (turning to the lovely matron at his side) why! I would go to hell with a woman like this——" But he never finished the sentence. Pandemonium vied with bedlam!

While Emerson was still a Detroiter, I wrote of him: "The services at North Congregational Church, Detroit, especially morning worship, indicate that the preacher there is something of a ritualist and keeps a watchful eye on every phase of the service, the music, the prayers, even the announcements, or more properly the 'notices.' Should you go to Emerson's church, nothing will grate harshly upon your sensitive ears. Everything will move with precision and velvety smoothness. From the time the preacher enters the pulpit until he pronounces the benediction, his mastery is everywhere evident, and his touch deft but sure. The sermon? Well, it will not be merely a polished essay. There will be vitality in it, beauty and color; and, what is more important, flashes of prophetic fire. You will enjoy Emerson, and his preaching sets your mind a-going. And this, I hold, is a very great deal."

An able contemporary who had for several years a church near Emerson's on Woodward Avenue, speaking of this preacher to a few intimates, observed: "Chester will probably spend all his ministerial days in Detroit. He has hosts of friends who would do anything for him, is a popular speaker in constant demand, versatile, well established; yet for his own sake it would be well if he finished in another church. It would stimulate his thought, afford him more time for study, test him as his present pastorate never could. Emerson has depths not yet sounded, resources as yet untapped. He will never be the preacher he might be, unless he tackles a new and harder field with possibilities, where the mettle of the man will be put to acid test."

The acid test has come. Just turned fifty, this preacher whom thousands thought a fixture in Detroit, has embarked upon a fascinating voyage on an unknown sea where perils lurk, and rich discoveries beckon. A less audacious and versatile person might be either appalled by the sense of risk, or dazzled by the splendor of the opportunity, but not so Dr. Emerson. He knows full well the difficulties and the dangers; he counted the cost of the adventure; he made the change with his eyes wide open. He has been called to one of the mightiest preaching centers in the nation where he will have to pioneer his way. Sobered by the responsibility, determined to make his way slowly but surely, he enters upon his new and untried venture with high hopes and courage unabated.

FREEMAN, Robert, clergyman; *b.* Edinburgh, Scotland, Aug. 4, 1878; *s.* Robert and Jemima (Rival) F.; came to America 1896; Heriot-Watts Coll., Edinburgh; A.B., Allegheny Coll., Meadville, Pa., 1904, D.D., 1912; grad. Princeton Theological Seminary, 1907; M.A., Princeton U., 1907, D.D., 1922; Litt. D., Coll. of Wooster, 1928; *m.* Margery Fulton (A.B., Vassar, 1909), of Buffalo, N. Y., July 14, 1909; children—Robert Gowans, Bertrice, Margaret, Fulton, David Guthrie. In mission work McKeesport, Pa., and Binghamton, and Buffalo, N. Y., 1896-1900; ordained Baptist ministry, 1900; preached in Bapt. Ch., Springboro, Pa., 1900-02, Presbyterian Ch., Erie, 1902-04, Lafayette Presbyn. Ch., Buffalo, during course at Princeton, and as pastor until 1910; pastor Pasadena Presbyn. Ch., since Jan. 1, 1911. Pres. bd. trustees Occidental Coll.; dir, San Francisco Theol. Sem.; moderator of the Synod of Calif., 1920-21, and of Los Angeles Presbytery, 1931; member Board of Missions of the Presbyn. Ch., Nat. Council Boy Scouts. Republican. Mem. Phi Delta Theta, Phi Beta Kappa. On leave in France as dir. 1st expeditionary div. of Y.M.C.A. and dir. religious work in France, July, 1917-July, 1918. *Clubs:* Twilight, Flintridge County, University, Princeton (Los Angeles), Canoe (Buffalo), Tuna (Santa Catalina), Kiwanis. *Author:* The Hour of Prayer, 1914; The Land I Live In (poems) 1921, 24, 28; New Every Morning, 1927; What About the Twelve?, 1929. *Address:* 675 Magnolia Av., Pasadena, Calif.

Chapter XXII

ROBERT FREEMAN

When Thomas B. Reed was Speaker of the House Representatives he happened to enter that historic chamber one day when an eloquent southerner was in the midst of a speech. Reed listened until the member from the Blue-Grass State had finished, then drawled to a colleague: "Say, don't they grow anything in Kentucky but orators?"

It was a fair question, and one familiar with the history of preaching is often moved to inquire, "Do they produce anything in Scotland so marvelous as their preachers?" For the roll is long and illustrious. There must be something in the lovely lakes, the heather-crowned hills, the old castles and famous shrines, that helps to develop the preaching genius of old Scotia's sons. From Scotland have come to our own land some of the shining lights of the pulpit. And from the counties of Chalmers, Whyte, Matheson, Drummond and Gossip came Robert Freeman by way of Princeton and Buffalo, to his pulpit throne in First Presbyterian Church, Pasadena, California.

What is it that inspires men to enter the ministry? Is it a family background of plain living and high thinking, devout parents? Or is it the lure of the Spirit when it is embodied in a grand prophet of the Word occupying a Presbyterian manse and unfolding the Scriptures Sunday after Sunday. Perhaps all of these influence lads of parts, together with the romance that haloes religion in the country of Scott and Burns. It is not easy to account for the promptings that surge in the hearts of youth and inspire those dreams that so often come true, and lo! another forthteller for God is here, trailing clouds of glory from God who is our home.

In the case of Dr. Freeman it was a business man, B. McCall Barbour, teacher of a Bible class of lads in Edinburgh who put the dream in his bosom. He belongs to the company of the saints of earth who are never canonized save in the hearts of those they touched for the radiant life of the Spirit. Under the influence of this just man forty or fifty young men went to the ends of the earth in Christ's name and for His sake. It is good to know that this teacher still carries on. Not even the coming of old age has dulled the luster of his contagious faith, if anything the years have but added to that luster and deepened a noble faith. Talk about crowns, scepters, emoluments, the baubles the world calls life's grand prizes, how they shrivel and pale into nothingness when compared with the spiritual jewels of such a blessed teacher of the school of Christ.

Dr. Freeman began as a Baptist and was ordained to the ministry of that aggressive denomination at the age of twenty-one. But he hankered for the old Presbyterian Kirk of his forebears and before he entered Princeton Seminary he had become a member of Erie Presbytery. Like Peter and John at the gate of the temple, young Freeman could say, "Silver and gold have I none," so he valiantly worked his way through college by preaching. He earned six dollars a week, lived on oatmeal and beans, keeping out of debt the while. Only a Scotsman could have accomplished this miracle. The last two years he was in Princeton he preached for the Lafayette Avenue Presbyterian Church in Buffalo, New York, at five thousand dollars a year! He traveled a thousand miles a week and carried on his studies. Graduating he became the settled pastor of the Lafayette Avenue Church and served five years. From Buffalo he went to First Presbyterian Church, Pasadena, where he has been the widely known and popular preacher for twenty-two years.

An intimate and admiring friend, Dr. Roy Ewing Vale, who was in Princeton several years later than Dr. Freeman paints this charming portrait of the Pasadenian:

"Freeman is about five feet, eight inches in height, perhaps a trifle less, neither slender nor stocky in build. His face is rounded in outline, his complexion florid with a tendency to freckle. His hair which is now quite scanty has been in hue between reddish and golden, though it is now showing marks of gray. His eyes are of average size, shaded by rather heavy eyebrows of the same hue as his hair. They are rather grayish blue and remarkably expressive. They can glow with great kindliness and warmth, or they can be chill and forbidding. At all times they betoken unusual intelligence, and power of imaginative vision. His nose is somewhat aquiline, his lips sensitive. His face is essentially Scotch. His forehead is full, with that width between the temples which phrenologists used to tell us indicated unusual leadership ability, a quality he certainly possesses.

"His voice has a remarkable carrying and penetrating quality without being in the least strident or harsh. It has the mellowness of a tuba horn with the flexibility of a slide-trombone. In speaking he does not open his mouth as widely as does the average trained public speaker, but his elocution and diction approach perfection.

"He has a quick sense of humor and a keen wit but does not permit himself to use sarcasm or to turn his wit to the embarrassment of any one else. Privately he is one of the most companionable of men. Publicly his power of humor and its twin of sympathy display themselves in the same sermon where frequently people are laughing or at least smiling audibly at some unexpected turn or flashing picture and within a few moments find tears on their faces.

"Theologically he would class himself as a liberal. The heart of the supernatural Gospel, however, is in his preaching and in his life. A deep current of personal spiritual cultivation and devotion is evident in all his work. Christ is his spiritual hero as well as Savior and Lord. He is a poet of no mean order. He has made his own in memory much of the great literature of the world as well as much of the Bible and of the hymnody of the church. At a communion service in San Diego which concluded the 1932 meeting of the Synod of California, he offered a prayer which began with the lines: 'For all the saints that from their labors rest,' and which was an interweaving throughout of Scripture and hymnal phraseology. As a brother minister said afterwards, 'Not more than one-seventh of it was Freeman's own language, yet it was all Freeman.' I think universal consent would have stated that it was the highest point of the five days of the Synod.

"He always speaks with a distinct Scotch accent which is of course native. In addition to this I have heard him speak the true Gaelic to a group about him whose faces were shining.

"He is a golf player who plays a remarkably good game but who regards it only as a game and has never permitted it to interfere with his chosen work. He has made his own way up from poverty and through his natural gifts and indefatigable industry, under the guidance of the providence of God who found in him a chosen instrument to herald the Gospel to great multitudes of people, he has become one of the outstanding preachers of our day, not only in the Presbyterian Church but in all the Christian Churches.

"His church in Pasadena, which is the First Presbyterian, seats, I should suppose from sixteen hundred to eighteen hundred people and in the winter season it is not possible for all to gain admittance who desire to hear him. Pasadena is one of the loveliest residence sections in the United States. It includes a great number of wealthy people of course as well as many in modest financial circumstances. There is a great deal of wealth in his church which has grown in membership very largely during his pastorate, and he has led his people in a program of very large missionary undertakings, for he is thoroughly missionary minded. He has also led in the erection of a magnificent educational plant which stands beside the church building connected with it by a covered passageway some forty or fifty feet in length, and he has developed a strong program of Christian religious education.

"His wife is one of the most charming women to be found anywhere. She is a graduate of Vassar College. She has been of exceedingly great help to him in all respects. They have five children. His wife is still very youthful in appearance. She combines unusual charm with unusually high intelligence.

"He was beloved by his associates as a student. He is beloved by his brother ministers who find him always kindly and not at all inclined to snobbishness on account of his high position. His bearing combines both modesty and the assurance of a man who knows what he thinks and why he thinks it. His church and his family absorb his attention, and so far as I know he has never been stung by the bee of desire to be Moderator of the General Assembly. He is one of the limited number of men in the Presbyterian Church upon whom Princeton University has conferred the degree of Doctor of Divinity. He is singularly free from foibles. Dr. Robert Millikan once said to me that he regarded him not only as a great preacher but also as a great teacher of advance in truth. He is truly 'a man of God.' "

One of Dr. Freeman's published volumes is a series of sermons on the apostles, bearing the title *What of the Twelve?* It is not a large book, only one hundred and seventy-six pages, yet the sermons are reasonably full and reflect the resourcefulness and versatility of the author. They are replete with carefully chosen poetical quotations, flashes of wit and chunks of pawky humor, numerous literary allusions, shrewd comments on character—an extremely readable volume. Take the sermon on "James the Less." Announcing the text which is the same as the title, he ranges alongside of it the phrase, "The least of things seem infinite," and is off at once with a discussion of the three Jameses of the New Testament and decides that probably James the Less is to be identified with James the son of Alphæus. He follows this with a paragraph in praise of the so-called trivial things of life.

"There are many things that we single out as trivial and inconsequential; but because a thing is little in size, occupies little space, makes but little noise, demands but little attention, does not prove that it is of no consequence. The poets write their sweetest lines concerning little things. Wordsworth's

" 'heart with pleasure fills,
And dances with the daffodils.'

Shelley listens to the skylark as it pours its

" 'full heart
In profuse strains of unpremediated art.'

Both John Keats and Leigh Hunt are caught by the charm of the smallest things, and write sonnets of the cricket on the hearth and his companion of the hillside.

" 'Sweet and tiny cousins, that belong
One to the fields, the other to the hearth.'

Longfellow drinks in the song of the mocking bird, to listen to whom the whole air and the woods and the waves become silent. Robbie Burns addresses the

" 'Wee, modest, crimson-tippèd flow'r . . .
There, in thy scanty mantle clad,
Thy snawie bosom sun-ward spread,
Thou lifts thy unassuming head
In humble guise; . . .'

. . . . . .

"What charm there is, what romance, about the humblest place and the humblest name! A certain editor approached Gilbert K. Chesterton with a volume entitled 'Mr. Smith,' or the like, remarking, 'There! you won't get any of your confounded mysticism out of that book!' But he had picked the wrong book, the wrong title. The response is too easy, too obvious. There are many names with no poetry in them. There may be little poetry in Thompson, or MacPherson, or in any of these that merely aver one to be the son of some one else, but Smith is full of poetry. The very name insists that he who bears it shall enter into arduous and heroic endeavours to live up to the poetry of it. It appears frequently in the Bible, it is respected by kings, it is full of musical and heroic connotation. . . . Why, if Mr. James Smith were to hand you his visiting card you might well project your imagination behind the short name, see the mountains of ore towering above it, the great flaming furnaces blazing behind it, and all the instruments of war and industry created because of it. Who can be blind to the poetry and romance bulking behind that humble name?"

Thus he continues, pleading for a just recognition of the wrongly called commonplace, praising the humble and the obscure, building up a case for James the Less. And in his ardent defense of the humble and obscure, he dares to quote dialect verses of one of the humbler American poets. Imagine, if you can, a dignified Scotch Presbyterian "meenister" standing in the pulpit of a wealthy church, with a sprinkling of the intellectuals, university professors and the like, in his audiences, and "spouting" this:

"De sunflower ain't de daisy, and de melon ain't de rose;
Why is dey all so crazy to be somfin else dat grows?
Jess stick to de place yo're planted and do de bes you knows;
Be de sunflower or de daisy, de melon or de rose.

Don't be what yo ain't, jess yo be what yo is,
If yo am not what you are den yo is not what yo is.
If yo're jess a little tadpole, don't you try to be de frog;
If you are de tail, don't yo try to wag de dawg.
Pass de plate, if yo can't exhawt and preach;
If you're jess a little pebble, don't yo try to be de beach;
When a man is what he isn't, den he isn't what he is,
And as sure as I'm talking, he's a-gwine to get his."

Ah, but this preacher can use powerfully such verses as these, imitating the southern negro's dialect to perfection, diverting and delighting his hearers one moment, only to turn the next to this sober passage:

"The little things determine our advancement. 'How do you come to have such good sheep?' the shepherd was asked. 'I take care of the lambs.' Yes, little is a relative term. There are some of us who think the big thing in life is making a living, who would doubtless receive the same rebuke from Samuel Johnson as that youth who, pleading excuse for certain conduct, said, 'But Dr. Johnson, I must live.' To this the wise old man replied, 'Sir, I see no necessity.' The big thing is not to make a living but to make life worth living. If the big thing in life be to make a living then let us have a saloon at every corner, a gambling hell half-way in every block; let us burn our Bibles and banish our ethics.

* * * * *

"James and you and I are just the little folk who determine the average, the average in work, the average in thought, the average in morality, the average in thrift. How easy, for example, it is for us to waste our substance on useless luxuries instead of joining the ranks of those who are making provision against the rainy day. Mandy, the negress, stood by the merry-go-round and watched them get on and off and then sagely remarked, 'You all have spent all your money and you gets on where you get off, and you gets off where you get on, and I ax you one question, Where you bin?' "

This sermon may not be wholly typical, nor present Dr. Freeman at his best, but it indicates his sprightly style and the versatile qualities that make his preaching so popular and interesting. I asked him for some hints of his methods and habits of study. Companionable and courteous as the man is he was reluctant to talk much about himself.

"It is like this," he explained. "You assign the kind of task I have no taste for, although I am naturally complimented by the demand. I don't mind seeing myself publicized, but am too Scotch to uncover what my kindly friends desire. To my doctors, I am sure I am the worst of patients, for I can never supply the symptomatic data they desire. But I'll try.

"Rarely do I plan my preaching ahead, though occasionally I follow a series. The volume *What About the Twelve?* illustrates the latter method. Ordinarily I let the reading and the experiences of the week determine my theme. While I like to preach expository sermons, I seldom do it. My besetting sin is letting all the fussing of the big job interfere with methodical and constructive study. I don't know how many books I read a year. Unhappily I am a slow reader, but I try to 'give every flying moment something to keep in store.'

"As for poetry. There is relatively little poetry which I see that I can use. It takes a lot of hunting. It has to be more or less commonplace and obvious to be effective in a sermon, or brief and surprising."

Dr. Freeman not only loves poetry but writes verses of merit and has published *The Land I Live In, and Other Verse.* Some of his poems have been widely quoted, as for instance, "In My Father's House." I had heard these verses recited before I ever read a sermon of Dr. Freeman's, and can readily understand their popularity. He told me how he came to write them.

"They were inspired," he said, "by Lyman Abbot's book *The Other Room,* and based on John 14. The book I knew would be read by few and I sought to put the essence of it in reach of many. Nothing I have done seems to have gone so far or accomplished as much as those very simple lines."

Quite appropriately, I think, the lines that have comforted multitudes of sorrowing men and women may close this chapter which has for subject one of America's most accomplished and gifted preachers, whose radiant personality inspires courage and faith in all who are so fortunate as to know Robert Guthrie Freeman, minister of Jesus Christ.

"No, not cold beneath the grasses,
Not close-walled within the tomb;
Rather, in my Father's mansion,
Living in another room.

"Living, like the one who loves me,
Like yon child with cheeks abloom,
Out of sight, at desk or school-book,
Busy in another room.

"Nearer than the youth whom fortune
Beckons where the strange lands loom;
Just behind the hanging curtain,
Serving in another room.

"Shall I doubt my Father's mercy?
Shall I think of death as doom,
Or the stepping o'er the threshold
To a bigger, brighter room?

"Shall I blame my Father's wisdom?
Shall I sit enswathed in gloom,

When I know my love is happy,
Waiting in the other room?"

Back of these lovely verses and inspiring theme are the deep well-springs of an undefeated faith; and back of this, the stream of a devout heredity and the mountains and lakes, the banks and braes of old Scotland!

STIDGER, William Leroy, clergyman; *b.* Moundsville, W. Va., March 16, 1885; *s.* Leroy Lester and Etta B. (Robinson) S.; Allegheny Coll. 3 yrs; Ph.B., Brown, 1912; theology, Boston U. 1 yr.; D.D., Allegheny Coll., Meadville, Pa., 1923; Litt. D., Kansas Wesleyan U., 1928; *m.* Iva Berkey, of Ligonier, Pa., June 7, 1910; 1 dau., Elisabeth Robinson. Ordained ministry M. E. Ch., 1914; pastor Calvary M. E. Church, San Francisco, 1913-16, First Ch., San José, 1916-19; publicity trip through Far East for Methodist Centenary, 1919-20; pastor St. Mark's Ch., Detroit, Sept. 1920-25; Linwood Boul. Ch., Kansas City, Mo., 1925-29; head of dept. preaching, Boston Univ. Sch. of Theology; preacher of Copley Methodist Church, (the old Edward Everett Hale pulpit). Served in France as truck driver for Y.M.C.A., 1918. Mem. Phi Delta Theta, Delta Sigma Rho, Pi Gamma Mu. Mason (32°), Odd Fellow, Republican. *Author:* Giant Hours with Poet Preachers, 1918; Soldier Silhouettes, 1919; Star Dust from the Dugouts, 1919; Outdoor Men and Minds, 1920; Standing Room Only, 1921; Flash Lights of the Seven Seas, 1921; Flames of Faith, 1922; There Are Sermons in Books, 1922; Henry Ford—The Man and His Motives, 1923; The Epic of Earth, 1923; That God's House May Be Filled, 1923; The Symphonic Sermon, 1923; Finding God in Books, 1924; A Book of Sunsets, 1925; Pulpit Prayers and Paragraphs, 1926; Building Up the Mid-Week Service, 1926; Building Sermons with Symphonic Themes, 1926; God Is at the Organ, 1927; The High Faith of Fiction and Drama, 1927; Personal Power, 1928; Preaching Out of the Overflow, 1929. Editor: If I Had Only One Sermon to Preach on Immortality, 1929; The Pew Preachers, 1930; Men of the Great Redemption, 1931. Contbr. chapters to Best Sermons of 1925; If I Had Only One Sermon to Preach; Great Southern Preaching, Contemporary Preaching, and many others. Mem. editorial staff and condr. column, "Conrad the Cobbler," The Christian Herald. *Home:* 99 Atwood St., Newtonville, Mass.

CHAPTER XXIII

WILLIAM L. STIDGER

HE IS superlatively unique—if it were grammatical to say so. Poet, preacher, journalist, publicist, traveler, litterateur, lecturer, advertising specialist, William L. (Bill) Stidger is in a way a combination of Walt Whitman, "Buffalo Bill" and Theodore Roosevelt. Stidger is a twentieth-century Peter Cartwright, sans sectarianism, sans the Democratic party. Punch he has a-plenty, brass in abundance, poetry drips from him, and a friendlier soul never lived. Built like a prize-fighter and blond of complexion, he gives the impression of perfect health.

Stidger is a West Virginian who arrived in Boston by way of California, stopping over for a season in Detroit and tarrying a while in Kansas City. He was overseas, heard the boom of the big guns, smelled powder and saw blood. Some think that his *Soldier Silhouettes* is the best thing he has written. He knows more celebrities than any other parson of my acquaintance, and all the way from Herbert Hoover to Jack Dempsey, from the W.C.T.U.'s to the I.W.W.'s. He is nothing if not versatile and expansive. He pals with bishops and policemen; he knows hoboes, prima donnas and many of the well-known actresses. He calls Ed Wynn and Fred Stone by their first names, and claims to have given Will Rogers some of his best jokes.

Not long after landing in Boston Dr. Stidger went after the Daughters of the American Revolution whom he dubbed "Daughters of Reaction." If Stidger does not make the front page of a city newspaper at least once a week something has happened to him; either he is out of the city or on vacation, which amounts to the same thing. After leaving Kansas City he became the minister of Copley Square

M. E., the church that once was Edward Everett Hale's, and widely famed. From that historic pulpit Dr. Stidger preached on Sunday mornings to capacity audiences. He had no Sunday evening sermonic responsibilities. More recently he has become the preacher of the Church of All Nations in the same city. He is in the faculty of Boston University's Theological Seminary, lives in Boston, but is anything but Bostonese.

Speaking of Boston! Meeting a widely known preacher acquaintance one day, he inquired: "Have you heard the latest limerick?" Now limericks are almost a weakness with me and I made swift reply: "No, but I want to hear it. Let's have it." Whereupon with mock seriousness he quoted, not an orthodox limerick, but the following quatrain:

"Here's to old Boston
The land of the bean and the cod,
Where the Cabots and Lowells are silent
And Bill Stidger plays vaudeville for God."

Clever? Yes, but not wholly fair. I quote it only because it reveals the human side of the ministry, the repartee of gentlemen of the cloth.

At Detroit Stidger inherited a debt-ridden church, the building having been constructed at war-plus plans, leaving an indebtedness of four hundred thousand dollars. Stidger used to boast of having the biggest debt in Methodism. I don't know about that, but anyway it was big enough. He was succeeded at St. Mark's by a Denver preacher who is also a personality. The first Sunday that the Denverite spent with his new charge, the church was closed and the congregation was locked out because of a past due interest item of twelve thousand dollars. The new pastor wired Stidger what had happened and received this answer:

"Dear Jim: you don't need a church to preach in. Take your congregation to the park across the street. Bill."

Stidger is typically midwestern in pronunciation, outlook, spirit, everything. He is as frisky as a calf, playful as a puppy, and if need be, bellicose as a bull in a beauty shop where the furnishings are all in crimson. And beneath all this there beats a warm heart in Stidger's bosom. Generally, too, this red-blooded preacher man who talks about a masculinity that is "able to spit over a box-car," is on the side of the angels. He is a prolific writer and for the last ten years has averaged a book per annum. He writes poetry that is genuinely poetic. Here his touch is so deft and sure that it seems out of harmony with the vigor, the unconventional speech and actions of the man. He edits a department in *The Homiletic Review,* another in *The Christian Herald,* and a third in *The Expositor.* He gives out numerous interviews, and everything he writes makes good "copy."

This parson is a voracious reader, remembers what he reads, and uses it effectively. I once heard him say that he read on an average two books a day, three hundred and sixty-five days of the year. It sounds incredible, but then he reads with great rapidity; I fancy he is a good "scanner," and knows how to skip where the skipping is good. I think it was old Dr. Johnson who counseled that there are very few books that deserve to be read closely and without skipping some paragraphs. Stidger goes in for author's autographed copies, and his shelves are lined with them. When he presents a copy of his own books to a friend, the inscription on the fly-leaf is usually characteristic. For example, in my copy of *There Are Sermons in Books,* written by W.L.S. in 1922, he penned:

> "To old man Jones—celebrating the first day I ever saw him with anything on save a 45° angle collar—
>
> "Fraternally & Faithfully,
>
> "Bill."

During Dr. Stidger's Detroit pastorate he was for some

time a feature writer on the *Times,* Hearst's daily, and also dipped a bit into local politics; made a number of political speeches and coined a cluster of epigrams. Some of the city's leading preachers were on the opposite side of the fence politically and these Stidger characterized as "the milk fed, hand led preachers on Woodward Avenue." He also labeled them "mama dolls" and a few other equally choice epithets. But it should be stated that he said these things "with a smile." When chided for those statements, Stidger replied that these same preachers were big fine fellows, big enough to take a joke like that and laugh about it. Alas, maybe some of them did not see the joke, or if so, didn't regard it as a laughing matter. But nothing fazes Stidger. He is generous, courageous, and lovable to boot. Methodism needs W.L.S., for he is unlike any other M.E. preacher of this generation, an oddity, unconventional, not a little spectacular, and kind to a fault. Stidger is a D.D. and a Litt. D.

Dr. Stidger claims to have put the idea in Sinclair Lewis' head to write a novel with a preacher hero. If this is true, then I suppose I shall have to take some of the credit, or discredit whichever way one may look at it, for his writing of *Elmer Gantry*. It happened this way; in 1922 I ran across Stidger in the lobby of a hotel in Terre Haute, Indiana. Mr. Lewis was also in the lobby, and having met him in Detroit a few months before, I renewed my acquaintance, introduced Dr. Stidger to him, and the three of us breakfasted together. It was during that meal that Stidger said to Lewis, "Why don't you write a book about a preacher?" Our famous guest remarked that he might think about it. Four years later, Dr. Stidger being then located in Kansas City, Sinclair Lewis took up his residence there and began work on *Elmer Gantry*. Stidger was a member of the group of preachers with which Lewis consorted frequently while he secured color and gathered data for a book that failed to achieve the success its author had hoped, and added nothing to his fame. It is only fair to Dr. Stidger to state that he most certainly did not have in mind the kind of a preacher book that Lewis wrote.

As a specimen of Dr. Stidger's poetry, read this exquisite thing which he wrote during his Detroit ministry. It has already appeared in one anthology and reappears from time to time in various periodicals throughout the country:

"I saw God wash the world last night
With His sweet showers on high;
And then when morning came
I saw Him hang it out to dry.

"He washed every tiny blade of grass
And every trembling tree;
He flung his showers against the hills
And swept the billowy sea.

"The white rose is a deeper white;
The red a richer red
Since God washed every fragrant face
And put them all to bed.

"There's not a bird, there's not a bee
That wings along the way,
But is a cleaner bird and bee
Than it was yesterday.

"I saw God wash the world last night;
Ah, would He had washed me
As clean of all my dust and dirt
As that old white birch tree!"

Of all my preacher friends and acquaintances, W. L. Stidger is the readiest to talk about his work. Nobody ever accused him of "lying awake at night hating himself"; but his frankness is refreshing and he has gifts that any minister might be proud to possess.

"Tell me, Bill," I urged, "how do you manage to accomplish so much with such apparent ease? How do you find time to write scores of sermons, a book or two a year, innumerable articles, lecture, preach, and for the better part of the year meet your classes five days a week? Say on, or better, dictate it?"

"That I'll do." Dr. Stidger sat down at his "portable" and typed off rapidly this breezy statement.

"The reason I get so much work done is summed up in one of Emily Dickinson's couplets:

"'Work is easy
When the soul is at play.'

All the work I do is play. I love to preach. It is never a chore. My church work—calling, business, financial work—is a pleasure. I go into my office and into my church whistling. I did not notice this until one day one of my secretaries called my attention to it. She said, 'You always come into the church whistling, no matter how hard things are going. It perks me up to hear you and to see the joy with which you approach hard problems.' That girl was right. I love to write. I never did a piece of writing in my life that seemed like work to me and which seemed hard to do. I like lecturing in the same way that I like preaching. I was trained in a newspaper office, and trained by an old newspaper editor who said to me early in life: 'You will have to learn two things on this paper; to work under fire, because your work will always have to be done quickly and under pressure; the pressure of the last edition going to press, the pressure of having thirty typewriters pounding around you. That means that you will have to learn to concentrate like the devil. Second: You will have to learn to write accurately in your first draft, for there will be no time for revision in a newspaper office. And why not learn to write the first draft as nearly perfect as it can be written? Why assume that you will have to revise it and do it over and over again? Learn to write correctly the first time.' In addition to having had that fine schooling in composition early in my career, I have also learned to husband my time.

"I do not waste time. I schedule my work for the day, then for the week, and generally for a month in advance. I know what I am going to write both in articles, books and sermons, a month in advance and plan everything to fit into my schedule. I read every night, every morning and on trains regularly. If I am waiting for my wife and she is half an hour late I have a book in my pocket. I have also learned to read by paragraph as Roosevelt, Bishop Quayle, and many a prolific reader has learned.

"I write out every sermon carefully on the typewriter. Then that sermon is permanently set aside. Its content may be used not only as a sermon, but also as a book chapter or an article in a magazine. Thus I make it do in a threefold way. I have written thirty-four books since the World War and some publisher has published them, AND publishers do not publish books for which there is no market. I have also written chapters in thirty-eight other books. During that period I have conducted eight different special columns in newspapers, magazines, etc.

"As to my method of sermon preparation: I get an idea and file it away in a carefully kept filing system. That idea gathers material like a snowball. It grows in my mind. In a few months it is ready to be written. I organize all of my material, find a text, write it out in full, following an outline. It is always written word for word, generally ten or twelve pages of typewritten matter. Then it is reoutlined on a single, folded letterhead and that outline is taken into the pulpit—but seldom used. You insinuate that I may be a genius but if I am I am a harnessed, disciplined genius, who knows that order, discipline and organization give me ten times the capacity for creative work that I would have if my office, reading, writing, were not organized. My sermons grow and ripen into being. Sometimes they ripen quickly, often not for months and some for years. But I want them all to ripen.

"I have tried everything else on earth, but preaching is the most satisfying thing I do. It gives me more joy than seeing an article appear in *The American Magazine, Good Housekeeping, Collier's, Ladies' Home Journal* or other magazines, in all of which I have appeared from time to time. To stand up before an audience, large or small, and deliver the Gospel of Good News, to talk about the Life Abundant, to feel that you are changing men's thoughts and view-points and lives; that is the greatest thrill that life has brought to me. To be friends with people; to know and love babies, to baptize them; to marry people, to make homes for them; to live with them in their troubles and to help them solve their problems; to be a shepherd, a friend whom they love, 'Oh, that will be glory for me!' To have influence in your city, in its political life; to know its business men, its preachers, its problems, and to help solve them; to be inside looking out rather than outside looking in; that is the big 'kick' of the ministry to me."

So this is William L. Stidger, who is the object of frank and nipping criticism on the part of his preaching brethren. His methods have been stigmatized as "sensational," "spectacular," "vaudevillian," "tending to lower the high standard of religious institutions." Yet nobody who knows intimately this preacher can deny his genius. And he is likable. There's something winsome about him in his best hours. One of his friendly critics remarked in my hearing, "I feel about Bill Stidger as Senator Jim Reed said he felt about Senator J. Ham Lewis."

"And how was that?"

"When I meet him I don't know whether to kiss him or kick him."

NEWTON, Joseph Fort, clergyman; *b.* Decatur, Tex., July 21, 1878; *s.* Lee and Sue G. (Battle) N.; student Hardy Inst. (now defunct) and Southern Bapt. Theological Seminary, Louisville, Ky.; Litt. D., Coe Coll., Cedar Rapids, Ia., 1912; D.D., Tufts Coll., 1918; LL.D., Temple University in 1929; *m.* Jennie Mai Deatherage, of Sanders, Ky., June 14, 1900; children—Joseph Emerson, David (dec.), Josephine Kate. Ordained Bapt. ministry, 1893; pastor 1st Bapt. Ch., Paris, Tex., 1897-98, asso. pastor non-sectarian ch., St. Louis, 1898-1900, founder and pastor People's Ch., Dixon, Ill., 1901-08, pastor Liberal Christian Ch., Cedar Rapids, Ia., 1908-16, The City Temple, London, Eng., 1916-19, Church of the Divine Paternity, N. Y., 1919-25, Memorial Church of St. Paul, Overbrook, Phila., 1925-30, St. James, Ch., Philadelphia, since 1930. Asso. editor Christian Century, Chicago. Served as Grand Chaplain Grand Lodge of Masons of Ia. *Author:* David Swing, Poet Preacher, 1909; Abraham Lincoln, 1910; Lincoln and Herndon, 1910; The Eternal Christ, 1912; Sermons and Lectures, 1912; The Builders, A Story and Study of Masonry, 1914; Wesley and Woolman, 1914; What Have the Saints to Teach Us? 1914; The Ambassador, 1916; The Mercy of Hell, 1918; The Sword of the Spirit, 1918; The Theology of Civilization, 1919; Some Living Masters of the Pulpit, 1922; Preaching in London, 1923; The Men's House, 1923; Preaching in New York, 1924; The Truth and the Life, 1925; The Religion of Masonry, 1926; God and the Golden Rule, 1927; Altar Stairs, 1928; The New Preaching, 1929; Things I Know in Religion, 1930; The Angel in the Soul, 1931; The Sermon in the Making, 1932; also many pamphlets on patriotic and Masonic topics, and numerous addresses and sermons. *Address:* St. James' Church, Philadelphia, Pa.

Chapter XXIV

JOSEPH FORT NEWTON

My first introduction to Joseph Fort Newton was through one of his sermons sent me from his church study at Cedar Rapids, Iowa. That was years ago, and ever since, up to this present time, sermons have been coming in a steady stream from the deep springs of his soul. Dr. Newton has done many things and done them well. He is an authority on Masonry and every Masonic honor has been heaped upon him. He has lectured and written upon many subjects, literary and historical. His book *Lincoln and Herndon* is an authority in that field. His biography of David Swing is ably written. His books number twenty-four volumes to date, yet preaching is Dr. Newton's supreme passion, and it is as a preacher he is best known to-day. I am inclined to believe that through twenty years Dr. Newton has been a more prolific producer of high-class sermons than any other preacher of the period.

Newton's career is unusual. His rise to international fame was sudden and spectacular. He is a southerner by birth and began his ministry as a Baptist. Four years later he founded the People's Church at Dixon, Illinois, stayed there seven years, then became pastor of the Liberal Christian Church at Cedar Rapids, Iowa, remaining there eight years. In 1916 he was called from that field to City Temple, London, as the successor of R. J. Campbell. It was a tremendous stride, and Dr. Newton was for weeks the most talked of preacher in the world. He spent three years in London, during the turbulent period of the Great War, returning to America to become pastor of the Church of the Divine Paternity, New York City. Then he was ordained in the Episcopal ministry, installed as Rector of the Memorial

Church of St. Paul, Overbrook, Pennsylvania, and only recently became the minister of Preaching at St. James' Church, Philadelphia. A Baptist, an independent, a Congregationalist and now an Episcopalian! Dr. Newton once wrote of R. J. Campbell that he looked like a man who had come a long distance and passed many graveyards on the way. Dr. Newton has come a long way also, but you do not think of graveyards when you look at him, listen to him preach, read his writings.

It is said that John Randolph, of Roanoke (himself an orator of no mean gifts), on hearing Daniel O'Connell exclaimed, "This is the man, these are the lips, the most eloquent that speak English to-day." I would paraphrase this utterance to express my own feeling after hearing Joseph Fort Newton preach, "This is the man, these are the lips that speak the most chaste and beautiful English in the Christian pulpit to-day." Dr. Newton is a lord of language, the master of a distinctive style. The literary quality of his sermons is opulent, and though saturated with the fragrance of belles-lettres is nevertheless marked by restraint. There is a suggestion in his style of Cardinal Newman, in serenity and purity, but it is much more alive and colorful than that of the renowned author of *Lead, Kindly Light.* If Dr. Newton has ever published a sermon or written a chapter in any of his numerous volumes that is marred by carelessness or unhappy phrasings, I have not come across it, nor expect to do so. As a preacher he is a rare combination of the mystic, the teacher and the prophet.

Dr. Newton's pulpit utterance is distinguished by a quiet, earnest, easy delivery. He is not so rugged of speech or so oratorical as his successor at City Temple, Dr. Norwood; nor is he so dramatic or rapturous in style as his immediate predecessor, Dr. Campbell. He is a handsome man, with fine eyes and a noble open countenance; one of the most companionable of men, urbane, and a charming conversationalist. Newton is a recognized authority on that finest of fine arts, the art of preaching. By "certain inalienable rights" he should appear in that great series known as *The Yale Lectures on Preaching*. At the zenith of his pulpit power Dr. Newton is disentangling himself from numerous activities in order to give the rest of his days to the high business of preaching the Word.

Not all eminent preachers are authorities on the sermonic art, but Dr. Newton is. His book *The New Preaching,* dedicated by the way to "A. Maude Royden, one of the greatest of the new preachers," is a work beyond praise. I engaged this master preacher in conversation on the subject he loves most of all. "Tell me," I pressed, "just what is this business of preaching?" He mused a bit before answering:

"As I see it, preaching, as Shelley said of life, is a dome of many-colored glass which stains the bright radiance of eternity. That is to say, it is the white light of God shining through the prism of a human personality, and its power to move and cleanse and exalt is measured by the purity, sincerity, richness and charm of personality through which the light shines. It is not the business of the preacher to prove things, but to make people *see* things which else are dim, if not unreal. As an old Eastern proverb puts it, "He is the true orator who can turn the ears of his congregation into eyes." Only, alas, oratory is dangerous; it is so easy for a preacher to say more than *he* sees, and that is fatal.

"In other words, the truth of the Gospel must be clearly seen, deeply felt, and dipped and dyed, in all the colors of human life, if it is to be made concrete and vivid. Much of our preaching, I am persuaded—my own too—is too abstract, and over the heads of folk. Guthrie, his biographer tells us, found this to be true when he asked the plow boys and country lasses in the afternoon what they had learned from his morning sermon. He was humiliated to discover that they had got little or nothing from it. So he changed his style of preaching, as Dale did more than once, made it simpler, full of shrewd practical remarks, and pictures of life as he himself had seen it, using imagery from country life and ways. Then the youths and maidens could tell him all about his sermon."

"Your own pulpit style is quite flawless," I commented. "How can a young minister acquire a style that is distinctive?"

"Intellect moves nothing," said Dr. Newton, quoting Aristotle. "Only when truth is linked with the will, by the power of emotion, does it release springs of aspiration and effort. We know as well as we feel, and we never do a thing until it is profoundly felt. One need not be a dealer in 'pocket-handkerchief rhetoric,' as the Germans say; but even that were better than the unimpassioned presentation of the Gospel of which Tennyson speaks in the Northern Farmer; 'He said what he 'owt to have said, and I come'd awa' '; and nothing happened. My late friend Baron von Hugel spoke of a French priest of rare force of mind, whose 'will of iron, by long heroic submission to grace, had attained to a splendid tonic tenderness'; and that is an ideal set up to be aimed at."

Dr. Newton paused, "Am I really answering your question, I wonder? But I am not through. To acquire a style that is at once lucid and attractive means devotion, it means hard work, and the most severe discipline of mind and heart and soul—and art. A young preacher ought to write his sermons for years—not read them in the pulpit—but write, if only to learn the weight, worth, color and music of words, and acquire a moral sense in using them. For sixteen years I published a sermon every week, and often two, written after they were delivered, as my habit is—if I write before, a paper flutters between me and my people—and it has helped me toward clarity, precision and concision, as well as in all sorts of ways. It clarifies thought to write it down—I am sure some of the earlier plays of Shakespeare were written for that purpose; to clear his own mind about the aims and issues of art."

"Do you recall that article by John Spargo many years ago on 'The Futility of Preaching,' Dr. Newton?"

"Indeed, I do. It was drastic, but not wholly fair. Whether preaching or any thing is futile depends upon what is put into a sermon, a picture, or a book. Emerson in an address to divinity students, complained that 'the soul is not preached.' If that be true, preaching is a failure and a futility. If the soul is to be preached, the preacher must dwell in the 'vale of soul-making,' as Keats called it. When the soul is preached men hear their own souls speak to them in the tones of the preacher, and they are moved as flame is moved to flame. Preaching is the greatest of all adventures and the finest of all arts—God make us men of soul force, that we may be helpers and healers of the souls of men."

Reference has already been made to Dr. Newton's interest in Lincolniana and his authoritative volume on *Lincoln and Herndon,* a work of rare beauty interpreting a famous friendship. Dr. Newton and I have exchanged many letters on the subject of preaching, Abraham Lincoln and books. He is the most rewarding of all my correspondents, the most fascinating letter-writer I know. I am making bold to insert just here a lovely little note of his—inserting it despite the all too complimentary notice of a modest sermon I had sent him. I may be pardoned for not deleting this section since the personal references afford an illustration of this premier preacher's generous attitude toward his lesser gifted brethren of the ministry. I cite this letter, principally because of the allusions to Lincoln and Herndon, especially the postscript with the Whitman episode.

"Dear Dr. Jones:

"A thousand thanks for your letter, and also for the clipping about Herndon, but most of all for the sermon, which went straight to my heart. I loved your sermon; it seemed, in parts, a transcript out of my own heart. It is exquisitely beautiful, searching, challenging, healing; I envy the folks who listened to it. Won't you let me see other sermons; they do me good, and I should like to review one of them in my sermon department in McCall's Magazine—giving you an audience of three million people.

"I am chagrined to think that I did not drop you a line of thanks for your generous, gracious appreciation of me in The Christian. It was just like you to praise your brethren, adding to their gifts out of your kindness. I have been having a spell of bad weather of late, owing to illness in my family, and some things have been neglected. I did appreciate your tribute more than I can tell.

"It is too bad that anyone should attempt to belittle Herndon; I hoped that my researches had made such a thing impossible. Such was my intention, but apparently I failed. My manuscript was read by the late Horace White—who thought that the characterization of Herndon on the second half of page eighteen was exact, and rather extraordinary, inasmuch as I had not known Herndon personally. Both Judge Zane and my old friend H. B. Rankin, who were students in the Lincoln and Herndon office, approved my record of facts and most of my interpretations. It does not exalt Lincoln to belittle Herndon; they were real friends—the lesser man one of the most self-effacing friends in our history. Yet no one near Lincoln has been treated more brutally—except Mrs. Lincoln! Mercy of God, what a story!

"I am, with brotherly love abiding,

"Yours in His name,
(Signed) "JOSEPH FORT NEWTON.

"P.S. Of late I have been having an interesting discussion with my friend Mrs. Morrow, about the mysticism of Lincoln. As you remember, toward the end of her story, 'The Last Full Measure,' she has Mary Harlan reading Whitman to Lincoln, and Lincoln quoting his great lines, and finding in them something profound—

satisfying. I had thought the dreamy mysticism of Whitman quite alien to the mind of Lincoln, and both Barton and Rankin agreed with me. The two minds were so utterly unlike; but Mrs. Morrow seems to have documentary evidence for her facts and her interpretation. It shows how fast, and in what direction, the mind of Lincoln was moving in those last six months. I yield to no one in my admiration of Whitman, who was the greatest mystic our land has known,—his vision turned, not upon another world, but like a transfiguring light upon our prodigal abundant America; and it does tie things together to know that even Lincoln was caught up into its ample vision. How does the matter lie in your mind? J.F.N."

Fort Newton varies his style, for even beautiful phrases become monotonous if marked by sameness. As a specimen not only of this master preacher's smooth flawless English, but also of his philosophy of life, I append the following:

"When is a man educated? When he can look out upon the universe, now lucid and lovely, now dark and terrible, with a sense of his own littleness in the great scheme of things, and yet have faith and courage. When he knows how to make friends and keep them, and above all, when he can keep friends with himself. When he loves flowers, can hunt the birds without a gun, and feel the stir of a forgotten joy in the laugh of a child. When he can be happy alone and high minded amid the meaner drudgeries of life. When he can look into a wayside puddle and see something beyond sin. When he knows how to live, how to love, how to hope, how to pray—glad to live, and not afraid to die, in his hands a sword for evil, and in his heart a bit of song."

An ornament indeed, is this preacher, to the ministry of the Word!

NIEBUHR, Reinhold, clergyman; *b.* Wright City, Mo., June 21, 1892; *s.* Gustave and Lydia (Hosto) N.; student Elmhurst (Ill.) Coll., 1910; Eden Theol. Sem., St. Louis, Mo., 1913; B.D., Yale Div. Sch., 1914, A.M., 1915. Ordained ministry Evang. Synod of N. A., 1915; pastor at Detroit, 1915-28; asso. prof. philosophy of religion, Union Theological Seminary, 1928-30, prof. applied Christianity since 1930; editor of World To-morrow. Mem. Alpha Sigma Phi. *Author:* Does Civilization Need Religion? 1927; Leaves from the Notebook of a Tamed Cynic, 1929; Contbg. editor, Christian Century, Chicago, also contbr. to Atlantic Monthly, etc. *Home:* 99 Claremont Av., New York, N. Y.

Chapter XXV

REINHOLD NIEBUHR

The author of *The Mirrors of Washington* avers that "pessimism and magnetism do not go together." Maybe not, but Reinhold Niebuhr can exude pessimism and magnetism at the same time. Niebuhr claims to be "a tamed cynic," but he is neither cynical nor tame. He is one of the few shining intellectuals among the preachers of America who are both radical and deeply religious. Professor Gaius Glenn Atkins once remarked to the writer, after listening to Niebuhr, "He can skin civilization, hang the hide up to dry, and offer prayer over the carcass." That, I hold, is a real accomplishment, for while there are a number who can do the skinning, and a multitude who can do the praying, only a few can do both within the hour.

Niebuhr is the most popular speaker among college groups on the American platform to-day. They fairly eat up his stuff, and after the fashion of Oliver Twist, ask for more. This young thinker is keen of mind and he loves to play havoc with the old formulæ of religion, the traditional prejudices, and particularly conventional piety when it is incarnated in the person of a "captain of industry." I recall hearing Niebuhr read an essay before a free-lance preacher's club, in which he said, "The lowliest peasant of the Dark Ages had more opportunity for self-expression than the highest paid employee in the Ford factory." He said this, mind you, in Detroit, and if Mr. Ford had been present Niebuhr would have said it just the same, and if possible made the statement stronger, although that were difficult.

Young Niebuhr came to Detroit in 1915 and took a small obscure church which grew slowly and solidly under his guidance. About this time he became a contributor to the chaste *Atlantic Monthly*. A new building was constructed on a thriving thoroughfare and Niebuhr's ministry went on the map in a more impressive fashion; and as his reputation grew his congregation increased accordingly. The new church building seats perhaps six hundred people, and with the rise of the youthful prophet's fame, his night audiences filled the place comfortably. It was not what would be called a popular assembly. The intelligentsia was well represented; radicals and liberals were there. Dr. Niebuhr conducted a forum at these meetings that was sprightly and occasionally distinguished by spectacular episodes. His morning congregations were more staid yet sprinkled with visitors in search of a thrill.

Bethel Evangelical Church has never been the same since Niebuhr left it. No evening congregation approaching the audiences that assembled there under his ministry has appeared since he resigned to become a professor at Union Theological Seminary. His first successor, a young man of fine spirit and much of Niebuhr's outlook, attempted to open the church rolls to a group of negroes who had applied for admission, made the thing a stirring issue, and went down to defeat. In turn he was succeeded at Bethel Church by a scholarly gentleman, possessing a shepherd's heart, who carried bravely on despite a good many difficulties, for the spell of the brilliant Niebuhr still hangs over the church, his first parish. The worshipers miss the suppressed excitement, the large audiences and the wide-spread interest that were inspired by their leader who had become a national celebrity.

Niebuhr is tall, slender, and boasts a peaches-and-cream complexion. His forehead is high, his hair thin and growing thinner. He would never take a prize in an oratorical contest. His delivery is careless; he "ahs" and "ers" a deal; and he is powerfully fond of the word "naïve." Occasionally he impinges a Germanism upon his English, but what of it?—the man's mind is quick as lightning, his ideas are fertile and fertilizing. He is a student, a scholar and very much a philosopher, often disturbing in public speech and in his writings, yet always stimulating, and to most minds vastly entertaining. With two books to his credit, one of them, *Does Civilization Need Christianity?*, a work that reveals an original mind; ten years of successful pastorate behind him; unusual platform opportunities pursuing him; membership in the faculty of Union Theological Seminary helping to give him a sounding board, Niebuhr has just begun to strike his pace. His future seems as rosy as his cheeks. As this is being written the critics are devoting columns to his latest volume *Moral Man and Immoral Society.*

A comparison of Dan Poling and Reinhold Niebuhr should be profitable, since they are the two most popular speakers at young people's gatherings in this country. Both are minister's sons, both have held pastorates, both are writing and speaking constantly, yet they are unlike in many ways. Poling is progressive but not radical; Niebuhr is recusant, an independent, a pathfinder. Poling can capture a crowd of church young people for a moral issue. Niebuhr can send a university crowd of young moderns into high-geared enthusiasm for radical economic ideals. Niebuhr loves to shock the complacent; Poling to inspire the indifferent. No one would think of calling Poling a "heretic"; Niebuhr invites that distinction or stigma, whichever you prefer, every time he speaks. Poling is a lesser Bryan; Niebuhr a more intellectual Debs.

Reinhold Niebuhr is the product of a home of plain living and high thinking. His father, a scholarly German preacher, died when his children were small. His mother is a dear serene soul of noble character. It is good to hear her address this son who has achieved a national renown as "Reinie." A brother, H. Richard Niebuhr, is a professor in Yale Divinity School, and author of one of the most thoughtful books that has yet appeared on the problem of Christian union, *The Social Sources of Denominationalism.* There is a sister, Hulda, who has published *Greatness Passing By,* and another brother, Walter, was in the newspaper business when I knew him in Illinois, and of promising personality.

Dr. Niebuhr tackles a lot of heavy reading with infinite zest. In hearing him speak, I have been impressed not so much with the sweep of his reading as the depth; so I made bold to ask him to name the books that had most influenced his thinking. Reluctant at first, he finally cited five authors who had helped him greatly.

"1. *Harnack's Essence of Christianity,* which first gave me a general statement of liberal Christianity in my college and pre-theological days.

"2. The various books of Carlyle which I devoured at college and between which I can not easily distinguish. I suppose *Sartor Resartus* might go down as the chief influence.

"3. Troeltsch's *Soccìallehren der Christlichen Kirche,* the study of which gave me historical support for the social task of modern Christianity.

"4. Schweitzer's *Civilization and Ethics* which convinced me that the social conservatism of the church was at least in part due to the monistic and deterministic character of orthodoxy and to the practical fatalism of professing Christians.

"5. The works of William James, particularly the volume *Will to Believe* which helped me very much in the readjustment of religious faith in theological school-days."

It is inevitable that a man of Reinhold Niebuhr temperament, daring, intellect and iconoclasm, should be regarded as dangerous in the more conservative church circles. He irritates a certain type of mind, and sometimes gives the impression that he enjoys doing so. He can be sarcastic; he frequently is caustic. A preacher acquaintance of mine who has heard Niebuhr in some of his slashing addresses before conventions or college groups, and who is, himself, quite widely known, commented freely in my hearing on

Niebuhr. "He has the freshest mind of any religious teacher among the younger men in America. He can cross swords with the British theologians and the Scotch professors. I have been listening to him for a half-dozen years, off and on. I wouldn't say that popularity has spoiled him, but I would say that it has not subdued him, nor yet inspired the best within him. He is almost too clever intellectually. A little more tenderness or downright compassion would help to balance his brilliance, and perhaps with the passing years such qualities will be more apparent in his teaching and preaching than they are now. I hope that such will be the case. The temptation of a clever mind is one of the subtlest that a teacher of religion can ever know." I let this stand for what it may be worth.

It is difficult to pick out a paragraph from Professor Niebuhr's writings that reveal his intellectual attitude, something of his prophetic passion, and at the same time the adroitness of his approach. But I fancy the following, taken from his *Leaves from the Notebook of a Tamed Cynic,* accomplishes this purpose as well as any other excerpt:

> "The old gentleman was there who wanted to know whether I believed in the deity of Jesus. He is in every town. He seemed to be a nice sort, but he wanted to know how I could speak for an hour on the Christian Church without once mentioning the atonement. Nothing, said he, but the blood of Jesus would save America from its perils. He made quite an impassioned speech. At first I was going to answer him but it seemed too useless. I finally told him I believed in blood atonement too, but since I hadn't shed any of the blood of sacrifice which it demanded I felt unworthy to enlarge upon the idea."

Niebuhr is a kind of spiritual mustard plaster on the body ecclesiastical. Strength to his hands and to the power of his poultices!

COFFIN, Henry Sloane, clergyman, author; *b.* New York, Jan. 5, 1877; *s.* Edmund and Euphemia (Sloane) C.; B.A., Yale, 1897, M.A., 1900; studied New Coll., Edinburgh, 1897-99, Univ. of Marburg, 1899; B.D., Union Theological Seminary, 1900; D.D., New York U., 1906, Yale, 1915, Harvard, 1922; LL.D., Amherst College, 1927; *m.* Dorothy Prentice Eells, Sept. 6, 1906. Ordained Presbyn. ministry, 1900; pastor Bedford Park Ch., New York, 1900-05, Madison Av. Ch., 1905-26; asso. prof. of practical theology, Union Theol. Sem., 1904-26; president of Union Theological Sem., 1926-. Annual preacher at Yale, Princeton, etc. Mem. Bd. of Home Missions Presbyn. Ch.; dir. Ch. Extension Com. of Presbytery of New York (Inc.). Trustee Atlanta (Ga.) U., Robert Coll., Constantinople, Turkey; fellow Corpn. Yale U. Mem. Delta Kappa Epsilon, Phi Beta Kappa, Skull and Bones, Chi Alpha. *Clubs:* University, Yale. *Author:* The Creed of Jesus, 1907; Social Aspects of the Cross, 1911; The Christian and the Church, 1912; University Sermons, 1914; The Ten Commandments, 1915; Christian Convictions, 1915; In a Day of Social Rebuilding (Lyman Beecher Lectures at Yale), 1918; A More Christian Industrial Order, 1920; What Is There in Religion? 1922; Portraits of Jesus Christ, 1926; What to Preach (Warrack lectures), 1926; The Meaning of the Cross, 1931. Co-Author: Some Social Aspects of the Gospel, 1912. Editor, Hymns of the Kingdom, 1910. *Home:* 80 Claremont Av., New York, N. Y.

Chapter XXVI

HENRY SLOANE COFFIN

The evening of June 15, 1910, I sat in the World's Missionary Conference, in the historic Assembly Hall in Edinburgh. It was a meeting long to be remembered. On the program, which continued for a week, appeared the names of the most famous preachers, scholars, missionaries and Christian laymen the world around. The Archbishops of Canterbury and York were present and spoke. The late Bishop Gore was one of the stars. Edinburgh was thronged with Christian leaders representing every communion in Christendom except the Roman and Greek Catholics. The first speaker that evening was the learned Professor W. D. Patterson, D.D., whose subject was "Christianity as Redemption." The professor delivered an able address, scholarly, a little erudite, perhaps, pitched upon a lofty level. He was followed by a young Presbyterian preacher from New York City, who took for his theme, "Christianity as an Ethical Ideal." This man appeared boyish as compared with the older and more mature speakers who graced that platform day after day, but he showed not a trace of alarm. I have never cared overmuch for the phrase, but this American preacher spoke that night with "holy boldness." He pioneered. He was in truth a voice crying in the wilderness. He suggested that Christianity had never been tried. He had the audacity to say, "Modern civilization is probably the greatest hindrance to-day to the proclamation of the Christian Gospel."

The speaker was the Reverend Henry Sloane Coffin, then the pastor of the Madison Avenue Presbyterian Church, New York City.

Most men of the ministry in this country are from the

humbler homes; homes that stand for something in faith and morals, but not homes of luxury. Dr. Coffin is an exception. He comes from a family of wealth and affluence. He has never known the pinch of poverty. He was born to place, prestige and plenty. He might have gone into business and become a captain of industry. He might have become a corporation lawyer with millionaire clients; he might have gone into politics and as a reward for his services been appointed ambassador to the Court of St. James'. Or, young Coffin might have become a gentleman of leisure, an elegant loafer dawdling away his days and living like a Prince of India on the fat of the land. Instead, he became a minister in the Presbyterian Church, received his A.B. at Yale, took Theology at New College, Edinburgh, Marburg, Germany, and Union Seminary, graduating from the latter in 1900. He began his first ministry in a hall above a butcher shop in the Bronx. Five years later he was the minister at Madison Avenue Presbyterian Church. Taking this church when it was at a low ebb, he thoroughly reorganized it, and in a little more than a decade made it one of the most influential churches in America, with a membership of two thousand and a Sunday-School of seventeen hundred, and a staff of twenty workers.

Not many men in the ministry are equally proficient as preacher, administrator, pastor and teacher. Henry Sloane Coffin is effective in each of these important leaderships, though Coffin the Prophet and Teacher out-tops, in my opinion, Coffin the Executive and Publicist. As a preacher, Dr. Coffin almost from the beginning has been popular in university circles. Excelling in the art of sermonic preparation and arrangement, the content of his preaching has always been to the foreground. This man is a clear thinker, a wise expositor, one who is never trite nor guilty of "elegant commonplaces." Listening to him one is impressed with his sincerity, sound scholarship, poise and sanity. An early and consistent exponent of the social gospel, he has never overlooked the great doctrines of Christianity or failed to do them justice. Living as he does in the rarefied atmosphere of the higher learning, he has preserved the common touch. Companying constantly with scholars, some of whom occupy cloud land, Dr. Coffin has not lost interest in the country pastor or the day laborer.

In 1918, Dr. Coffin delivered the Yale Lectures on preaching, the forty-fourth in that notable series. Imagine appearing in that long and illustrious line at the age of forty-one and in the midst of the World War. What a test! The ordinary man would have flattened and gone down to defeat, but not so Dr. Coffin. He produced a set of lectures worthy the occasion and shot through and through with prophetic fire. He took for his theme *In a Day of Social Rebuilding,* and his first lecture was entitled "The Day and the Church." I secured a copy of Dr. Coffin's Yale Lectures as soon as they came off the press and during those disturbing days of the winter of 1918 and 1919 this volume was often in my hands. The book shows much usage and the margins are marked with many penciled comments. I began purchasing the Yale Lectures early in my ministry and thirty-six of these volumes form my Shelf Supreme. I unhesitatingly put Coffin along with the leaders in this series—Beecher, Brooks, Jowett, Horne and Jefferson. The timeliness of these lectures is astonishing; their simplicity alluring; their optimism heartening. I have contrasted this volume with that of Dr. John Kelman, who followed Coffin in this historic course the next year. Dr. Kelman took for his theme, *The War and Preaching.* His lectures are creditable and in places he rises to extraordinary heights; but Dr. Coffin's chapters, I hold, have a more direct appeal, indicate a closer relation to things as they are, reveal a warm and generous heart, and make the reader feel that the ministry in all periods of history is the grandest vocation known to man.

Dr. Coffin has published much, and not a single unworthy volume, or one that shows slovenly preparation. His *Ten Commandments, Portraits of Jesus Christ in the New Testament, "What to Preach, What is There in Religion?, Some*

Christian Convictions, University Sermons, are strong, engaging, stimulating. His little book, *A More Christian Industrial Order,* published in 1920, is an example of *multum in parvo.* There are five meaty chapters, to wit: "The Christian as Producer," "The Christian as Consumer," "The Christian as Owner," "The Christian as Investor," "The Christian as Employer and Employee." Here indeed is a social gospel attractively, convincingly, set forth. The little work is an immense advance over the ordinary work on Stewardship. Then there is Dr. Coffin's *The Meaning of the Cross*—brief, fresh, rewarding. Every preacher in the land might read this little book on the heart of the Gospel with very great profit. The author is not a slave to any school of theology, though possibly a debtor to them all.

The Meaning of the Cross is a little book, only one hundred and sixty-four pages, four chapters, bound in red. It is filled with such thoughtful sentences as these: "The cross does not cancel sin; it does something far better. It transfigures the sin-distorted character so that the remembrance of sins and their very consequences become factors in the new life. . . . The cross of wood on which Jesus was nailed is the symbol of an eternal cross in God's heart and conscience. . . . There is no cleansing blood which can wipe out the record of what has been. The past has been built into the fabric of our spirits. The cross of Christ leaves suffering still a mystery, but he shows us what to do with it. . . . We must make plain that, by no artificial legal transaction, but by the solidarity of our sin with the factor which crucified Him, what we are today in our selfishness is 'that Christ's loss.' . . . The cross is a family catastrophe, in which the actors are our kinsmen, and the blood of the victim stains us as sharers in our brothers' crime. . . . Men of awakened consciences, faced with Christ on the cross, feel themselves involved in that tragedy. . . . At present our churches draw and hold the settled and cramp or repel venturesome which is precisely the reverse of the New Testament church. The appeal to enter the church should be a summons to risk everything for Christ's sake. . . . That was the appeal of Jesus to His followers, a call which won home with added realism after Golgotha."

It is time to look at a sermon by Dr. Coffin. Here is a typical discourse with the text taken from II Corinthians 13: 13, "All the saints salute you," used also as title. Wherever a text will serve in this dual way, it can be used effectively. Sitting in their pews, worshipers are measurably prepared for the sermon since they have time and opportunity to reflect on the text as they read it announced in the title. The introduction is very brief and pictures vividly a miscellaneous company of first-century Christians, mostly slaves and working men gathered in the large room of a well-to-do Christian's house. There are five divisions to the sermon in which the word "Salute" is utilized to the fullest. Thus, First: "The Saints Salute You with *Sympathy*." Second: "The Saints Salute You with *Their Witness to the Reality* of Him Whom They Believed." Third: "All the Saints Salute You with *Guidance*." Fourth: "All the Saints Salute You with *Expectation*." Fifth: "All the Saints Salute You with *Present Fellowship*."

This is the sermon of a shepherd, a teacher, a friend. Nobody would call the sermon "learned," but it is scholarly in the good sense of that word. Homiletically the progressiveness of the thought is noteworthy. It moves forward like the current of a river which gains in depth and strength because it is fed by many tributaries. There are many historical allusions, very brief, but striking, and as follows: the downfall of Jerusalem; the period of the Jewish-Christian Church when Ambrose and Augustine flourished; the puritans of New England, the "great awakening" under Jonathan Edwards and George Whitefield; the far-away time when Abram left Ur of the Chaldees; the Reformation under Luther, and Melancthon; the work of John Calvin; the rise of the Liberal party in England and the dwindling of its power. There are two illustrations employed with fine restraint, the first refers to a visit the preacher made to

Japan, and the fact that while there he was always in sight of Mt. Fuji, yet he failed to see its snowy crest. The rainy season came on during his stay, and a thick atmosphere obscured all views. He was obliged to leave the country without having had a glimpse of Fuji, but he never doubted that the mountain was there. Its snow-capped summit was the motif of designs on china, fans and screens. Hotels and tea houses proclaimed its existence, trips to it and arrangements for climbing it were advertised. It was impossible to believe that so many thousands of people had in so many different ways been victims of delusion, "There are periods in an individual's life and periods in the life of humanity, when God—God as seen in the face of Christ—is obscure . . . but God's reality is too widely apprehended and relied on to be denied. In certain situations we find Him mirrored—mirrored imperfectly in some disturbed human life at our side, mirrored perfectly in one serenely confident and untiringly loving life. We lift up the eyes of our hearts, and for us, too, God is there in His august and ennobling goodness."

The above is taken from the second division, but the preacher returns to the same thought in the fifth and last section and concludes with this serene and lovely illustration:

> "There is a very beautiful lake in the Adirondacks about which the camps have been built so that they are almost completely concealed by the forest from any one on the water. Unless some other canoe is in sight, one paddles along with a sense of solitude amid the mountains and the woods. But when night comes, the glow of the camp-fires touches one with an awareness of comradeship.
>
> "The absorbing interests of our days usually claim our attention so fully that invisible presences remain unrealized. But when darkness falls as it does in bewildering and confusing times, light gleams out for us

and we become aware of the communion of the faithful in God. 'All the saints salute you.'"

And this is the man who heads Union Theological Seminary, where young ministers from the various communions go to top off in theology. Is not the portrait attractive? What a boon to have as president of that famed institution a man of such culture, such charm of literary expression, such serenity and poise, a fascinating and powerful exponent of the Christian faith!

MORRISON, Charles Clayton, editor, clergyman; *b.* Harrison, O., Dec. 4, 1874; *s.* Hugh Tucker and Anna Jane (Macdonald) M.; A.B., Drake U., 1898; fellow in philosophy, U. of Chicago, 1902-05; D.D., Oberlin Coll., 1922; Litt. D. from Syracuse U., 1927; D.D., Chicago Theol. Sem., 1928; *m.* Laurel Scott, of Springfield, Ill., Oct. 3, 1906; children—Jane, Helen. Ordained ministry Disciples of Christ, 1892; pastor, Clarinda, Ia., 1892-93, Perry, Ia., 1894-98, Monroe St. Ch., Chicago, 1898-1902, First Ch., Springfield, Ill., 1902-06; editor Christian Century since 1908; professional lecturer on Christianity and world peace, Chicago Theological Seminary since 1931. Delegate World Missionary Conf., Edinburgh, 1910; editorial sec. Regional Confs. in S. America, 1916, and editor of Proc. same; mem. deputation Am. religious press, invited by British Gov't. to visit Eng. and France, 1918. Pres., The Christian Century Press, Inc. Mem. Phi Beta Kappa. Republican. Mason. *Club:* Union League (Chicago). *Author:* The Meaning of Baptism, 1914; The Daily Altar, 1918; The Outlawry of War, 1927. Compiler: Hymns of the United Church, 1916. *Home:* 6144 Kimbark Av. *Office:* 440 S. Dearborn St., Chicago, Ill.

Chapter XXVII

CHARLES CLAYTON MORRISON

When first I knew Dr. Morrison he was hypothecating his life insurance and holding out his salary checks in order to keep *The Christian Century* off the rocks. Believe me, it was no small job. Those were the days when the editor's manly brow was corrugated with troublesome worries and his face a little drawn by the strenuous life of keeping a struggling weekly religious journal three jumps ahead of its creditors. About that time I overheard somebody say something to Dr. Morrison regarding "the editor's easy chair." It is unnecessary to chronicle his reply to that "wise-crack." However, those days have gone for ever. *The Christian Century* has a place in the sun, a subscription list in which the celebrities of all the denominations appear, and a sprinkling of the English nobility to boot. Furthermore, Morrison is an international figure.

C. C.'s smashing success as an editor is not an accident nor a matter of luck. He worked hard for it, coupling with a good mind a stout heart and a spirit of "never say die." Morrison's journalistic instinct is basically good and he has a nose for news. He is resourceful, adventurous, audacious. Also, he has a faculty for gathering about him other men who have ideas and know how to write. The editor of *The Century* is a fighter who is at his super-best when facing a real battle. He fairly loves a scrap where the issue is sufficiently large and something important is at stake. He is a valiant champion of world peace, but were there no more battles of any kind, Charles Clayton Morrison, like Othello the Moor, would be a gentleman without an occupation.

Morrison the preacher interests me even more than Morrison the editor. It is, I hold, a misfortune that his fame as an editor has dwarfed his reputation as a preacher. Actually he belongs within the small circle of great contemporary preachers, and I happen to know that he is at his happiest when he is in the pulpit and has let himself go in the full passion of the preaching ministry. His pulpit style is a diverting study. He begins in so low a tone that only those sitting well up in the front can hear him. Gradually he gathers vocal strength until his strong and resonant voice completely fills the church and even "the deaf hear." His vocabulary is distinctive and he is never satisfied until he finds the right word. It is habit to sacrifice fluency for the sake of accurate speech. A connoisseur of words, this editor-preacher loves with a very great love the word "inhibition." He hesitates occasionally in delivery—hesitates and halts until the word comes, and it is always the right word, the one word above all others for that particular place. I am never quite sure whether Dr. Morrison actually has to wait and feel for the right word or if it is a deliberately chosen method for effective appeal at strategic moments. In either case he makes an impressive use of what might be to some speakers a grievous fault.

Most eminent preachers have made their reputation by a few famous sermons—sermons into which they have crowded their best thought and illumined them with rich illustrative material. Dr. Gunsaulus, for example, had a noted sermon based upon the words found in the thirteenth chapter of John's Gospel, the fourth verse, "And [he] took a towel." He had another, not quite, but almost equally famed, on the superscription that Pilate wrote and which was attached to the cross where Jesus died. The text was John 19:20, "And it was written Hebrew, and Greek, and Latin . . . The King of the Jews." Dr. Stephen H. Tyng, who flourished in the middle part of the last century, a very eloquent Episcopal clergyman of New York City, had a sermon on "Lot's Wife." It was original, pictorial, and the Doctor preached it with fine effect. He was asked to repeat it so many times that he once remarked, "That woman will be the death of me yet."

Now Clayton Morrison has a half-dozen sermons so striking in content and application that once heard the thoughtful hearer will never forget them; not only so, but every time he reads or hears quoted the text upon which these particular sermons were based he will think of Morrison's sermon. I recall that he has a remarkable discourse on the mighty affirmation of Job, "The Lord giveth and the Lord taketh away. Blessed be the name of the Lord." He has another, a luminous discourse, on John 7: 17, "If any man will do his will, he shall know of the doctrine," a penetrating handling of this familiar text, fresh and invigorating withal. For myself, I should regard Morrison's sermon on the words of Jesus spoken in the upper room, "The hour cometh and now is," as the finest of this select group. In the latter sermon he makes a magnificent plea for unity, chides us for postponing union to some distant date, calls upon us to quit talking about unity and begin to practise it now.

This preacher needs plenty of time if he is to achieve the best results oratorically. It takes him actually ten minutes to get started, sometimes fifteen; and he requires forty-five minutes to an hour to round out a powerful sermon. One church where Dr. Morrison was supplying the pulpit for several Sundays was a little troubled by the famed editor's disposition to preach forty-five minutes as a minimum. Finally, a member of the staff hit on this device—a small clock was installed at the back of the pulpit in plain view of the preacher and under it in fair-sized letters was tacked this inscription, "Preach not over thirty minutes." But all in vain! When Dr. Morrison preaches he preaches and a little thing like a clock and an inscription warning him to stop in thirty minutes is as futile as a snowball in the tropics.

The first time the Doctor preached for me in the beautiful new Gothic structure known as Central Woodward Christian Church, an odd thing happened, and amusing as well. As usual Morrison carried into the pulpit three or four sheets of note-paper containing the outline of his sermon. Now it happens that the stone pulpit in this church is without a desk, although there is a fairly wide ledge which answers the purpose. Dr. Morrison laid his notes on this ledge and in the course of twenty-five minutes of splendid preaching he consulted the sheets perhaps three times. Then in shifting them the sheets fluttered to the floor apparently unnoticed by the audience. A little later, perhaps five minutes, Dr. Morrison closed the sermon impressively—the shortest sermon, however, I had ever heard him preach. Later he explained to me that he had left off the last division of the sermon on account of the loss of his notes. Knowing the impatience of the average American audience with a sermon that goes beyond forty minutes, no matter how powerful, I remarked to this dear friend of many years' standing: "You will be the most popular preacher that ever comes to this church if you will arrange to lose your sermon notes each time before you reach the fourthly and fifthly." Personally I relish an hour's preaching from this prince of the pulpit any time, but to a host of church-goers the day of long sermons is past, and I am not sure it will ever come back.

Morrison's method of sermonic preparation is simple. He rarely writes out a sermon but makes generous notes, broods over the subject and trusts the occasion to produce the inspiration necessary to fire his imagination and give potency to speech. And he is seldom disappointed, nor is his audience. He puts a great deal of vigor in delivery, perspires freely and invariably wilts down his high collar. I recall his wife remarking that by the state of her husband's collar after preaching she knows whether he has been at his best or not. I have never heard him fail in the delivery of a sermon but he is more impressive and gripping at some times than others. Once or twice I heard him when he "labored" and once when Bryan was to follow him with a fundamentalist speech the Chicagoan appeared to be a little nervous. Little wonder! I can think of only one experience more difficult than preceding the "Commoner" on the platform, and that would be to follow him.

Dr. Morrison has an address, or sermon (he can make it either, and equally effective by the setting he gives it), on "The Higher Sacerdotalism," and sometimes he calls it "The Priestly Function of the Minister." Like most of his productions, it is forthright, keeps out of well-worn paths, is fresh, penetrating and immensely stimulating. There is not an illustration in it, nor a poetical quotation. It is critical as is the case with many of his best pronouncements, yet constructively so. He begins by describing the wide-spread custom among Evangelical Protestants of contrasting the priest and the prophet to the former's discredit. He claims that in such comparisons the priest is shown at his worst, the prophet at his best, and proceeds to defend the priest, and by a somewhat oblique approach makes a magnificent plea for the priestly function in modern Protestantism. He holds that it is the presence of the prophet among us that now makes this work of a priest necessary. He pleads for a revitalizing of a priesthood that is adequate for our modern day. He pokes slyly a little fun at the efforts of the Protestant ministry to "enrich" the order of services in their churches, and the hodge-podge of amateurish attempts at a denatured liturgy. I think the word "denatured" is my own, not his, but it describes the preacher's attitude as he attempts in a noble address to correct certain deficiencies in contemporary worship, and fire the imagination with new possibilities of the priestly task.

The bone-work of this sermon is not in evidence. It is covered up with the flesh of close thinking and meaty paragraphs that do not indicate clearly the divisional points. But they are there all right, though you have to feel for them as an osteopath searches out the ribs of a fat patient. Now this is not always the case with Dr. Morrison's sermons and speeches. Sometimes they fall into their divisions with Maclaren-like precision. It is not easy to quote from Morrison and do him justice. You miss the resonance of his voice, the flash of his eyes, the tense energy of his body, all of which supply passion to his delivery. I venture however a brief excerpt from this sermon on "The Priestly Function of the Minister."

> "I am sure that you have felt the incongruity between the sermon of a modern prophetic preacher and the context of liturgy in which it was set. In my capacity as a sort of editorial circuit rider I preach in many churches all over the land, and I am depressingly struck with the fact that our churches are compelled to make the bricks of worship without the straw of any consistent liturgy. The situation is pathetic. Most of our Protestant denominations, reacting from a decadent priesthood and a decadent liturgy, flung all ceremony out-of-doors and sought to make religion support itself in terms of preaching alone. For a certain length of time religion did support itself in these terms. But to-day it will not do so. It is a fallacy to assume that it should do so. Religious ideas are not self-supporting. They depend for their support upon ceremony, that is, upon liturgy. The refinements of our theological thinking are not transferable to the lay mind of our time. That mind calls for a more gross, more objective, more visible setting forth of its deeper aspirations. It demands pageantry, drama, movement. It hungers for truth expressed in art, in music, in more sensuous forms than wordy arguments of a preacher. Or more precisely, it hungers to express *itself* in such forms."

Dr. Morrison's voice in behalf of world peace, like the shot of those embattled New England farmers, has been heard the world around. On the platform and in the editorial pages of *The Century* he did magnificent service in behalf of the Paris Pact outlawing war. Dr. and Mrs. Morrison spent the summer of 1928 in Europe, and the editor of *The Century* made seventy-one speeches in England and Scotland on his favorite theme. The Morrisons were guests of some of the leading statesmen and journalists. By the eloquence of the one and the charm of the other this husband and wife made many and influential friends. Were I a politician, and my word counted for anything at Washington, I should whisper in the president's ear the advice to appoint Charles Clayton Morrison as Minister Plenipotentiary and Envoy Extraordinary to the Netherlands and Luxemburg. The doctor has the eloquence and the dash, his wife the grace and the diplomacy for just such a high mission. Between the two what a success they'd make!

BUTTRICK, George Arthur, clergyman; *b.* Seaham Harbour, Northumberland, Eng., Mar. 23, 1892; *s.* Tom and Jessie (Lambert) B.; grad. Lancaster Independent College, Manchester, 1915, Victoria U. (honors in philosophy), 1915; D.D., Hamilton Coll., 1927; *m.* Agnes Gardner, of Chicago, Ill., June 27, 1916; children—John Arthur, George Robert, David. Ordained ministry Congl. Church, U. S. A., 1915; pastor First Union Concl. Ch., Quincy, Ill., 1915-18, First Congl. Ch., Rutland, Vt., 1918-21, First Presbyn. Ch., Buffalo, N. Y., 1920-27, Madison Ave. Presbyn. Ch., New York City since 1927. *Author:* The Parables of Jesus, 1928; Jesus Came Preaching, 1931. *Home:* 124 E. 71st St., New York, N. Y.

Chapter XXVIII

GEORGE A. BUTTRICK

It was at a National Convention of one of the large communions the strength of which is mostly in the Middle West and the South. The occasion was the Preachers' Breakfast, an annual event at which eight hundred pastors sat down to break their fast and later listen to a sermon by a guest speaker. In due season the speaker was introduced, a good-looking fellow; scarcely middle-aged, smooth shaven, dark of hair, tense with vitality, yet of marvelous poise; straight and tall, he stood there with not a note of manuscript before him, facing an expectant gathering of his fellow-ministers. It was the Reverend George A. Buttrick, minister of the Madison Avenue Presbyterian Church, New York.

The preachers greeted the speaker with a salvo of generous applause and settled back to listen, all the while taking the man's mental and sermonic measure. The best audience in the world to preach to, if the preacher has a real sermon, is a company of parsons, and the worst, if the speaker has nothing to say but platitudes. Dr. Buttrick quoted Hebrews 11:13, "These all died in faith, not having received the promises, but having seen them afar off, and were persuaded of them, and embraced them, and confessed that they were strangers and pilgrims on the earth." Then he began:

> "'But you can not speak about that,' said a friend. 'Why not?' he asked. 'Oh, it is too pessimistic. "These all died . . . not having received the promises."' 'But it is true,' we insisted; 'it is life! What preacher has ever reached the end of the road feeling that all his hopes were fulfilled?' 'I know,' came the rejoinder; 'but it is too gloomy. Better cut out the depression: there's enough of it already!'

"But if he was sure, we were obstinate. As a matter of fact this verse is not a fit of the blues; it is more like a triumph-shout: 'These all died as they lived—in faith! Their hopes were not compassed, but they saw their goal and hailed it as voyagers nearing the port wave their hands to friends on shore. And they declared that what is never was their fatherland: they were pilgrims of the ideal!' How can such a word be turned into an attack of the mopes? But in any event the word is written, and it is obviously true. There is a school of modern thought which charges Christianity with being wishful thinking: God is a fiction (it suggests), and religion is only believing what we wish to believe. Let the charge pass. It may itself be wishful thinking: the psychologist himself is not free from repressions and complexes. Certainly the charge can not be brought against the religion of the Bible. 'These all died, not having received the promises'—what could be more starkly and nobly honest?

"The happy ending is taboo to this generation. It is too sweet. Besides, it is not true; events do not soon conspire so that the preacher or any one else lives happily ever after! But our current despair is not true either: the journey need not end in a slough of despond. 'These all sought a city; and they died in a wilderness. But they caught on the horizon the gleam of towers; and they died as they lived—adventurers still! Beyond the tavern of death they would travel on to that homeland of the soul.' All of which seals this Book as the Book.

* * * * *

"This is not said to spread a gloom, but to face a fact. Here is a mocking question which plagues all of us. Unless I mistake, it is the root of many a preacher's skeptic moods. We must find answer. Old Dr. Johnson quoted Pope's rather melancholy lines:

"Hope springs eternal in the human breast:
Man never is, but always to be blest,"

and some one challenged him: 'Is none genuinely happy in this present time?' 'No,' he grunted; 'nobody, except when he's drunk.' But even in that exception the Doctor was 'way off'; a man is not happy when he is drunk, for then he is not a man. He may be happy as a beer-keg or with a half-animal intoxication; but he has not reached a genuine human joy. He has only sunk in the scale. But even the great hearts have not found the climax of peace; they have stood a-tiptoe at the last, and with arched hand over peering eyes they have caught a glimpse through parted rifts of 'the hid battlements of eternity'; but they have died 'not having received the promises.' And—brutal truth—that is how we shall die. There is the problem for the preacher. We have stated it in its sharpest thrust, and the thrust in these times is made sharper by the prevalent skepticism, the poverty, the indifference and the fear! The preacher always lives and dies 'not having received the promises.' "

I looked about me. Across the table sat the minister of a county-seat town, where the going was hard, the task grinding. His eyes were shining. By my side sat the able minister of a strong city church; his face was aglow. A little farther away was a county preacher whose parish covered a section or two on the wind-beaten plains of Nebraska. He sat enraptured. I glanced toward an old preacher to my left, wrinkled of face, hair white, cheeks sunken, no longer much in demand, serving as supply as opportunity came. His eyes were brimming; his cheeks wet. I looked—but the sermon was going on. My wondering gaze returned to the preacher. He spoke with quiet force, noble dignity, now and then increasing the vigor of his voice.

"Well, there is the interpretation (blunderingly, but as well as I can make it) of such a word as you will not find for stark honesty outside the Bible. Will all your hopes be fulfilled on earth? They will not! Is there guarantee that your hopes will be fulfilled in heaven? There is not—at least, not what the world calls guarantee! You will die, as all the Christian company have died, 'not having received the promises.' Jesus died amid the jeers of the foes who had compassed His death. To cleave to one's hopes does not mean the early realization of one's hopes; the hopes themselves grow as we travel. 'Died—not having received the promises.' *But it was great fun to have lived that way!* There was zest in it, and persuasion, and comradeship; and such flashes of light that ever and again they saw the mists wash away to reveal the shining of minarets and the gleaming of rivers. And they died with a shout on their lips, for their hope had conquered even the contradiction of death.

"The courage of it; the zest of it; the conviction of it; and look at the *comradeship* of it. 'Wherefore God was not ashamed to be called their God,' which is a magnificent understatement, meaning, 'Wherefore God was proud to be called their God.' *'Wherefore':* because they had dared to live in their deepest hopes, and dared to die hoping still; therefore God was eager to claim them as friends. Do you understand? We look through a telescope and can not see the trailing robe of the Eternal—and we say there is no God. We look through a microscope and can not see the busy fingers of the Most High—and we say there is no God. Sinclair Lewis blasphemes deliberately on a public platform and dares God to strike him dead for it, and, because God does not strike him dead, there is no God—as though God's mercy were not doubly shown in the fact that He permits that kind of nonsense to go on living!

"That, if you please, is being Christian. They died, not having received the promises. But they saw them afar off. They hailed them with a cheer. They were persuaded of them. They confessed that hope as their true fatherland. And God claimed them for His own! Go thou and live likewise."

The breakfast was over. The preachers were leaving quietly, talking in subdued tones. The city pastor plucked at my sleeve. "That's what I call preaching," he commented.

Dr. Buttrick was born in Northumberland, England, and educated in Independent College, Manchester, and Victoria University. He began as a Congregationalist in Quincy, Illinois, going from there to First Congregational Church, Rutland, Vermont, and thence to First Presbyterian Church, Buffalo, New York. In 1927 he succeeded Henry Sloane Coffin in the ministry at Madison Avenue Presbyterian Church, one of the largest and most influential of New York congregations. Rapidly this minister, English-born, has forged his way to the front, and in New York City, once described as the graveyard of preachers, he is the wise administrator of a church that is like a city set upon a hill, the patient shepherd of a strangely varied and diverse flock, the very rich and the very poor, the prophetic visioned preacher whose pulpit rings with a clear high note of victorious faith.

Buttrick is a preacher who combines artistry with sound interpretations; the expositor who uses freely the garlands of literature and the freshest of illustrative material. It is profitable to study his sermons as they appear in *The Weekly,* published by his church. These sermons have not received final revision according to Dr. Buttrick. They are printed as prepared for immediate delivery, yet very little polishing would be necessary. The workmanship is excellent and the phrasing unhackneyed, often striking. The quality that most impresses me in the preaching of Dr. Buttrick is what I could call "aliveness." His sermons suggest both the midnight study lamp and something of the freshness of the morning dew. Rooted in the Scriptures they partake freely of current history, literature, drama; if they begin away back in ancient days, they end in the all-absorbing present.

Take his sermon "The Beloved Leader," based on John 12:1, "Jesus . . . having loved His own that were in the world, He loved them unto the end." And Luke 22:28, "Ye are they which have continued with me in my temptations." He plunges headlong into his subject. In a single short paragraph Jesus' relation to His disciples is pictured, thus: "He went—by the black door of a Cross. They stayed—in the world which had dealt with Him so cruelly. He loved them beyond His time on earth. He loved them 'unto the end,' the end of love which has no end." This is the thought of that introductory paragraph. The sermon has five divisions and it marches straight to the climax, what the preacher terms, "a confession of faith." There are quotations ranging from Donald Hankey's *A Student in Arms,* to a novel, *Father Malachy's Miracle.* There are allusions to James A. Garfield, Sinclair Lewis, Kipling and Dr. Oman.

The preacher pauses to consider scientific doubt, which he says does not "trouble me much more. God is not found in a test tube." The real doubt, he avers, is "in baleful moods, in the sharp inroads of tragic sorrows, in the stubborn fact of human inequalities." The preacher hammers the thought of Jesus loving us to the end, hammers it home, persistently. His hearers must get that thought if they miss everything else. Thus he maintains: "There seems to be a Voice in it, saying 'you have stayed with me to the end'—a Voice that rings true, and eyes that shine clear. That is heaven enough—here or hereafter. Golden streets would not be heaven in any event, and much less heaven if He were not there; and Hell would not be Hell with Him. . . . 'But,' some one urges, 'you do not know.' That is where the risk comes in. We would not wish to know—except in the surmises of the soul! What soldier wishes his victory handed him without wounds or adventure?" And again he turns to Donald Hankey and closes the sermon with a paraphrase of one of the most poignant paragraphs from the chapter, "The Beloved Captain":

> "But he lives, somehow he lives. We feel his eyes upon us. We work for that wonderful smile of His and to hear Him say, 'You have stood with Me.' Anyway in that faith let us live and die, and so I think we shall die content."

"Tell me," I queried of one who knows Dr. Buttrick, "has the man any foibles or eccentricities?" He mused a while before replying, "I do not know him intimately. I think I should answer in the words of his book. 'The preacher is never a spectator, but always a participant.' Buttrick forgets himself when he preaches. He twists his legs together, stands on one foot and pours out his soul. He charms me with his spiritual and mystical attitude. He is a lover of folk. He preaches not only from books but from his intimate contact with human life. His little strain of satire is subtle but redeeming. Of course, Buttrick is young. The question is—is he at his peak? With all the preachers the question is, what will the years do with them?"

I gather the impression from ministerial colleagues of Dr. Buttrick that few know him intimately. One fellow New York Presbyterian preacher of parts, said that he had spoken to him only once and that by telephone. Another waxed eloquent in praise of Buttrick's excellent reputation but declined to comment in an interpretative way of the man, fearing, he explained, that he might do Dr. Buttrick an injustice. If I did not know both of these preachers so thoroughly I might suspect a possible strain of professional jealousy, of which I believe them incapable. May not the explanation of such an attitude be that Dr. Buttrick is an Englishman with that natural reserve which can be so easily misunderstood? Most Americans simply can not understand an Englishman, and frankly admit it. And as for an Englishman understanding an American, the average Britisher is quite sure that he knows us better than we know ourselves. It may be so. Anyhow if Dr. Buttrick is difficult to get acquainted with it is probably due to his native reluctance to wear his heart upon his sleeve. Nor is it a matter of much importance. He is the student type, intellectual and more at home among his books than at a Monday morning minister's meeting, unless he is on the program for an address. Few men can be all things to all men. Saint Paul was, but he was an exceptional character. Dr. Jowett was one of the finest preachers of his day, but he was anything but a hale fellow well met, and of infinite jest. The good God did not make us all alike.

I questioned Dr. Buttrick on aspects of his ministry such as interest every aspiring preacher. When a master craftsman arrives, we all wish to know how he prepares his sermons, what are his habits of study, pastoral visitation and views on things ministerial. Sermonic shop talk never fails to delight the comrades of the high calling. The answers reveal a great deal of this man who, just turned forty, has climbed to far heights in the Christian ministry.

"My method of sermonizing is described in chapter six of my Lyman Beecher Lectures, entitled *Jesus Came Preaching*. The specific title is *The Craftsmanship of the Preacher*. That chapter in particular is autobiographical though the book itself makes no such admission.

"I carry a full manuscript into the pulpit, but refer to it only infrequently. For years I have written out every sermon in full. The manuscript is read several times on Saturday night and Sunday morning. In the pulpit I trust it to 'come again.' There is no attempt to memorize, but I find that the crucial passages (as for instance the all-important 'transitions') return almost word for word as they were written.

"I try to keep the morning hours for study. Latterly the needs of the tremendous program of relief that this church is conducting have broken the rule. But somehow I manage to keep my four hours a day.

"I try to make from twenty to twenty-five pastoral calls a week. Usually they are made in the afternoon, but some of them necessarily fall in the evening.

"I do not know what is the besetting sin of the ministry. I do not think I would wish to talk about it even if I knew. But I could tell you a good many besetting sins of my own!"

The minister of Madison Avenue Presbyterian Church has two notable books to his credit. The first of these, *The Parables of Jesus,* was published in 1928. The dedication throws light upon the background of the author.

To my
Father and Mother
Who by Word and Life
Taught their children to cherish
The Parables of Jesus,
This Book is Dedicated
in
Gratitude and Love.

This work on the Parables will be found in the library of most preachers who keep their shelves fresh and down to date. It is a meaty volume, thoughtfully worked out, exhibiting a fine painstaking scholarship and wide literary associations. The annotations are useful and the index adequate. It is the work of a preacher who knows how to preach and the homiletic value of the work is considerable. Most ministers whose literary opinions are worth weighing rank this to be the best book on the subject that has appeared in twenty-five years on this side of the Atlantic. There can be no question but this first book of Dr. Buttrick increased his influence and made him many friends and admirers. Few things so add to the reputation and usefulness of a minister as the publishing of a book of recognized merit.

In the spring of 1930 Dr. Buttrick delivered the Lyman

Beecher Lectures on Preaching at the Divinity School of Yale University. To be chosen for this lectureship is the highest honor of the kind that can come to any minister. It is at once a heavy responsibility and a vast opportunity. In the company of the immortals who are in this noble series—Beecher, Brooks, Gordon, Watson, Jowett, Home, Parkhurst—Buttrick is not ill at ease, but proves himself worthy a place in such high company. Taking as his subject *Jesus Came Preaching,* he produces eight brilliant lectures, to wit: "Is There Room for the Preacher Today? 2. Is Christ Still the Preacher's Authority? 3. Preaching Christ to the Mind of Today. 4. Preaching Christ to the Social Order. 5. Preaching Christ to the Individual of Today. 6. The Craftsmanship of the Preacher. 7. The Personality of the Preacher. 8. The Preaching of the Cross." Perhaps I could not close this appraisal of a mighty prophet of our times better than to submit a passage from his last chapter in his Yale Lectures on "The Preaching of the Cross." It is shot through and through with the vital stuff of the best preaching, the kind that lifts human beings out of their lower self to the highest things.

> "The Cross—God's power! But power for what? If God's purpose is to make men and women kind and true, then removing mountains into the sea and plucking stars from the sky (such wonders as the world has always required of its Messiahs) are a waste of time. New battle-ships are worse than a waste of time. What will make people Christlike? The Cross, for instance! There is always the Cross! Love laying down its life—parents for their children, patriots for their country, laborers doing it for us at what seems the price of their nobler growth, poets scorning surface gains and living deep, philanthropists pouring forth their gifts, doctors and prophets and teachers. On all these there is the mark of the Cross—love laying down its life. To make people Christlike there is no other power—only the

power of loving life laid down. If that is God's purpose then the truest sign of God's strength will be the *sign of God's own life laid down.* Therefore we preach Christ crucified the power of God."

Thunder of God!

MORGAN, G(eorge) Campbell, clergyman; *b.* Tetbury, Gloucestershire, Eng., Dec. 9, 1863; *s.* George and Elizabeth Fawn (Brittan) M.; ed. Douglas Sch., Cheltenham, Gloucestershire, and by pvt. study; D.D., Chic. Theol. Sem., 1902; *m.* Annie Morgan, of Gloucestershire, Aug. 20, 1888; 7 children. Ordained Congl. ministry, 1889; pastor Stone Ch., Staffs, Eng., 1888-92, Rugeley Ch., 1892-94, Westminster Rd., Birmingham, 1894-97; New Court Chapel, London, 1897-1901, Northfield Conf. extension lecturer, U. S., 1901-04; pastor Westminster Chapel, London, 1904-17; also pres. Chestnut Coll., Cambridge, 1911-14; Y.M.C.A. work, London, 1917-18; preacher Highbury Quadrant Ch., London, 1918-19; lecturer at Bible confs. in U. S. several years; pastor Tabernacle Presbyn. Ch., Phila. since 1929. *Author:* Discipleship, Malachi, Life Problems, 1897-98; God's Methods with Man, 1899; Practice of Prayer, 1899; Hidden Years of Nazareth, 1901; Ten Commandments, 1901; First Century Message to Twentieth Century Christians, 1903; The Crises of the Christ, 1903; Evangelism, 1904; Analyzed Bible (10 vols.), 1905-10, Messages of the Books of the Bible (2 vols.), 1909-10; The Bible and the Cross, 1910; The Parables of the Kingdom, 1911; The Missionary Manifesto, 1911; Simple Things of the Christian Life, 1912; The Ministry of the Word, 1919; Acts of the Apostles, 1924; Searchlights from the Word, 1926; The Gospel According to Mark, 1927; The Gospel According to Matthew, 1929; Categorical Imperatives, 1930; Studies in the Prophecy of Jeremiah, 1931; The Gospel According to Luke, 1931. *Address:* Tabernacle Presbyn. Church, Philadelphia, Pa.

CHAPTER XXIX

G. CAMPBELL MORGAN*

IN THE year 1901 a tall, slender, lean-faced, non-conformist preacher came from London to conduct a series of preaching missions in America. He arrived bearing the reputation of a brilliant sermonizer with unique gifts as an expositor of the Holy Scriptures. But lately out of college, I heard with avidity and delight this English preacher in a half-dozen memorable sermons delivered in the Ninth Street Baptist Church, Cincinnati. His sermons were forty-five minutes to an hour in length and nobody went away before the benediction. The preacher was G. Campbell Morgan, who later returned to this country to make his home and to preach from one end of the land to the other; and nearly always to crowded churches.

Campbell Morgan is a scholar who loves his Greek New Testament, and a preacher of marked speaking ability. His voice is cultivated and while not considerable in volume is rich in timbre and exceedingly flexible. Dr. Morgan is the teacher in the pulpit. He is always unfolding, interpreting and illustrating religious truth. He can be cutting, and frequently is, and he also possesses a delicious brand of humor. His descriptive powers are extra good, and there is a dramatic quality about his preaching that magnetizes. One who heard Dr. Morgan remarked to me, "Morgan can get more out of a familiar passage of Scripture that I didn't know was there, and some things that I am not yet certain are there, than any man I ever heard preach." Truly, this man's mastery of Biblical material is marvelous. And with what zest he preaches!

* Dr. Morgan has returned to England, but his long American residence and extraordinary ability entitle him to recognition in this work.

I heard Campbell Morgan preach on "The Fall of Simon Peter," in the series referred to above: and his divisions, the several stages of the Apostle's temporary apostacy, are as clear in my memory as though I had heard the sermon recently. His texts were the confession of Peter of Jesus as Christ, taken from Matthew the sixteenth chapter, and the strange and pathetic denial that he even so much as knew Jesus, found in the twenty-sixth chapter of the same Gospel. The divisions, as I recall them, are as follows: (I have never read the printed sermon and my wording is not meant to be exact).

1. He refused to Follow Where He Could Not Understand. Matthew, 16:21-24. Jesus had announced that he must go to Jerusalem, suffer many things of the elders, chief priests and scribes, be killed and the third day be raised up. Peter was offended by this. He could not understand it. Therefore he balked, took Jesus to one side and began to rebuke him, saying, "Be it far from thee, Lord: this shall not be unto thee." This was the beginning of Peter's fall. In the life of faith it becomes necessary to follow Jesus even when we can not fully understand.

2. His Boastfulness. The preacher enlarged upon the incident recorded by St. Luke, chapter twenty-two, where Peter made a great show of courage, and said to Jesus, "Lord, I am ready to go with thee, both into prison, and to death." When a man begins to boast, look out! He is already slipping. In his long experience as a pastor, Dr. Morgan said he made it a rule to offer special prayer for anybody who boasted of spiritual strength. He quoted Paul, "Wherefore let him that thinketh he standeth take heed lest he fall."

3. His Unwatchful Prayerlessness. The scene was the garden. Jesus had requested the three, Peter, John and James, to watch and pray while he went a little farther on to struggle alone. But Peter and the others fell asleep. Jesus returned and finding his friends sleeping, awoke them, and said unto Peter, "What, could ye not watch with me one

hour?" Three times this happened. To be unwatchful at so hazardous an hour, to be prayerless at so crucial a period, means defeat. A man is slipping fast when he quits praying and ceases to be watchful. Peter was now far gone.

4. His Zeal Without Knowledge. When the enemies of Jesus came to take Him prisoner Peter drew a sword, smote the servant of the high priest, and struck off his ear. Jesus bade him put up the sword. Here was zeal but not knowledge. The world suffers from over-zealous people who know not what they do.

5. Knowledge Without Zeal. Having been rebuked, "Peter followed him afar off." He had knowledge now but his zeal was gone. He was ready to quit, give up, resign. Dr. Morgan held that there is one rule that ought to be followed, whenever a resignation is presented—always accept it.

6. The Open Disavowal Accompanied with Oaths. Peter's fall was complete. He denied that he had ever so much as known Jesus. He went on record not only openly, but in the coarsest manner, accompanying his denial with oaths. Mark it well—his fall was gradual. There were definite steps in it, gradations, not suddenly or all at once.

Thus Dr. Morgan climaxed an hour's sermon, contrasting sharply the Simon Peter of the sixteenth chapter of Matthew, with the Simon Peter of the twenty-sixth chapter, the open denial accompanied with oaths. This is great preaching and while there are some who would say the analysis is too finely drawn and in one or two instances possibly not warranted, the fact remains that such handling of a theme fixes it indelibly in the minds of his hearers. He is the teacher in the pulpit, combining pedagogics and homiletics in an original manner.

During the International Christian Endeavor Convention which met 1901 in Cincinnati, I listened to Campbell Morgan in a series of sermons given in Central Christian Church, opposite the City Hall. He spoke at noon each day, and despite the strongly doctrinal cast of his sermons, or maybe because of it, crowds attended. I can see him now, his tall spare figure bending low over the pulpit desk, his voice sinking at times to a dramatic whisper, again rising in intensity. His long artist-like hands were ever in action, now clasped, now gesturing, always eloquent hands.

In one of these sermons he purposely misquoted from the Second Corinthian letter, fifth chapter, reading it thus: "God was in Christ reconciling *Himself* unto the world." The preacher leaned far out over the pulpit and in a low penetrating tone exclaimed: "If I believed *that,* I would never preach another sermon. I'd quit the ministry. But the Scripture does not say that. On the other hand it says, 'God was in Christ reconciling the *world* unto *Himself.*'— Aye, that is different, that is the Gospel, that is the love that will constrain me to preach as long as I have life and strength."

I recall another sermon by Dr. Morgan, this time on "Job's Comforters." He introduced the subject with a few vivid verbal pictures. You saw these distinguished personages traveling across the desert by camel to commiserate with their afflicted friend. Another vivid sentence or two and you saw poor Job sitting in torture, alone and aloof, an outcast, an object of abhorrence. You beheld his comforters taking their places silently about him, visibly affected by what they saw, weeping and wailing, sore at heart. Then Campbell Morgan came to the defense of Eliphaz, Bildad and Zophar. He conceded that they had been severely criticized, but there were at least three things that might be said in their behalf and to their everlasting credit. In the first place, it was remarkable that they came to see Job at all, considering how disreputable and God-forsaken he appeared. In the second place, what these three men said, they said to Job's face, not behind his back. They were not two-faced men, thank God! In the third place—oh, marvelous restraint—they kept their mouths shut for seven days and seven nights, and for this they deserved unstinted praise. There is a cleverness in such dealing with Scriptural narrative, which together with a very human flavor helps to account for Campbell Morgan's long-time popularity as a preacher and teacher.

Replying to my inquiries as to his sermonizing methods, Dr. Morgan cited an address on "Fifty Years Preaching—And More," which he gave in the chapel of the Eastern Baptist Theological Seminary, copy of which he handed me. Two or three excerpts from this informal talk will serve to show Campbell Morgan's conception of the ministry and how he goes about preparation to preach.

> "If I am to talk about fifty years and more of preaching it may be well to go back to the beginning. I was born in 1863. In the year 1876 I preached my first sermon in public. I played at preaching long before that. My sister, four years older than I, used to put her dolls in a row and I conducted services regularly, and preached to my sister and her dolls. There is a philosophy in that. I have been playing at preaching ever since. Preaching to me is the biggest fun in the world. I would rather preach than do anything else.
>
> * * * * *
>
> "I have never found an hour—I am now thinking of things in life generally, quite apart from the individual—I have never found an hour in my ministry in which the Bible has had no message. It never was my habit in pastorates, and never will be wherever my life may be cast, to preach on current events. But there have been hours when it was necessary that from the pulpit there should sound the prophetic voice to some national or international situation. I never found an hour when I had to go anywhere except to my Bible to find the message for such an hour. The Bible is the most living literature, absolutely up-to-date—I apologize to it—ahead of any date man has ever reached, waiting for us, guarding and keeping us in the true perspective, if we are

familiar with it. But if a local situation occurs, and a man thinks he ought to preach on it, and desires to preach on a text from the Bible, God help him if he goes to the concordance to find out what to say! There must be familiarity. We must live in the literature all the time, if we are to be ready when the special occasion arises.

"Still further, I have tried to remember that a phase of truth is not the whole of Truth. I do think that is important. I need not stay to stress it, but so many men I have known have squinted at one thing, and seen nothing else. There are some men who think if you do not say something about the premillennial Coming every time you preach, you are unsound! I think I will take my courage in both hands and tell you a story. A good brother, Baptist, gave out his text one morning, 'Adam, where art thou?', and he said, 'There are three lines we shall follow. First, where Adam was; secondly, how he was to be got from where he was; and thirdly and lastly, a few words about baptism'!

* * * * *

"The question is sometimes asked, How do you make your sermons? Do you ever find a man who can tell you? It is a difficult question. I can only give some very general statements as to my methods. Two things are vital: first, personal first-hand work on the text; and then, all scholarly aids obtainable. I never take down a commentary until I have done personal, first-hand work, and have made my outline. Sometimes after consulting scholarly aids I have to alter the outline; but at any rate I have had the benefit of first-hand work. We make a mistake when we have a text that has gripped us, or better, that has found us; and turn to commentaries first. To do that is to create a second-hand mentality. The first thing is to work on the text itself.

"Then sometimes I am asked about methods of delivery. Well, all I can say is, as a rule, I have a brief. I never prepare sentences. I do not know when I rise to preach what my first sentence will be as to form. I know what the thing I want to say is. I speak from a brief most carefully prepared, and give myself freedom of utterance.

* * * * *

"The last thing I want to say is this. There is a sense in which preaching is a conflict, a conflict with your hearers. I do not like the word conflict, but I do not know a better. The preacher is not merely asking a congregation to discuss a situation, and consider a proposition, or give attention to a theory. We are out to storm the citadel of the will, and capture it for Jesus Christ. Whether evangelizing or teaching does not matter. The appeal is the final thing. The sermon powerful in its matter and delivery up to a certain point demands application. So many preachers fail in that they say to their congregations, 'But, beloved, I am persuaded better things of you.' Then the people go home comfortable in their self-satisfaction, when they ought to be groveling in the dust, as they have been brought back to the point, 'Thou art the man.' 'Thus saith the Lord.'

"Thus I have tried to talk out of my experiences through the years. I have always felt, and never more so than to-day that the work of preaching is not that of debating difficulties, or speculating, or considering philosophies; but that of proclaiming the Word of God."

This English preacher, now considerably Americanized, is a spirited person. He shows a flash of temper when the occasion seems to require it, as for instance at Northfield when in a series of sermons, an ardent anti-tobacconist publicly and drastically criticized Dr. Morgan's habit of smoking. The doctor, smarting under the caustic slashing, prefaced a sermon one morning with an allusion to the criticism then proceeded to declare his personal independence on questions of this sort, and very distinctly informed his critic to mind his own business. Once when preaching in Detroit and the attendance seemed not up to the standard, he warmed up vigorously and attacked the American habit of non-churchgoing and fairly blistered the stay-at-home brethren, who unfortunately were not present, and since it was before the general use of the radio, were not even listening in. These little human touches, if anything, endear Morgan to us, and are comparable to spots on the sun.

Dr. Morgan has written many books, running expositions for the most part, of the Scriptures. He is the author of a good solid work on preaching, *The Ministry of the Word*. He holds many Bible conferences and preaching services. He is a theologian of the conservative school and, while dogmatic, gives the impression of breadth of view and tolerance of spirit. He has traveled much, read prodigiously, is a man of mark, a celebrity to whom preaching is a passion. His hair is white now, his face furrowed, the years are telling on him. His career is crowded with honors, and as the gloaming begins to steal upon him I love to think of that noble phrase, "A good minister of Jesus Christ." One other thing deserves mention, and may properly stand at the end of this sketch. Dr. Morgan has four sons in the ministry and occupying influential pulpits. Only a preacher father who exalted his vocation could achieve so enviable a distinction as this.

In his seventieth year, the snows of many winters on his head, this mentally youthful preacher has gone back to his former charge in the heart of old London town, Westminster Church. There he shares the ministry with the Rev. Hubert Simpson, a much younger man, and also marvelously gifted. Dr. Morgan's work at this notable preaching center has begun with record-breaking crowds, a packed church in foggy and rainy weather. In truth, weather conditions have little effect on audiences in England when this veteran is announced to preach. Thus he continues at the very eventide of life, unveiling the Scriptures, original, powerful, flashing his wit and genius of exegesis upon the Scriptures, always the Scriptures—a commanding and unique preacher of the Word!

TRUETT, George W., clergyman; *b.* Clay Co., N. C., May 6, 1867; *s.* Charles L. and Mary R. (Kimsey) T.; A. B., Baylor Univ., 1897; (D.D., 1899); *m.* Waco, Tex., June 28, 1894, Josephine Jenkins. Projected Hiawassee (Ga.) High Sch. and was its prin. 1887-89; financial sec. Baylor Univ., 1890-92 (elected to presidency but declined); ordained to Bapt. ministry, 1890; pastor at Waco, 1893-97; First Baptist Ch., Dallas, since 1897. Ex-pres. Southern Baptist Conv. *Address:* 5105 Live Oak St., Dallas, Tex.

Chapter XXX

GEORGE W. TRUETT

Thirty-five years as preacher and pastor of the same church and still going strong, is a record. One must have a wealth of sermonic ability and a world of character stuff to stand the strain. In three decades the pastor of a large church would preach between three and four thousand sermons, marry about two thousand couples, conduct about the same number of funerals, hold thousands of conferences, attend myriad committee meetings, make annually a multitude of calls. Any way you look at it, here is a man's job; and Dr. George W. Truett, minister of First Baptist Church, Dallas, Texas, has to his credit this shining record.

Dr. Truett is numbered among the small group of powerful preachers in America. Some say he is the brightest star in the galaxy of sermonic geniuses among the Baptists. They are proud of him; no wonder. He is the preacher always, and a preacher of Christ. He never preaches any special sermons, or sermons to special groups. Not only so, but he never announces any subjects. It is enough to know that Dr. Truett will preach. What he preaches on or about is a secondary matter. His sermons are distinguished by clarity, earnestness, excellent illustrative material and evangelical fervor. He has been known to use the same sermon before thousands of a city's most representative citizens in the municipal auditorium, before concourses of students and before humble folks gathered in groves.

The people of Dallas generally call him "Dr. Truett," but his own people usually address him as "Pastor." He is away from home a great part of the time preaching, always preaching. He holds many evangelistic meetings. He has an iron constitution, appears to be in excellent health, is a tireless worker. His church is marvelously loyal both to him and the missionary interests of the whole wide world. His annual church budget prior to the depression was about two hundred and twenty-five thousand dollars and nearly two hundred thousand dollars of this amount goes for missions, benevolences and educational work. Dr. Truett frequently preaches on giving. The doctrine of trusteeship is generally accepted by his congregation. They are a generous people and the spiritual pulse of the church is healthful. Prayer is stressed in this church; probably one out of every ten of the huge membership is competent to lead in public prayer.

Pastor Truett is a serious man but not austere or "bleak." Brother ministers in Dallas call him "genial," say he is an interesting conversationalist but not jocular and never frivolous. As he walks down the streets of Dallas, the citizens think, if they do not say it, "There goes a man." Dr. Truett rarely speaks on civic affairs or takes part in meetings of a general interest, but when he does it is an event, and Dallas listens. A man who preaches year in and year out in the same city, who holds many evangelistic meetings, must study, reflect, meditate. Dr. Truett does not have a study at the church and is seldom seen about the building except at the hour of services. He rarely attends the Sunday-School but occasionally he speaks at special meetings of the various groups of the congregation, and always on religious themes.

Returning to the gravity of Dr. Truett's demeanor: a prominent deacon in one of the leading Baptist churches of the South is authority for the statement, "Dr. Truett has never been seen to smile." Literally this is not true, but there is some truth in it, and hereby hangs a story of heart-break. Nearly everybody who knows Dr. Truett intimately is aware of the tragedy that came into his life when he was a young preacher and shortly after he went to Dallas. He was out hunting with one of the officers of his church and accidentally shot and killed him. He brooded over the accident, took it terribly to heart, and made his adjustment by way of a high resolution that he would abandon himself to just one thing—the preaching of the Gospel with every ounce of his strength, every atom of his personality. Such is the tragedy in the background of Dr. Truett's life, the explanation of his serious face, and a certain noble somberness that distinguishes him from his fellows, his soul "a star that dwells apart."

George W. Truett is a loyal Baptist, in a section where Baptists *are* Baptists. He believes without gainsaying that the Baptists have a special mission. But the man is greater than a denomination. He belongs to the Church Universal. One of his friends remembers having heard him say that he would get up in any hour of the night to defend any man, Jew, Catholic or what-not, whose religious liberty was being encroached upon. This same friend expresses the belief that Dr. Truett would like to see every man, woman and child in the world in the Baptist Church, and is doing all he can to bring that about. In times like the present it is refreshing to find so sturdy a defender of his own particular interpretation of Christianity, who at the same time finds something divine in every man, woman and child, and is measurably helping to usher in the great consummation.

Truett's printed sermons have a wide sale, especially through the South. In the homes of many humble believers will be found Truett's books, and in the library of ministers who preach for the so-called fashionable churches, the sermons of this renowned Baptist preacher are often found. Preachers who pay a great deal of attention to sermon-making are eager to learn the secret of Dr. Truett's power. The published sermons of Dallas' premier preacher are not nearly so literary as those of Joseph Fort Newton or Frederick Shannon, nor have they the clever modernness and arresting human touch of Burris Jenkins, but great sermons they are, in all verity.

It is rewarding to leaf through Dr. Truett's most recent volume, *Follow Thou Me,* running through the pages rapidly, stopping now and then to read a paragraph, or muse over an illustration. Those sermons were taken down in shorthand by a court reporter and are, for the larger part, a series preached in brief revival services at the Immanuel Baptist Church, Nashville, Tennessee. Some are college chapel talks, and there is one address to a group of Nashville preachers. The titles are not especially striking, some of them are commonplace yet they deal with the mighty verities of the faith.

Especially enjoyable is Dr. Truett's informal address to the preachers of Nashville, following a noon-day luncheon—the closing chapter. It is delightfully done and exalts the minister's calling from beginning to end. That Dr. Truett can make wise use of an occasional amusing incident is evidenced by this fragment in his talk to the parsons.

> "The story is widely told of a preacher who spent nearly all of his time in going from one business house to another in his town, writing promiscuous letters, wherever he paused, and then hurrying to the depot to mail them when he heard the sound of the coming train. One day, this same preacher declaimed loudly against the indifference of his people, vehemently asked them: 'What more can I do, in this town, than I am doing?' To which question, one of the men present made the blunt reply: 'Nothing more, unless you meet all the freight trains too!' The preacher is never to be a trifler for one hour with his incomparable task. He is to be the most indefatigable toiler in his community. It is said that Whitefield preached eighteen thousand times ere he reached the age of fifty-six. Certainly the preacher is one man who should be utterly unwilling to eat the bread of idleness."

This new volume of Dr. Truett's includes, among other sermons, one of his best known, and perhaps most typical deliverances, a sermon that he has preached from one end of the country to the other. The subject is "Our Adequate and Abiding Gospel," and the text Romans 1: 16, "I am not ashamed of the gospel of Christ: for it is the power of God unto salvation to every one that believeth." It is full length, covering nearly twenty pages. Let us see how this master preacher goes about this sermon.

He introduces his theme in a paragraph of a personal nature, intimate and direct, informing his audience that he has come to talk to them about Christ and His great salvation. He refers to "the multitude of faces in this hall," (bear in mind these sermons were stenographically reported). His second paragraph deals with the unrest and uncertainty of these present times, the instability of things that were thought to be unshakable, and then he asks the question, "Have the people of God an adequate remedy for the world situation as it is to-day?" Dr. Truett is absolutely sure that they have. That remedy is stated by the Apostle Paul in the text announced. Next the speaker enlarges upon the Apostle Paul as a preacher; then follow his points in this order: 1. Paul was not ashamed of Christ. 2. He was not ashamed of Christ's Gospel. 3. The Gospel of Christ is the one adequate remedy for every need and condition of mankind. 4. The crowning glory of Christ's Gospel is that it may be fully tested and proved in the crucible of experience. 5. The vital question inevitably emerges, for every person now assembled in this hall: What are our personal relations to this adequate and abiding Gospel of Christ? Conclusion:

> "What shall I say to souls here who are ashamed of Christ. . . . Remember, you must do something with Him, you must do one of two things with Him. You must confess Him or deny Him. Neutrality respecting Him is utterly impossible. Oh, come to Him, without further delay. Publicly register your unreserved surrender to Him to be your Savior and Master to-day and for evermore. Let your hearts give their unreserved 'Yes' to be expressed by your public confession of Him, even now as we sing our closing hymn:

"'Jesus, and shall it ever be,
A mortal man ashamed of Thee?
Ashamed of Thee whom angels praise,
Whose glories shine through endless days.'"

"Old stuff," commented a preacher acquaintance of mine after reading this sermon. Old stuff, yes, and powerful stuff, the stuff that tens of thousands of troubled souls under this man's preaching have found to be saving stuff, food for their souls, light for their eyes, healing for all their hurts. Yet it should be remembered that part of the power of this sermon, and a good part of it, resides in the preacher, Truett of Texas. Put these same words on the lips of a personality thin in character values, anemic in the rich blood of the spirit, and they will lose more than half of their potency. For no man can give out to others what he himself does not possess.

It was not possible for me to have a personal visit with Dr. Truett, but I wrote him requesting that he tell me something about his methods of sermon-making and pastoral visitation. His reply is so characteristic I am moved to include it just as he wrote it. If it be true that letters are an index to the soul of the letter-writer, and I think it is, here is a portrait of one of the most famous preachers of our day. It should be noted too that this letter was not typed, but written in longhand, as is the case with most of Dr. Truett's correspondence.

"Your letter of the 29th ult. came recently to hand and has been carefully noted.

"Replying, I beg to say, first of all, that I am deeply touched by your kindly thought of me in connection with the chapter in your forthcoming book on preachers. Poignantly conscious as I am of my unworthiness of any such recognition at your hands, yet, your suggestion intensifies my desire and purpose, God helping me, to strive still more earnestly, through the days ahead, to be a faithful and helpful witness for Christ to our needy world.

"Briefly answering your questions, I will say: as to Sermon Preparation. Texts and material for sermons are unceasingly suggested to me in manifold ways. These sermonic suggestions come supremely from Bible reading, and also from personal contact with the people with their manifold questions, needs and experiences. A note-book is ever with me, in which are jotted down beckoning texts, with seed-thoughts thereon, to be amplified, sooner or later, as these thoughts *live* and *grow* and *unfold*.

"As to Pastoral Visiting: in a large down-town church of several thousand members as in the case of our church here, the pastor's visiting must be largely limited to cases of actual and urgent need, very much like the visitation of the physician. Very much of a pastor's wisest and best help is given in personal counsel with the people, in his study at home, or in his office in the church building, or in both, as is the case with our work here.

"The pastor must hold himself in readiness to visit the people, wherever and whenever they need him. Exceptional cases of need call for extra pastoral consideration.

"In our work here, our Church Visitor, whose time is given wholly to visiting the people, is of unceasing and untold help in aiding both pastor and people in the matter of pastoral visitation and personal conferences. Indeed, all our paid church workers, together with our many unpaid and voluntary officers and teachers in our various church organizations, give much time to personal visiting, and in enlisting others to visit.

"Let me add that my work seems of such humble consequence, whether, as preacher or pastor, that acute embarrassment is given me, when I am asked any questions concerning it.

"Faithfully yours,
(Signed) "George W. Truett."

If Dr. Truett has any weakness, foibles or faults, they are certainly not known to his congregation or his fellow-ministers. Nor has he any critics worth noting, if we except an extreme individualistic fighting fundamentalist parson in the Lone Star State, who has publicly attacked Truett for his "modernism," of all things. I questioned Dr. Dawson as to any possible weakness of this preacher-celebrity.

"None," he replied, "unless it is his love for apples. He munches apples most of the time." Which is delightful and reassuring.

This title "Pastor" as applied to George W. Truett and used quite generally among his own people has puzzled me. For it is as a preacher that he is preeminently known. He is preaching all the time, preaching in his home church, preaching in conventions, preaching in evangelistic meetings throughout the land, and yet they call him "Pastor." Why? Resolved to make some investigation, I turned to Dr. J. M. Dawson, of the First Baptist Church, Waco, Texas, from which Dr. Truett was called to Dallas. Dawson and Truett are warm friends. They cross each other's paths frequently. They are intimates. Said Dawson:

"Dr. Truett has the shepherd heart. He is naturally a pastor. By the very nature of things he can not to-day do much house-to-house visitation, but he manages to keep in contact in one way or other with his large membership. He has never lost the individual in the mass. He writes in his his own hand a volume of letters annually—to every home in his congregation where there has been a bereavement, a birth, a son or daughter graduating from school or college. He especially loves to write a happy little note of congratulation to a wife whose husband has come into the church, or vice versa. No honor ever comes to one of his members but Dr. Truett calls up by telephone, or writes a letter of congratulation. No adversity overtakes any one of his flock without a friendly and comforting letter from the pastor. But of all the letters Dr. Truett writes he has never written one that he wouldn't face all the world with on the judgment day. Nothing could induce him to write a letter that would be a sword in a wound, or a sword in the hand of an enemy."

A venerable Texan who has been a member of the First Baptist Church, Dallas, during Dr. Truett's entire ministry loves to reminisce after this manner:

"It was a few years after he became our pastor in Dallas, thirty-five years ago on a Saturday, one of the bleakest of wintry days, that a call came for him to hold a funeral in the country fifteen miles out. 'You must not go, my dear,' his wife began to remonstrate gently. 'It is a hard all-day trip in the buggy, and you know how much is dependent upon you to-morrow.' 'I understand,' he demurred, 'but I must go. I was entertained in that home when I held the country meeting; they are my friends, and they need me.' She protested more vigorously, but to no avail. Over her entreaties he started, and to protect him, I went along with him. I saw him comfort that stricken family where the little wife and mother had died; I heard his words of consolation and courage in the church by the cemetery; I watched him as he put his arm around the broken-hearted husband while they lowered the coffin of the little woman into the grave that was as big as a cavern; I heard his benediction and tender farewell words as he took leave of the loved ones—I tell you George Truett was the greatest man that day I ever saw!"

"Pastor" Truett then is not a misnomer. He deserves this eloquent title, more eloquent, I hold, than "preacher," "clergyman," "dominie," "rector," "chaplain," or "minister." Curious is it not, and praiseworthy altogether that a man known throughout America as a preacher of unusual gifts, should be known best in his home city as a shepherd of souls, a friend of suffering human beings? And the explanation is at hand—the man, the man is greater than any sermon he ever preached. Truett is like that!

CADMAN, S(amuel) Parkes, clergyman; *b.* Wellington, Salop, Eng., Dec. 18, 1864; *s.* Samuel and Betsy (Parkes) C.; ed. Wesleyan Coll., Richmond, Surrey; D.D., Wesleyan (Conn.) and Syracuse Univs., 1898, Yale and New York U., 1925; S.T.D., Columbia, 1913; L.H.D., U. of Vt., 1913; Litt. D., Dickinson Coll., 1916; Ph.D., Wesleyan U., Bloomington, Ill., 1920; LL.D., Syracuse U., 1922, Muskingum Coll., New Concord, O., 1927; *m.* Lillian Esther Wooding, of Buxton, Eng., 1889; children—Frederick Leslie, Marie Isabel, Lillian Esther. Pastor, Metropolitan Temple, N. Y. City, 1895-1901, Central Congl. Ch., Brooklyn, since 1901; acting pres. Adelphi Coll., Brooklyn, 1911-13. Pres. Federal Council Chs. of Christ in America, 1924-28; radio minister of same since 1928. Has served as spl. lecturer Yale Div. Sch.; Shepherd lecturer Bangor Theol. Sem.; Carew lecturer Hartford Theol. Sem.; Earl Lecturer U. of Calif.; Cole lecturer, Vanderbilt U. Del. to Gt. Britain for Tercentennial of Mayflower's Sailing, 1920; rep. of clergy of New York, at 300th anniversary of founding of the first Christian Church of that city, 1928; chmn. Am. sect. of Stockholm conf. on Life and Work, 1925. Pres. British Schs. and Universities Club, 1930-, Golden Rule Foundation, 1930-31. *Author:* The Victory of Christmas, 1909; Charles Darwin and Other English Thinkers, 1911; The Religious Uses of Memory, 1911; William Owen, a Biography, 1912; The Three Religious Leaders of Oxford, 1916; Ambassadors of God, 1920, 2d. edit., 1921; Christianity and the State, 1924; Lure of London, 1925; Imagination and Religion, 1926; The Christ of God, 1929; Every Day Questions and Answers, 1930. *Clubs:* Union League (Brooklyn), Clergy (New York). Collector of English china and antique furniture. *Home:* 35 Prospect Park W., Brooklyn, N. Y.

Chapter XXXI

S. PARKES CADMAN

Dr. Cadman is an institution. He is the best known clergyman in America, not excepting Dr. Fosdick. One thinks of him along with Will Rogers, Henry Ford, Amos 'n' Andy. He has lived a full and many-sided life. His ministry began in England, is international in scope. He started out as a Methodist, but in a little while was numbered among the Congregationalists. Never a narrow denominationalist, the radio has made his voice and messages known to millions. His capacity for work is prodigious. He is always preparing, writing, speaking. The springs of his resourcefulness never go dry. His sermonic barrel, like the widow's cruse of oil, never fails. Slightly above medium height, Dr. Cadman has become a little corpulent and achieved a double chin.

Thirty-two years ago I heard Cadman lecture in old Morrison Chapel, Transylvania College, Lexington, Kentucky. He was something of a newcomer then and his star was blazing its way toward the meridian. His subject, "Street Life in London," was graphic, picturesque, enchanting. He called Shakespeare "Will" and armed old Doctor Johnson and his circle about with great gusto. Famous Fleet Street came to life. Oliver Goldsmith, Sir John Hawkins, Joshua Reynolds—they were all there. It was great! He spoke an hour and a half without a scrap of paper or a note. Professor and students reveled in the joy of that lecture. They liked it so well Dr. Cadman was asked to stay over and give his lecture on Robert Burns the following night. It was a new composition and he used manuscript. The contrast was marked. Cadman seemed like a chained eagle as compared with the previous lecture.

Dr. Cadman's fluency is equaled only by his encyclopedic knowledge. He knows something about everything, and not merely a smattering. His memory is marvelous. Names, episodes, dates, roll off his tongue unhesitatingly and with accuracy. Some say he is too fluent, too voluble. I wonder. He is a liberal in theology. He simply couldn't be anything else. He is built on the liberal scale. His preaching is characterized by directness of thought, and his style, though voluble, is not without perspicuity. His much reading is indicated by his wealth of allusion, although his quotation is by no means excessive. Take his book on preaching, entitled *Ambassadors of God*. It is not exactly light reading, neither is it ponderous, but some of its long paragraphs are a little diffuse. There is a suggestion in some of the sentences of Gunsaulus, who loved to run his phrasings into long, involved and sometimes tortuous windings, to a climax.

Some one with a flair for the epigrammatic has set going a clever critique of S. Parkes Cadman and Joseph Fort Newton. It runs something like this: "Cadman is essentially a speaker, Newton a writer. Cadman should preach exclusively; Newton devote himself wholly to writing." The trouble with this epigram is that it is too clever; nor is it exactly fair to either of these men. For my part, I prefer to take Parkes Cadman and Fort Newton as they are. I would not make them over if I could. Something would be lost, something distinctly fine and worthful, if either of these accomplished gentlemen ceased both to write and to preach.

The newspaper columnists have poked a lot of fun at Dr. Cadman's "Questions and Answers." They accuse him of omniscience. They love to burlesque his column. All the same, Dr. Cadman is adept at the question and answer business. His counsel is sound, wholesome and practical. He speaks out of a background which warrants a little of the oracular; but his newspaper critics have not accused Cadman of bigotry, intolerance or sectarianism, and they never will. The man is a wonder who can keep as intellectually fresh as does Dr. Cadman. He has been in the public eye for more than thirty-five years as author, preacher, lecturer, administrator, publicist, and shows no signs of going stale.

Speaking of Dr. Cadman's expertness in answering questions upon almost every subject under the sun, study this rejoinder to the query by a fellow-minister, "Does not the layman have an equal responsibility in creating the environment in which alone the preacher can come to his best?"

> Answer: "No people are so exorbitant in their demands upon the clergy as the American people are. The English clergyman has a more peaceful time; so does the German clergyman; so do all the Continental clergy. They are not called on as we are to be guide, philosopher, friend, and moral mechanician of a general sort to the whole community.
>
> "It will be a sorry day for the minister when he is not required to solve any problems. Nevertheless, you can carry a good thing too far. The toll we pay for the habit of driving ministers, rabbis and priests, is a high one. Churches would do well to release a minister with a great message to the business of preaching, provided he saturates his message with actual contact with the people of his parish. Then it will not lose the note of actuality. Allow other men to do the work which they can do without requiring him to serve tables. The idea from the early days of New England that the minister must take the entire care of souls for a given district has been rather thrust aside by the implacable circumstances of modern life. A man who can induce people to hear divine truth, as he believes and understands it, is a godsend and should be carefully shielded on his task by those fortunate enough to possess him."

S. Parkes Cadman is the pioneer radio preacher of America. He was the first to broadcast a religious address. Moreover when first invited to use the radio he declined.

He didn't think it practical. Then, too, he fancied that for him to broadcast at the hour of regular service might seem unfair to his ministerial brethren in other churches. He consented however to try the experiment in the Bedford Y.M.C.A. Sunday afternoon service for men, where he had been speaking to large audiences. So the trial was made and it was an astounding success. But before Dr. Cadman's radio preaching was perfected he had to undergo some amusing disciplinary measures and was obliged to change his platform habits. For years it had been his custom to pace back and forth in front of his pulpit, to turn aside and address persons on the platform, and to aim his voice at various sections of his audience as he pleased. Naturally he forgot the microphone, and the unseen listeners caught only fragments of his first addresses over the air. Something had to be done. The difficulty was dissipated in this way; one of Dr. Cadman's friends took a seat just back of him during the broadcasting and when the preacher got out of range of the microphone, he would tap him gently on the right or left leg, as the need might be, with the toe of his shoe. It was something like guiding a horse by means of reins. The plan worked admirably for a time but shortly they built a special pulpit for the Doctor and so hedged him in by a railing or bar that he was obliged to stand still and talk straight into the "mike." Thus gradually this pioneer broadcaster of sermons subdued his physical energies, concentrated them on the business at hand and became in a little while the most effective radio preacher in the land. He still is that. Nobody listening in loses a word of his sermons. He speaks with marked clarity as well as fluency. He makes almost constant use of the short sentence. His diction is chaste and beautiful, yet he never sacrifices vigor of thought or pungency of expression for mere rhetorical charm.

What Mr. Arthur Brisbane is to journalism in amazing fecundity of expression and encyclopedic range of interest, Dr. Cadman is to the pulpit. The amount of work he does is almost unbelievable. He reads constantly in most any place and under unfavorable surroundings. When he goes on vacation, quite regardless of the distance or the place, he soon surrounds himself with books, magazines and papers. He is the only man, as far as I know, who took the *Encyclopedia Britannica* on a vacation trip for recreational reading. He preaches as many as four times a Sunday and lectures throughout the week, keeps up an immense correspondence. Mention has already been made of his memory, which is a thing of wonderment to all who know him. At the least sign of a slip in his memory he takes himself in hand, checks up his facts, concentrates anew and appears fresh, buoyant and fluent at the very next speaking engagement. He reads rapidly yet is able to give on a minute's notice a summary of any book he has read. He likes detective stories, but he can devour a heavy scientific tome with zest at any old time. He is extremely fond of poetry. Great reader that he is however, Dr. Cadman has no time for literary trash.

I could wish to ask Dr. Cadman a hundred questions bearing upon the Christian ministry; I actually asked him only three. Perhaps it was to be expected that my first question took this form: "How did you acquire so delightful a style and so rich and varied a vocabulary?"

"From my youth up I have disciplined myself in reading the prose of the English Bible, Bunyan's *Pilgrim's Progress.* Under my father's guidance I read Addison and Scott, Thackeray, Dickens, and in my later years Walter Pater, and George O. Chevalier. I could name a dozen others but these are enough, are they not?"

"Thousands of preachers would like to know your method of making a sermon. Do you write it in full or simply outline what you wish to say?"

"I write in full all my sermons and then make careful notes of the manuscript. These notes I take to the pulpit, but seldom use them, and the better time I have the more I am free of them."

"You read omnivorously. How do you find the time?"

"My time for study has been greatly helped by the habit formed early in life of reading in bed. I now take at least a couple of hours at night and sometimes as many in the morning, and have a pile of books at my bedside ready at hand."

Many stories are in circulation that cluster about Dr. Cadman—his jests, repartee, amusing experiences. Dr. Burris Jenkins gave a dinner in Cadman's honor at Kansas City not so long ago, to which a dozen or so of the local clergymen were invited. Dr. Jenkins' account of that event is rich. Here is a fragment of it:

"I sat beside him. A friendly fellow! That is about as good a thing as you can say about a preacher. Soon he was calling several of us by our first names. He looks rugged and fine and strong; and I couldn't see that he dieted any in particular. He took out a cigar and lighted up, before he had finished his coffee, saying, 'Burris, do you smoke?' Various others around the table followed his example. Then he told how he had been in a company of ministers who most of them were smoking after dinner when one of them said:

"'I find that a good cigar relaxes my nerves at the end of the day, helps me to rest, and gets me in good shape for a night's sleep.'

"Another one ventured, 'Yes, smoking is the best thing that I find for brain fag.'

"So it went round the circle, each one making his apology. One man kept still. Finally they asked him why he smoked.

"'Well, I've got corns. And I find it the best thing for them.'"

Cadman is in truth a friendly man and loves to stretch out his legs and talk it out with his cronies. A metropolitan minister, who has known him for years, was called to the telephone at ten-thirty o'clock on a certain Sunday night. It was Cadman. He was at a down-town hotel two miles away. He was lonely and would like to see his friend. He was told to take a taxi and come right away. He arrived in twenty minutes. Effervescent with lively good humor, he sat with that friend until after midnight, conversed in a steady stream on books, poetry, preachers, politics, and would you believe it—roses. Reluctantly he said good-by away past midnight, returned to his hotel, off the next day for a series of speeches, then back to New York, speaking, writing, dictating, correspondence, broadcasting. What a life! What a life!

The great old guard of preacher-lecturers famous twenty-five years ago is fast fading out. Hillis is gone; Gunsaulus is gone; Robert McIntyre is gone; "Sunshine" Willitts is gone; Cadman still survives, virile, versatile, eloquent, voluble, loving and lovable. May he be spared us for a decade or more! America and the world have need of S. Parkes Cadman.

HOLMES, John Haynes, clergyman: *b.* Philadelphia, Pa., Nov. 29, 1879; *s.* Marcus Morton and Alice F. (Haynes) H.; A.B., *summa cum laude,* Harvard, 1902, S.T.B., 1904; D.D., Jewish Inst. Religion, 1930, St. Lawrence University, 1931; *m.* Madeleine H. Baker, of Brooklyn, June 27, 1904; children—Roger Wellington, Frances Adria. Ordained and installed as minister Third Religious Soc. (Unitarian), Dorchester, Mass., Mar. 2, 1904; pastor Ch. of the Messiah, New York (now called The Community Ch. of N. Y.), Feb., 1907-. Pres. Unitarian Fellowship for Social Justice, 1908-11; v.p. Middle States Unitarian Conf., 1908-19; chmn. Gen. Unitarian Conf., 1915-17; pres. Free Religious Assn., 1914-19; pres. Unitarian Temperance Society, 1917-18; dir. Am. Civil Liberties Union, 1917-; chmn. City Affairs Com., 1929-; v.p. Nat. Assn. for Advancement of Colored People, 1909-; pres. All World Gandhi Fellowship since 1929. On spl. mission to Palestine for the Jews, 1929. Left Unitarianism and became independent, 1919. Mem. Delta Upsilon and Phi Beta Kappa. *Author:* The Revolutionary Function of the Modern Church, 1912; Marriage and Divorce, 1913; Is Death the End? 1915; New Wars for Old, 1916; Religion for Today, 1917; The Life and Letters of Robert Collyer, 1917; Readings from Great Authors, 1918; The Grail of Life, 1919; Is Violence the Way Out?, 1920; New Churches for Old, 1922; Patriotism Is Not Enough, 1925; Palestine Today and Tomorrow, 1929; The Heart of Scott's Poetry, 1932. Editor, Unity, Chicago. contbg. editor The World Tomorrow, New York. Lecturer. *Home:* 26 Sidney Pl., Brooklyn. *Office:* 12 Park Av., New York, N. Y.

CHAPTER XXXII

JOHN HAYNES HOLMES

WHEN America swung into the World War in the spring of 1917 thousands of ministers of the Gospel of Christ went into Gethsemane and a few went all the way to Calvary. Can I ever forget my own experience? I had hoped and prayed that America might make her contribution to the peace of the world as a friendly neutral. I was conducting Lenten services in Indianapolis the week that President Wilson in a memorable speech informed the Congress that a state of war existed between the United States and Germany. The excitement was intense along the street fronting the theater where I was preaching the love of Christ and that peace that passeth all understanding. Khaki-clad men tramped to the time of martial music, the crowds cheered. It was with a heavy heart that I carried on my Lenten addresses. The minds of the people were on the war not Lenten subjects. At the close of the service one of these trying days, just after the benediction had been pronounced, an old man, a veteran, I think, of the Civil War, stood up and calling me by name cried, "Jesus said, 'He that hath not a sword, let him sell his coat and buy one.'" A salvo of cheers followed his challenge. I returned to my home Easter morning, ill and unable to take the services, took to bed, and was out of the pulpit for two weeks. In that time I made my decision, and supported the nation in its war with Germany.

Not so the Reverend John Haynes Holmes, minister of the Community Church, New York City. The Sunday before Congress formally declared war on Germany, he delivered a sermon from his pulpit entitled, "A Message to My People on the Eve of War." It was a dramatic occasion.

An audience was present that taxed the capacity. The air was vibrant with excitement. Minister after minister of prominence had declared his purpose to stand by the government should war come. War madness had come to America. Dr. Holmes spoke that day under great emotional strain, reminded the people that throughout his ministry he had preached the spirit of Christ, had been unalterably opposed to force and armed conflict, and now that a war was impending, he could not for the life of him see any reason why he should desert his principles simply because the nation would declare war and that was the popular side. Squaring his shoulders and lifting his head high he said to his congregation:

> "I am opposed to war in general and to this war in particular. Other pulpits may preach recruiting sermons; mine will not. Other parish houses may be turned into drill halls and rifle ranges; ours will not. Other clergymen may pray to God for victory for our arms; I will not. In this church, if nowhere else in America, the Germans will still be included in the family of God's children."

Then the fur began to fly. John Haynes Holmes was on the front page of every newspaper in the country. He was savagely assailed, engulfed by denunciation. His mail swelled overnight with vitriolic attacks by known and unknown correspondents. His name was anathema on the lips of thousands. His case was all the more damnable in the eyes of his critics because he was an American of the Americans, his ancestors having come over in 1630. He was a blue-blood and a Bostonian to boot. What was the matter with this man? Was he mad? Where was his patriotism? He was disloyal, and still the battle waged about him and few there were to come to his defense. But one miraculous thing happened—his church stood by him.

I remember with what astonishment I read at the time

the Associated Press dispatch to the effect that the trustees of Dr. Holmes' church did not propose to demand his resignation. Not that they agreed with his views, at any rate the majority did not. The trustees issued a statement explaining that Dr. Holmes' views regarding the war were not theirs, but that their regard for him and their belief in his sincerity was unchanged, and that they desired him to remain as their minister. Somehow I fancy that nearly every preacher who read this heaved a sigh and said to himself, "I wish I had a church like that." Yet I may be mistaken. Perhaps only a few felt that way and most of the parsons who saw that item exploded and gave utterance to an expression of disgust and disappointment. For thus does the war spirit work havoc in the hearts even of those who are called to preach the unsearchable riches of Christ.

Still it is not wholly true that all of Dr. Holmes' parishioners stood by him in this painful ordeal. Some left in a fine frenzy, breathing maledictions against so pestiferous a pastor, and one so "unpatriotic." Yet these were the exception, and the Community Church remains as almost the solitary example of a congregation that kept its head when all around were others losing theirs. Throughout the war, Holmes kept flying at the masthead his flag of conviction. He was, in truth, to his fellow-churchmen, what Senator LaFollette was in the same period to his political associates. A friend of Dr. Holmes who is in a position to know avers that he has probably been denounced more often and in more violent terms than any other man living in New York to-day. Thus *What's What,* official publication of the Industrial Defense Association, Inc., a Boston patriotic society, declares him to be one of the most dangerous persons in America; the Lusk committee which investigated "seditious activities" in New York State some years ago condemned both him and his church; and Holmes' name is said to be written on the D.A.R. blacklist so that all who run may read.

Three years after his graduation from Harvard University

Divinity School, Dr. Holmes was called to the Church of the Messiah, famous because of the ministerial leadership of such eminent preachers as Robert Collyer, Orville G. Dewey and Minot J. Savage. Dr. Collyer was still living when Holmes came on the scene as his successor. He was a grand old warrior and he gave the full measure of his loyalty to his young and radical successor. Within a brief period young Holmes exhibited an independence and a liberalism beyond anything the church had hitherto known. He struck out boldly, slashed right and left, made membership in his church as wide as humanity, drawing not a single line of color, class or creed. In 1921 he resigned from the Unitarian ministry, changed the old name "Church of the Messiah" to "Community Church," carried with him the majority of his congregation despite the objection of some and the dismay of others.

New York is the home of many eloquent and brilliant speakers and John Haynes Holmes is accorded a place in the inner circle. His oratory is dramatic, persuasive, vivid, entertaining. His literary style is alluring. His words flare into flaming sentences. He is good to look upon, of commanding presence, charming and gracious in manner. Coupled with such assets of voice, manner and fire, is his radical utterance, daring, utterly unorthodox, spoken with the utmost sincerity. Here indeed is no "man afraid of his shadow," but instead an audacious defender of the underdog, eulogist of Eugene V. Debs, friend of Gandhi, champion of the poor and the disinherited. Here too is a prohibitionist who defends his belief in the righteousness of the Eighteenth Amendment with the same vigor and ardent enthusiasm that he brings to his anti-war crusade.

As a specimen of this fiery prophet's iconoclasm, ponder this paragraph:

> "The truth is that our nation, like all nations of our western world, has never been Christian, but frankly and brutally pagan. Nor am I sure that it is worth

while at this late date that this nation, or any nation, should try to be Christian! Perhaps the very fact that men have professed to be Christians, and thereupon have found it necessary to invent easy signs and symbols of their Christian character, has diverted their attention and energy from the real task of human living, and thus betrayed them. For Christianity, as set over against some other type of religion, must be distinctive. Hence the creeds and rites and ceremonials, the elaborate theological definitions and ecclesiastical organizations, which have been imposed upon Christianity, like royal regalia upon a king, to mark its identity and glorify its authority! To believe this doctrine or to practice that rite, to belong to a church or an order or a holy brotherhood, to observe Sunday and partake of sacraments and support foreign missions, these and a hundred other performances have been regarded for centuries as the stigmata so to speak, of Christian loyalty. They are the 'mint, anise, and cummin' of the law, obedience to which has justified faith and vindicated character."

Out of the pulpit and off of the platform, Holmes is a human being of simple tastes, kind and courteous, considerate of the least of these his brethren. He is a collector of first editions, and autographs of celebrities. Sir Walter Scott is his favorite author. His library as a whole is notable, though his shelf supreme holds a delectable array of highly prized editions of Sir Walter. The rare book shops of New York are acquainted with the minister of Community Church, and love to have him browsing over their stock. He is a book lover with a wide range of author's first printings, and no end of literary topics. His conversation on these subjects is delightful and informing. It is perhaps to be expected that this lover of Victorian writers cherishes no high opinion of some of these latter-day novelists, such as Sinclair Lewis and Theodore Dreiser. For this preacher, radical though he be, has a great deal of the Puritan in him, and is free from the so-called small vices which he probably overlooks in others, although he does not condone them.

Dr. Holmes' intimate friends are not blind to his defects. One of these who admires him extravagantly says that when he takes a position he does so with almost fanatical fervor, becomes an extremist, makes no allowances for extenuating circumstances, "fights for peace with his fists clenched." The same criticism has been made of many another reformer, William Lloyd Garrison, for instance, likewise Wendell Phillips. Was it not Dr. Eliot of Harvard who, writing of Woodrow Wilson, referred to a fierce side of Wilson the reformer? Of "gentle cynics" there may be many but of mild and ladylike reformers I can recall not a single one. They are simply not made that way.

I have been profitably engaged in reading a sermon by Dr. Holmes entitled, "My Twenty-Five Years in New York," "Preached on the Twenty-Fifth Anniversary of His Ministry at the Community Church." It is intensely interesting, and also revealing, being largely autobiographical. Holmes' account, for instance, of his elation when he discovered Mahatma Gandhi in 1919, is thrilling. Unable to find words to express his emotion, he made effective use of the words of John Keats to describe his discovery of Chapman's *Homer*—

"Then felt I like some watcher of the skies
When a new planet swims into his ken;
Or like stout Cortez when with eagle eyes
He star'd at the Pacific—and all his men
Look'd at each other with a wild surmise—
Silent, upon a peak in Darien."

The temptation to quote further from this remarkable sermon is strong, but I must resist it if I can. Holmes' picture of himself as he appeared in the pulpit of the Church of the Messiah, in February, 1907, is vivid. He sees himself across the quarter of a century, that day of days, lean and lithe, and tall, proud of his fine head of hair. He was at the same time eager, confident, bumptious, arrogant and self-entered. He contrasts that picture with this, the man who is: hair thin and gray, figure no longer erect but stooped, face looks tired, his heart very heavy, yet inexpressibly happy in his family, his friends, his fortune. But he still believes, believes in man, believes in God, believes in "the ultimate destiny of good."

Thus I have quoted from that sermon after all, but how could I help it?

What a preacher! What a man! What a voice in the wilderness!

THE END